REDBACK

GRAPHIX

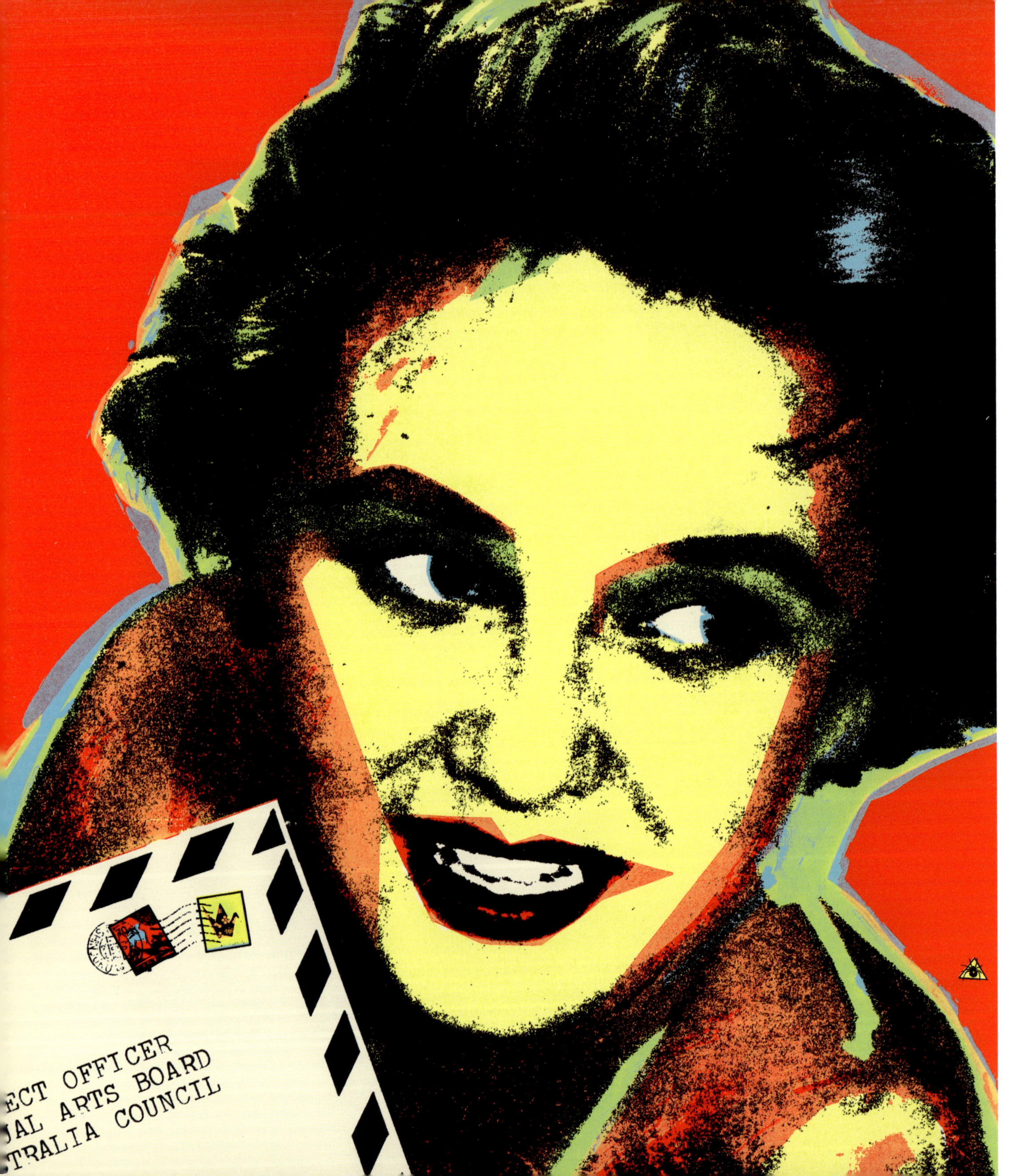
ECT OFFICER
UAL ARTS BOARD
TRALIA COUNCIL

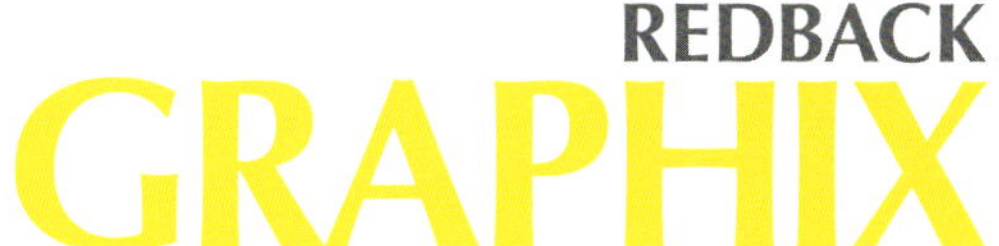

# REDBACK GRAPHIX

Anna Zagala

■ national gallery of **australia**

Produced by the Publications Department
of the National Gallery of Australia
nga.gov.au
The National Gallery of Australia is an Australian Government Agency

Editor: Margaret Trudgeon
Design: ZOO Design
Printer: Blue Star Print

National Library of Australia Cataloguing-in-Publication entry

Author: Zagala, Anna.
Title: Redback Graphix / Anna Zagala.
Edition: 1st ed
ISBN: 9780642541987 (pb)
Notes: Includes index.
Bibliography.
Subjects: Posters—20th century—Australia.
Posters, Australian.
Other Authors/Contributors:
National Gallery of Australia.
Dewey Number: 769.994

Distributed in Australia by
Thames and Hudson
11 Central Boulevard Business Park
Port Melbourne, Victoria, 3207

Distributed in the United Kingdom by
Thames and Hudson
181A High Holborn
London WC1V 7QX, UK

Distributed in the United States of America by
University of Washington Press
1326 Fifth Avenue, Ste 555
Seattle, WA 98101-2604

**Acknowledgments**

I would like to thank Redback artists Michael Callaghan, Gregor Cullen, Marie McMahon, Alison Alder and Jan Mackay, who spoke with me about their experience of working at the Redback Graphix studio, as well as their clients and friends who shared valuable impressions.

National Gallery of Australia curator Jaklyn Babington sourced additional Redback posters, as did curator Sarina Noordhuis-Fairfax who was also instrumental in bringing this project to completion.

My appreciation also extends to Roger Butler at the National Gallery of Australia for giving me the opportunity to pursue my long-held interest in Redback Graphix. I'd also like to acknowledge the support of Gordon Darling, the Gordon Darling Australia Pacific Print Fund and The Gordon Darling Fellowship program.

Thank you to Peter Vandermark and Marie Hagerty for their hospitality while I was in Canberra and to Maria Zagala for her expertise and enthusiasm. Finally, I would like to thank my husband Stephen for being there from the very beginning

*The printed image* Australia · Asia · Pacific
Series editor: Roger Butler
An access initiative of the
Gordon Darling Australia Pacific Print Fund.
printsandprintmaking.gov.au

In the same series:
*Australian Artists Books* by Alex Selenitsch
*Papua New Guinea prints* by Melanie Eastburn

(Front cover)
**Michael Callaghan** (designer and printer)
*If the unemployed are dole bludgers, what the fuck are the idle rich?* 1979 (detail)

(Inside cover)
**Leonie Lane** (designer and printer)
*Hatstand* 1985

(Title page)
**Alison Alder** (designer and printer)
*Visual Arts and Crafts Board* 1984 (detail)

# CONTENTS

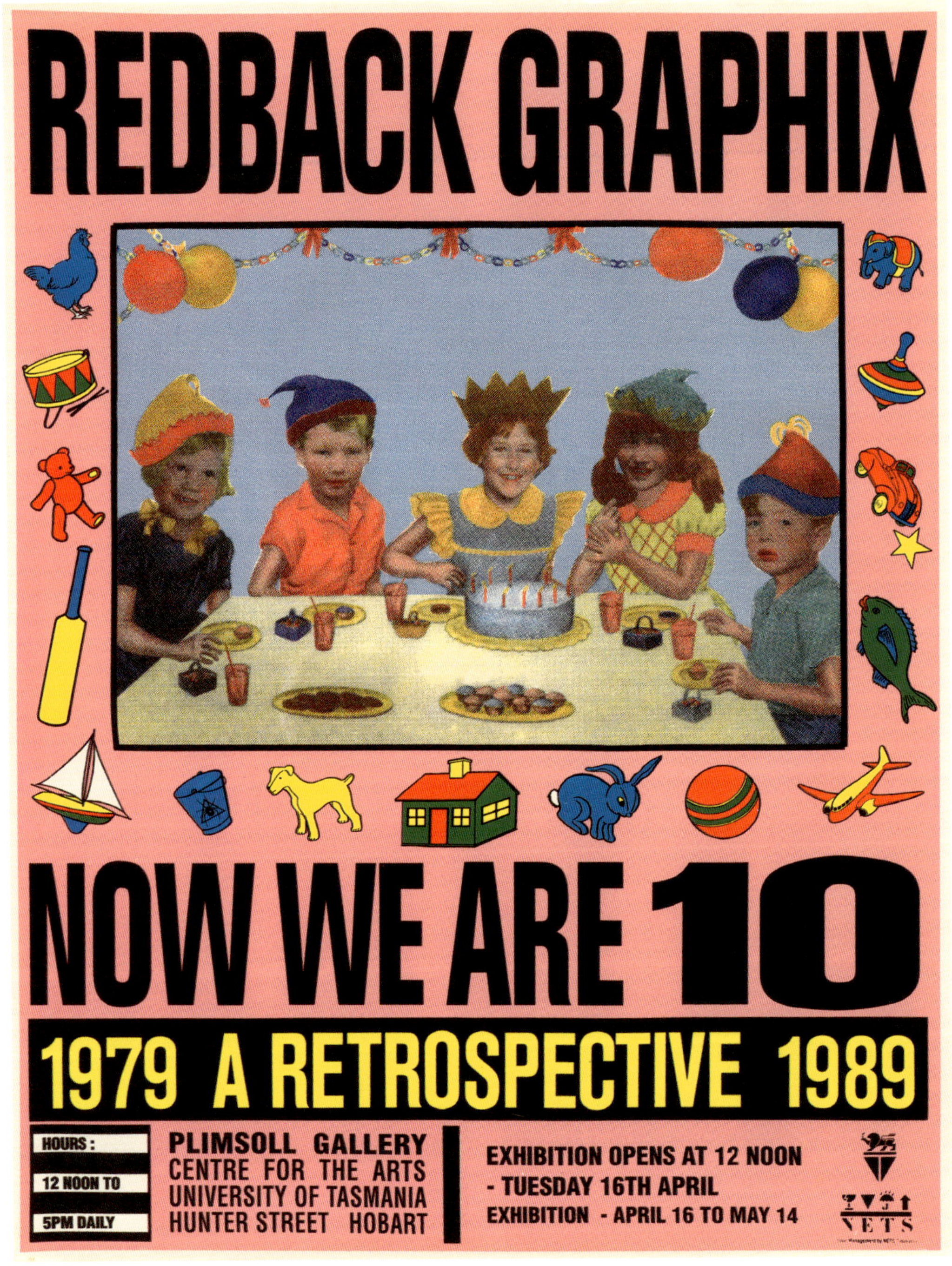
REDBACK GRAPHIX
NOW WE ARE 10
1979 A RETROSPECTIVE 1989
HOURS :
12 NOON TO
5PM DAILY
PLIMSOLL GALLERY
CENTRE FOR THE ARTS
UNIVERSITY OF TASMANIA
HUNTER STREET HOBART
EXHIBITION OPENS AT 12 NOON
- TUESDAY 16TH APRIL
EXHIBITION - APRIL 16 TO MAY 14
NETS

## Director's foreword

The impact of a printed poster, placed on the street or in a public space, can be vast. Posters have the capacity to reach large audiences and can often have a powerful effect on individuals and the collective conscience. Since the 1970s, printed posters have played a vital role in influencing the Australian political climate. Perhaps nowhere more so is the power of the printed poster as a social and political tool more strikingly evident than in the works of the 1980s poster collective, Redback Graphix.

The publication of the *Redback Graphix* book forms part of the National Gallery of Australia's twenty-fifth anniversary celebrations, which focus on highlights from the Gallery's permanent collection. The Gallery's remarkable collection of Australian prints, posters and illustrated books is unrivalled in its breadth and depth, amassing over 40 000 works on paper. These works have been assembled by Senior Curator of Australian Prints and Drawings, Roger Butler, and supported by the Gallery's previous directors, Council, artists and donors and through the Gordon Darling Australia Pacific Print Fund.

Since 1981, over 400 political posters and assorted ephemera from Redback Graphix have been collected. Over time this collection has been augmented by donations from artists and printers employed by the workshop. The Redback Graphix archive now encompasses the majority of the workshop's varied output, including posters, banners, t-shirts, stickers, cassette covers, wrapping paper and publications. These vibrant works document a series of significant social movements of the twentieth century.

Anna Zagala was the third recipient of the Gordon Darling Fellowship, which provided the opportunity to research the Gallery's holdings of screenprinted posters and ephemera from Redback Graphix. Drawing upon her background as an artist and freelance writer, Anna has produced a thought-provoking insight into the legendary print workshop. This publication is the third in *The printed image* series which publishes the wide-ranging research of Gordon Darling Fellows. I congratulate Anna on her thoughtful examination of this dynamic area of contemporary art practice, and her significant contribution to the appreciation of Redback Graphix.

Ron Radford AM
Director
National Gallery of Australia

(opposite)
**Michael Callaghan**, **Paul Cockram**,
**Leonie Lane** (designers)
**Alison Alder** (designer and printer)
*Now we are ten* 1989

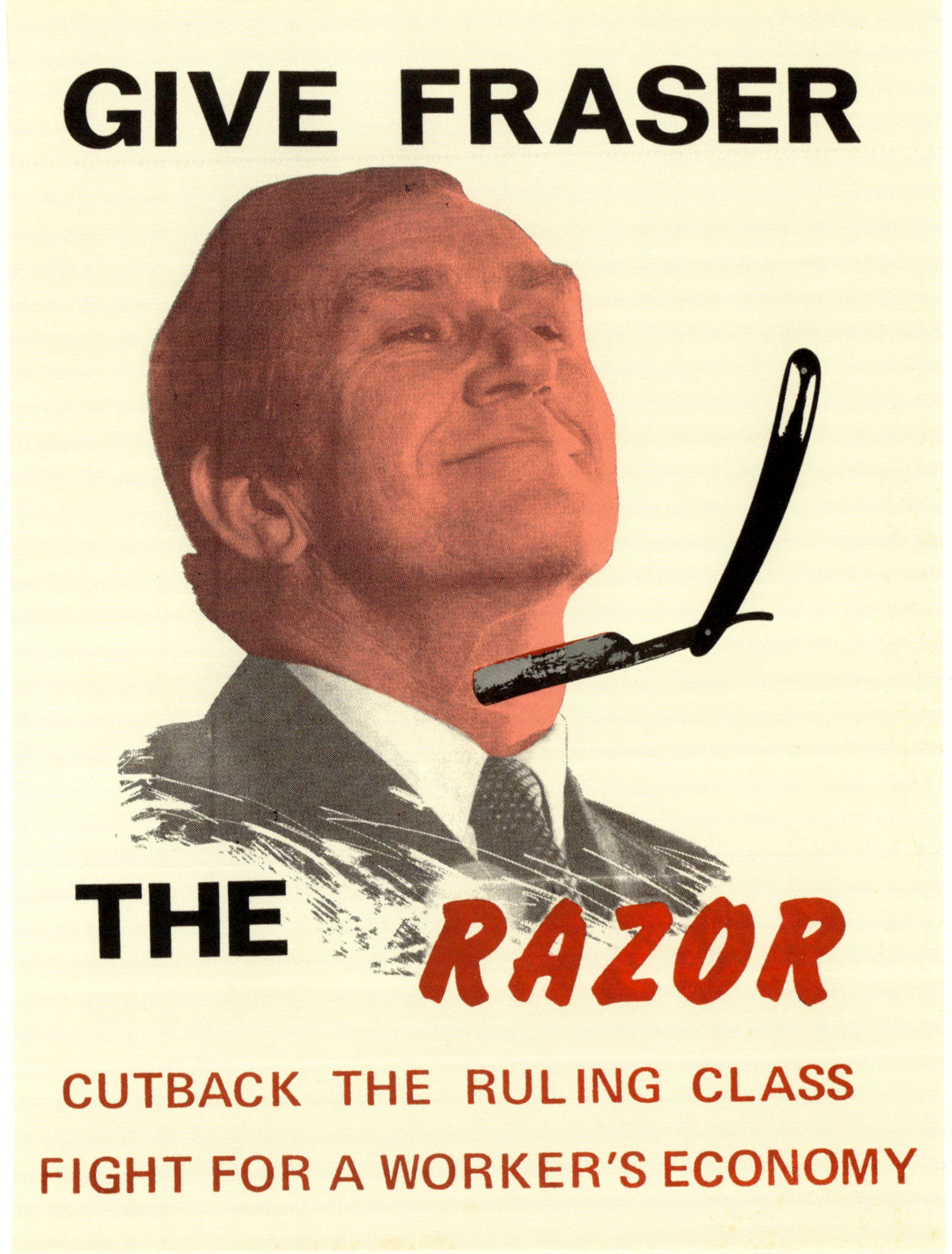
GIVE FRASER
THE RAZOR
CUTBACK THE RULING CLASS
FIGHT FOR A WORKER'S ECONOMY

# INTRODUCTION

With the emergence of social movements in the late 1960s, such as women's liberation, gay and lesbian rights, environmentalism and nuclear disarmament, people began to take to the streets. In Sydney many of these protests were promoted through the Earthworks Poster Collective, a screenprinting poster workshop founded in 1972 on the grounds of the University of Sydney. The collective produced hundreds of vibrant posters to raise awareness and advertise events in the city, matching arresting images with memorable slogans: 'Give Fraser the razor', 'Every mother is a working mother', 'Keep warm this winter – make trouble'. By the decade's end, many of the causes so passionately fought for by students and radicals had moved from the fringes into the general public consciousness. Out of this socially engaged environment sprung a different kind of print workshop called Redback Graphix. Redback continued the tradition of Earthworks, printing socially engaged, eye-catching posters, but it instituted a different work culture in line with the changed political, social and economic circumstances that now existed.

Taking the technical screenprinting skills learnt while at Earthworks, Redback's founder, Michael Callaghan, established an alternative advertising agency for the left in 1979. Founded in Brisbane, Redback moved initially to Wollongong, where it was situated for five years before relocating to Sydney for the next decade. Aspects of the communal ethos of Earthworks, including its non-hierarchical organisation and principle of equal pay for all workers, were implemented by Redback. The studio, however, rejected open access in favour of a business model that operated on a commission-only basis. Redback Graphix brought its distinctive aesthetic – an amalgam of images raided from popular culture and history reproduced in bumped-up colours – to a range of issues for local and national clients. The studio's broad appeal and uncanny ability to harness support from diverse sources ensured its longevity, while also accounting for its strangely indeterminate status. It straddled the two very different worlds of art and advertising. For almost fifteen years the studio received state funding and operated as a private business. Redback posters, designed for both private and community organisations, found an audience beyond its client base. They were collected by state and regional galleries, exhibited internationally, and won accolades in both the design and advertising industries.

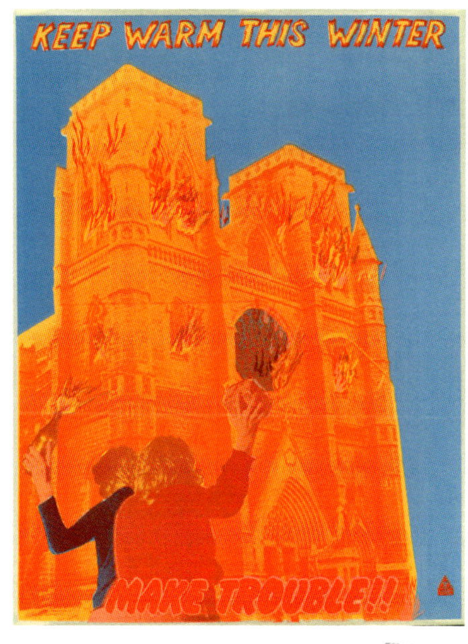


(opposite)
**Earthworks Poster Collective**
Australia 1972–1979
**Michael Callaghan**
*Give Fraser the razor* 1977
screenprint, printed in colour,
from four stencils
68.2 x 53.2 cm (printed image)
Gift of Marie McMahon, 1994
94.305

**Earthworks Poster Collective**
Australia 1972–1979
**Marie McMahon**
*Keep warm this winter – make trouble!!* 1978
screenprint, printed in colour,
from five stencils
99.4 x 73.2 cm (printed image)
National Gallery of Australia, Canberra
Purchased 1982
82.930

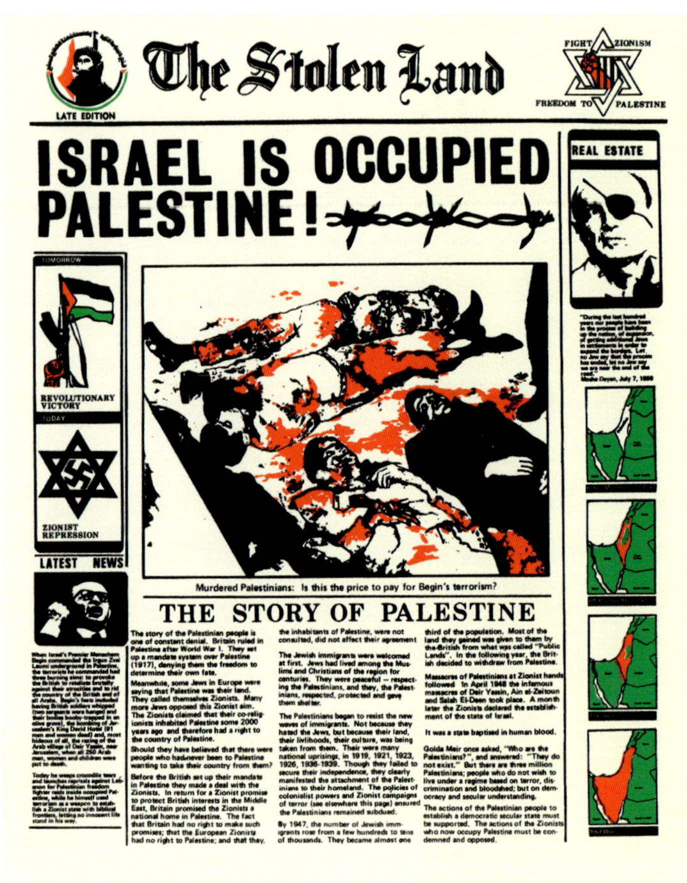


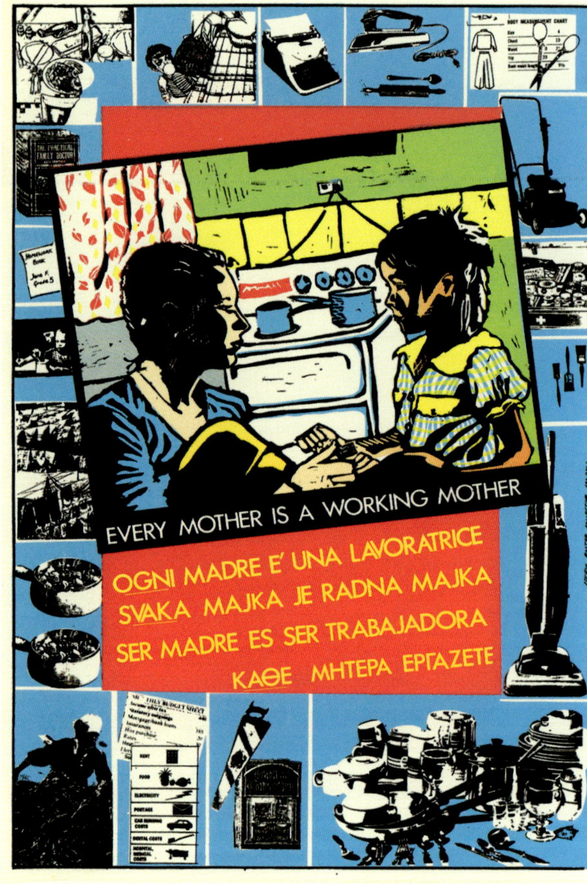


(above)
**Earthworks Poster Collective**
Australia 1972–1979
**Michael Callaghan**
**Kerry Woodhill** born Australia 1950
*The stolen land* (English version) 1978
screenprint, printed in colour from multiple stencils
53.0 x 41.6 cm (printed image)
Gift of the artist, 1989
89.1169

(above right)
**Lucifoil Posters**
Australia 1980–1983
**Jan Fieldsend** born Australia 1951
*Every mother is a working mother* 1981
screenprint, printed in colour, from five stencils
74.2 x 49.2 cm (printed image)
National Gallery of Australia, Canberra
Purchased 1990
90.1311.93

Over the years, some twenty individuals worked at Redback. They found their way to the studio through a loose network of contacts linking screenprinting studios around Australia, stretching as far north as Bathurst Island. Photographic stencils, a vital part of the early posters, gave way to hand-rendered illustrations as artists brought new design skills, fresh perspectives and different printing techniques to Redback. The advent of personal computers opened up new possibilities for reproduction. And while Redback is largely known for its posters, which had the broadest appeal and were the most visible items produced by the studio, it also produced a variety of promotional material ranging from publications to banners.

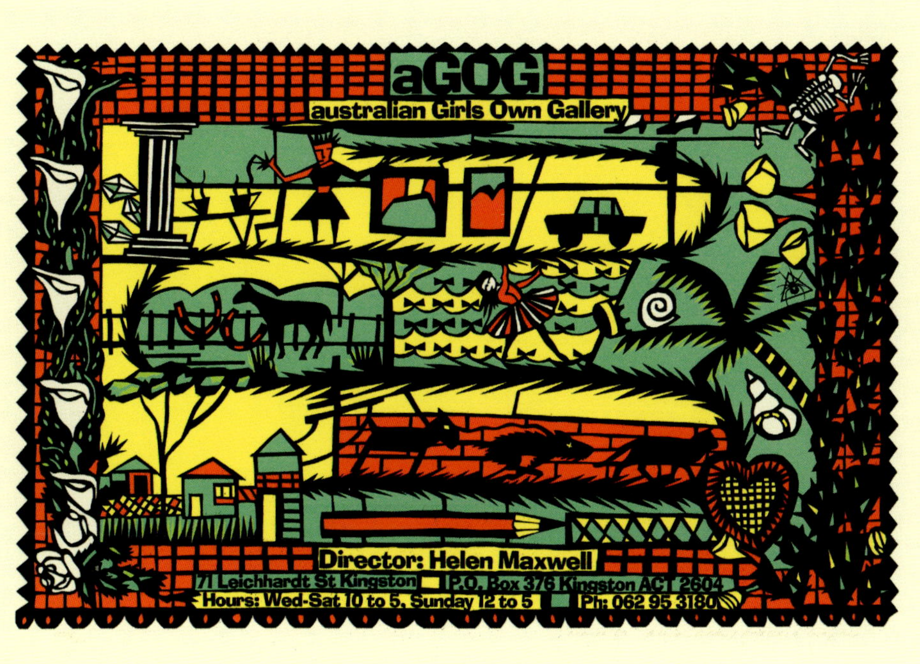


In the late 1980s Redback continued to expand its output, printing directly onto T-shirts, creating wrapping paper and designing corporate identities in step with the constant changes that were occurring in both the marketing and communications industries. The studio rode the wave of 1980s affluence and survived several economic downturns until the recession of 1994 forced the closure of the screenprinting workshop. By this time graphic communication had changed immeasurably; the poster, so popular with clients fifteen years previously, had begun to fall out of favour with both designers and clients. The proliferation of personal computers and the relative ease and affordability of desktop publishing enabled designers to produce offset printed material without the exertion or the associated health risks of screenprinting.

Offset printing techniques cannot reproduce the vibrant colours and velvet sheen of screenprinted posters. Those days have passed. The posters of Redback Graphix belong to a historically specific moment – brief in its duration – but volcanic in force.

**Alison Alder** (designer and printer)
*aGOG – Australian Girls Own Gallery* 1988

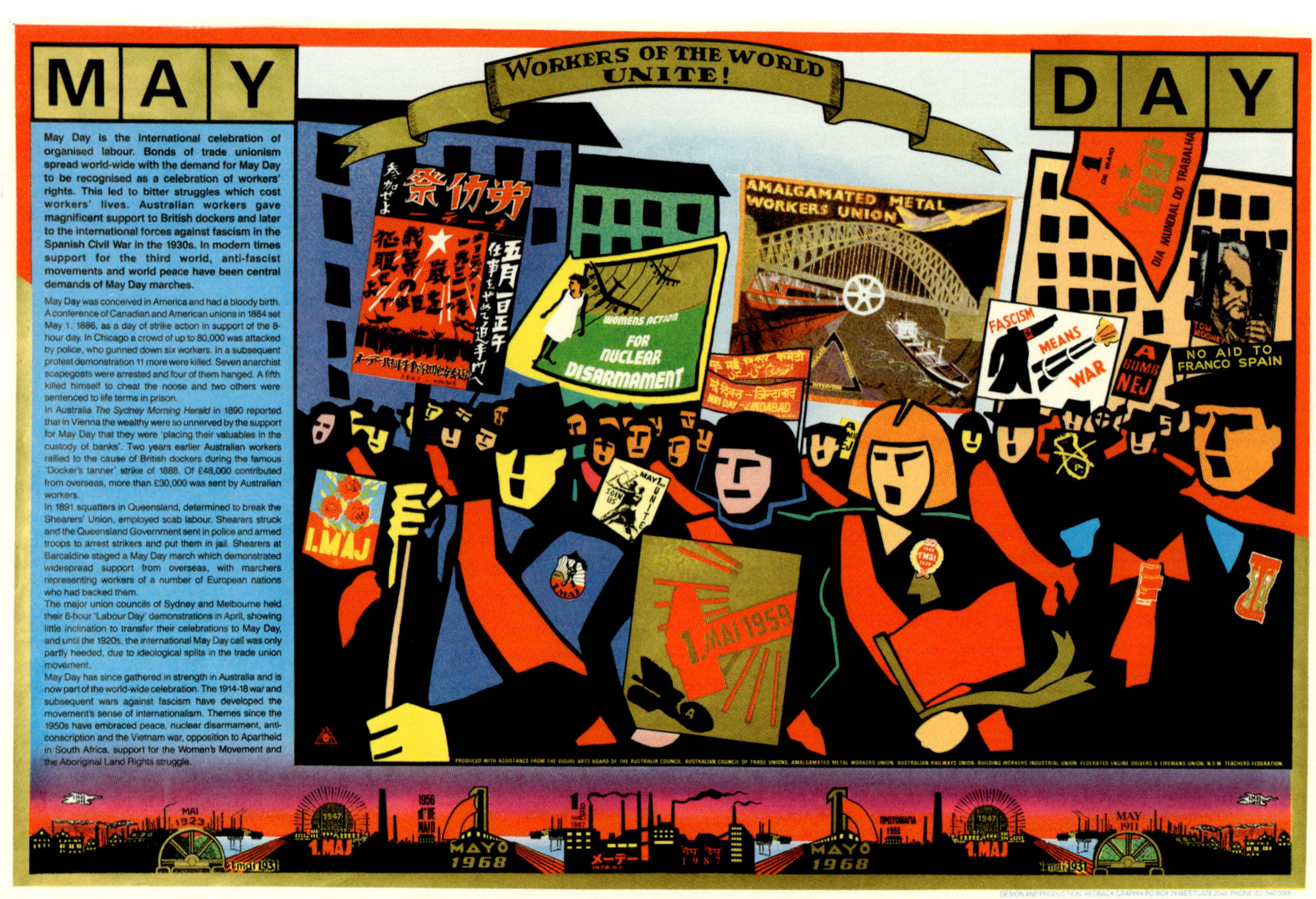


**Marie McMahon** and **Michael Callaghan** (designers)
**Ann Stephen** (research)
**Paul Cockram** (film planning)
**Peter Curtis** and **Ray Young** (printers)
*May day* 1986

## Street days

As a printmaking technique, screenprinting was developed at the turn of the 20th century in the United States and applied in a commercial context until the 1930s when the US government established a poster workshop as part of the United States Works Administration for unemployed artists.[1] While screenprinting became a popular medium in Britain and the United States through which social and political issues were raised, in Australia, with the exception of Noel Counihan, who created several portfolios of linocuts with a strong leftist message including *The miner* 1947 and *War or peace* 1950, printmaking did not seek to address social and political issues until the early 1970s. By then, screenprinting was being taught in art schools around Australia; activists and students involved in anti-Vietnam War protests seized on the technology, since screenprinted posters were relatively cheap to make, enabled the fast production of multiple copies, and could be printed by activists themselves. Moreover, the group effort required in the screenprinting of posters appealed to the communal ethos of the movement and engendered a strong sense of grassroots participation.

Globally, the counter-culture of the 1960s was anti-authoritarian in spirit and radicalised along various lines. In Britain anti-nuclear protests galvanised the population, while in the United States the Civil Rights movement demanded increased power and recognition for minorities.[2] Around the world, young people rallied against the Vietnam War. In Paris, students revolted against the government, occupying the Latin Quarter and organising strikes that called for an end to capitalism and consumerism. They founded the Atelier Populaire at the École Nationale Supérieure des Beaux-Arts; students and activists would meet daily in a general assembly to plan happenings, print newspapers and produce posters. The posters were intended as a form of public protest to counter de Gaulle's attack on the students through mainstream communication channels. Simple designs, the torn shape of a raised fist or rudimentary illustrations coupled with punchy slogans carried the Atelier's revolutionary message.[3] And the production process, and the use of one or sometimes two colours, reflected the activists' sense of urgency. Posters were screenprinted, distributed and posted up on the streets in secret. Their presence was a provocation, a means of resistance and a demand for action.

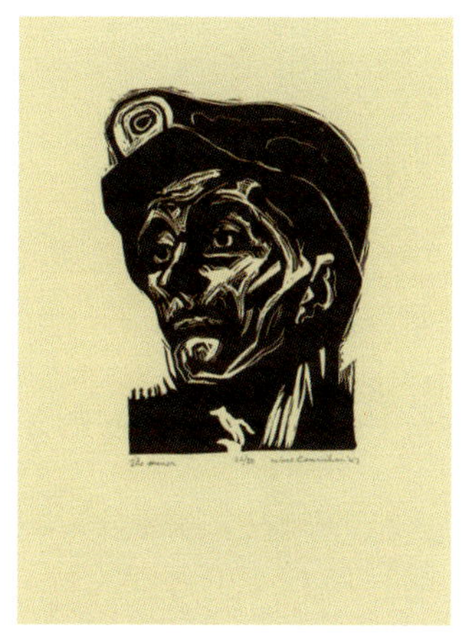

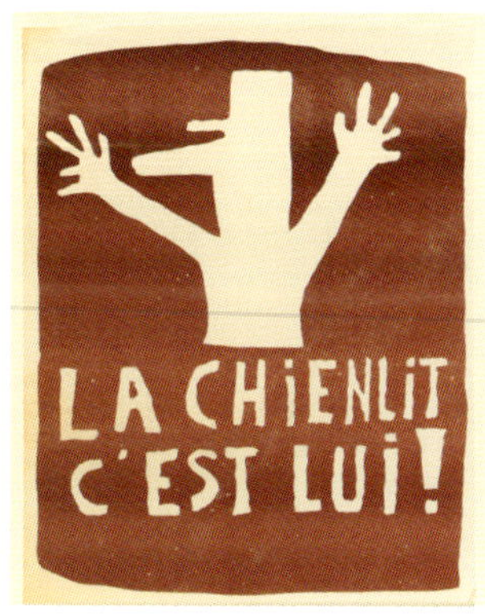


(top)
**Noel Counihan** Australia 1913–1986
*The miner* Melbourne 1947
linocut, printed in black ink, from one block
23.0 x 17.0 cm (printed image)
National Gallery of Australia, Canberra Purchased 1974
74.170

**Atelier Populaire**
*La chienlit c'est lui* France 1968
screenprint, printed in red ink,
from one stencil on thin white paper
37.0 x 28.7 cm (printed image)
National Gallery of Australia, Canberra Purchased 1985
85.2001

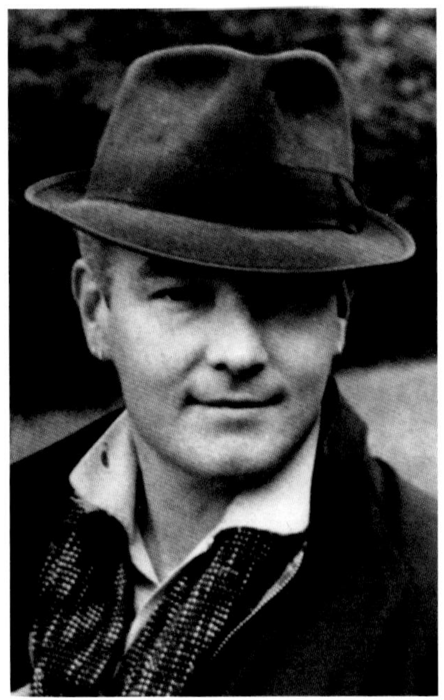

Michael Callaghan 1982
Photograph courtesy of Bronwyn Barwell

Television brought pictures of these revolutionary occurrences to Australia. Thousands attended protests being staged in the state capitals against the Vietnam War, ushering Australians into the loop of global events. These demonstrations changed the social climate and created an atmosphere that was charged with possibilities. The potent combination of optimism and dissatisfaction directed at institutions gave rise to the emergence of social movements. Curator Charles Merewether wrote of this time:

> They were street days, of occupying the public space as a site where real life was still lived and waged, days of demonstrations, rallies, marches, of people taking over the streets.[4]

Michael Callaghan, founder of Redback Graphix, was a high school student at the time in Wollongong, and remembers attending demonstrations in Sydney and distributing *Students for a Democratic Society* (SDS) bulletins at Wollongong schools. This early political action resulted in his suspension from secondary school. As well as an interest in politics, Callaghan discovered the early twentieth century art movement, Dada, at school.[5] When Dada emerged in Europe following the First World War it challenged the traditional concept of the valuable art object and sought to reconnect the artist to society. Artists used found objects, collage, text-based works, and performance to produce deliberately discordant, asynchronous effects. Influenced by its ideas, Callaghan, along with school friend Phillip Batty, who would later establish CAAMA (Central Australian Aboriginal Media Association), founded a poetry magazine, *Box*, and performed simultaneous poetry performances around Sydney. Collaborative relationships, political agitation and a distinctively Dadaist sensibility would become the hallmarks of Redback Graphix.

Callaghan's interest in Dada so early in life seems prescient given the strong connections between that art movement and Callaghan's own involvement in politically engaged art. Dada's importance to modern graphic design is also worth noting. Artists Kurt Schwitters, Tristan Tzara and Ilia Zdanevich designed and printed Dada posters, poems and invitations. Schwitters, known principally for his paper collages and wild performances, actually ran an advertising agency by day. Dada posters explored the limits of the structured grid of the letter press by playing with scale, mixed type and incorporated ornament and dingbats into the design. Graphic design historian Ellen Lupton describes them as possessing an 'aesthetic of commercial quotation', drawing as they did on advertising, street signs and found commercial objects.[6] Redback posters would similarly borrow from the world around them.

Callaghan attended art school, completing a diploma in sculpture at the National Art School, East Sydney Technical College in 1974. Here he met Aleks Danko and Mike Parr, and participated in a number of performance works with Danko at Central St Gallery, along with Noel Sheridan, who was a teacher at the school at the time. Callaghan continued his association with Danko and Parr after finishing his studies, teaching a Post Object art class at the Tin Sheds Art Workshops and collaborating on Parr's film *Rules of displacement activities* 1975. The Tin Sheds were a collection of abandoned Second World War corrugated iron huts on the grounds of the University of Sydney that were built in a E-shaped configuration. They housed a printing and etching workshop, a painting studio, ceramic studio and facilities for a street theatre group. The East Sydney Technical College was criticised for its teaching methods and conservative curriculum.[7] Graduates and dissatisfied students from disciplines as diverse as sculpture and engineering gravitated to the Sheds. This group of students and artists included Lloyd Rees, Imants Tillers, Joan Grounds, Mike Parr, Tim Johnston, Tim Burns, Vivienne Binns and Ian Burn, working across a range of practices from painting and sculpture to photography and craft. Many of them became increasingly interested in conceptual, performance and language-based art.[8] Artists and writers were interrogating the function of art; discourse centred around the validity of an art practice that focused on the art object at the expense of process. Artist Bert Flugelman and several students formed a collective called Optronic Kinetics, which explored the relationship between electronics and movement. They staged conceptual installations and experiments at the Arts Workshop and around the city.

The year after Callaghan finished his course he took part in the group show, *Performance, documents, film, video*, at the Art Gallery of New South Wales and the National Gallery of Victoria, and received funding from the Experimental Film Fund to make a short film based on the work of Italian Futurist F.T. Marinetti. One of the collaborators on this project was Marie McMahon, also a former art student at the National Art School. More than a decade later, McMahon would bring her strong print and illustrative abilities to Redback Graphix.

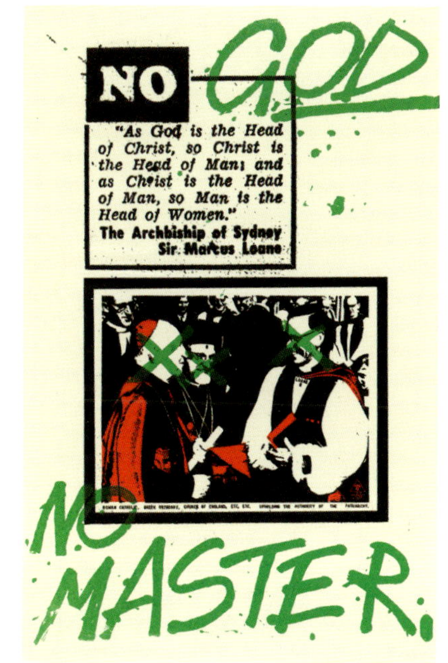


**Earthworks Poster Collective**
Australia 1972–1979
**Michael Callaghan**
*No God no master* 1977
screenprint, printed in colour, from three stencils
92.0 x 58.0 (printed image)
National Gallery of Australia, Canberra
Purchased 1982
82.933

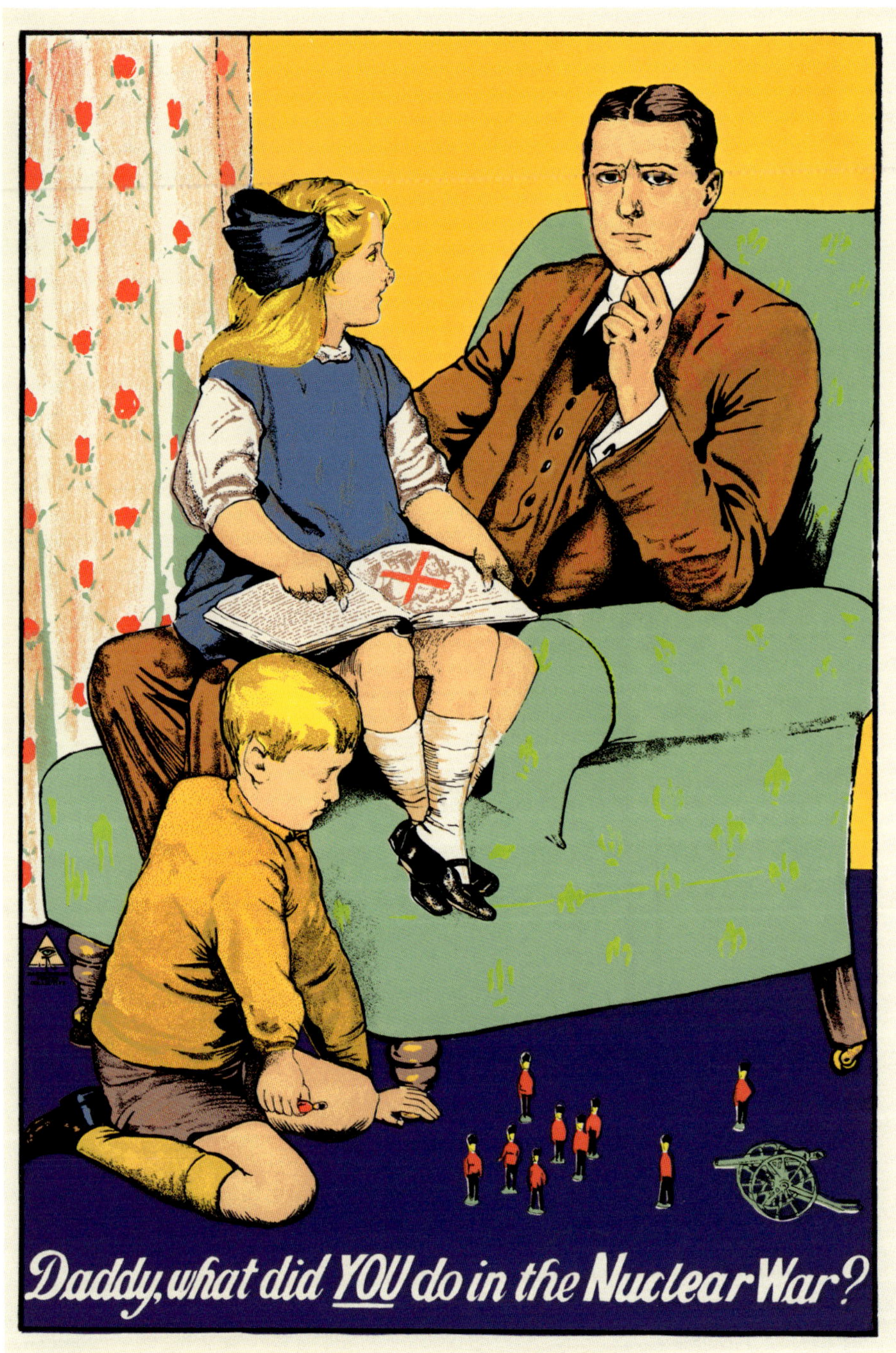
Daddy, what did YOU do in the Nuclear War?

## Earthworks for the good of the community

In 1971, Colin Little founded Earthworks Poster Company at the Tin Sheds with the help of Vicky King. Little was a first-year engineering student who had dropped out of his course to pursue an interest in alternative lifestyles and Eastern religions. The following year the facilities were expanded and it became a collective, changing its name to Earthworks Poster Collective in the process. In the early years its principal members were Little and Mitch Johnston, a fine arts student and activist, but the group grew in 1974 to include Chips Mackinolty, Mark Arbuz and Toni Robertson. Many people who used the facilities at Earthworks never officially joined the Collective. Some of the people who used the facilities had formal art training while others were self-taught. The Collective's symbol – a triangle, based on the Egyptian pyramid containing the all seeing eye – identified Earthworks posters. In accordance with the principles of the Collective, no individual credits appeared on any of the works; each member was paid equally and the work was shared among them. Printed on cheap paper, sometimes recycled cardboard or discarded computer printout paper, Earthworks posters featured strong slogans, forceful imagery and vivid colours, and were designed as immediate attention grabbers, pasted up around the city where the public would see them.

The hundreds of posters printed at Earthworks over the years gave expression to a wide range of concerns and hopes and documented the rich fabric of social and cultural life of the university and the city. Posters ranged from advertising the Art Workshop's annual Christmas party, film screenings or lectures, to raising awareness about international causes such as the cyclone-affected Dominican Republic, the need for reconstruction in Nicaragua, Indonesia's invasion of East Timor or human rights atrocities in Chile. Posters printed in response to local issues were inspired by feminist beliefs, gay and lesbian rights, anti-nuclear issues, unemployment and the environment. They reflected a passionate concern for the state of the world, coupled with a genuine belief in the ability of the individual to effect change.

Callaghan formally joined Earthworks in 1976, the same year as Marie McMahon and Jan Mackay. They were joined by Ray Young the following year and by Jan Fieldsend in 1978. All but Fieldsend would work at Redback Graphix. Speaking of his decision to join the Collective, Callaghan said:

> Around this time I was becoming increasingly disillusioned with the mainstream art world and eventually decided to reject it as an inappropriate conduit for my work. I was looking for a more politically direct means of engagement … the reason I got involved in making posters was that I wanted to use my skills in some way that I considered politically viable.[9]

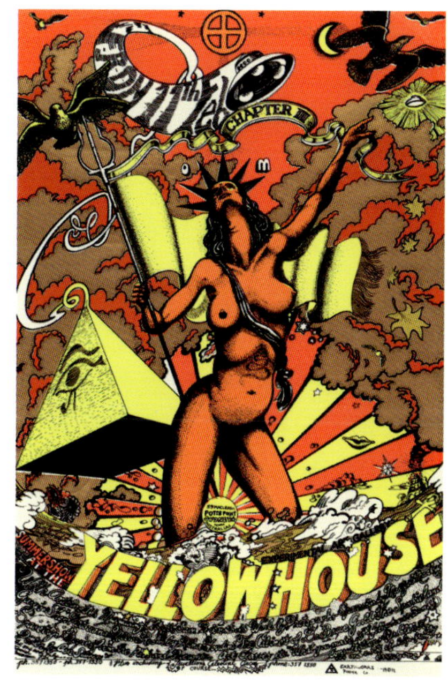


(opposite)
**Earthworks Poster Collective**
Australia 1972–1979
**Toni Robertson** born Australia 1953
**Chips Mackinolty** born Australia 1954
*Daddy what did you do in the nuclear war?* 1977
screenprint, printed in colour,
from multiple stencils
73.4 x 48.2 cm (printed image)
Given in memory of Mitch Johnson, 1988
88.549

(above)
**Earthworks Poster Collective**
Australia 1972–1979
**Asko Sutiner**
*Summer show at the Yellow House* 1972
screenprint, printed in colour,
from five stencils
75.0 x 50.3 cm (printed image)
National Gallery of Australia, Canberra
Purchased 1975
85.978

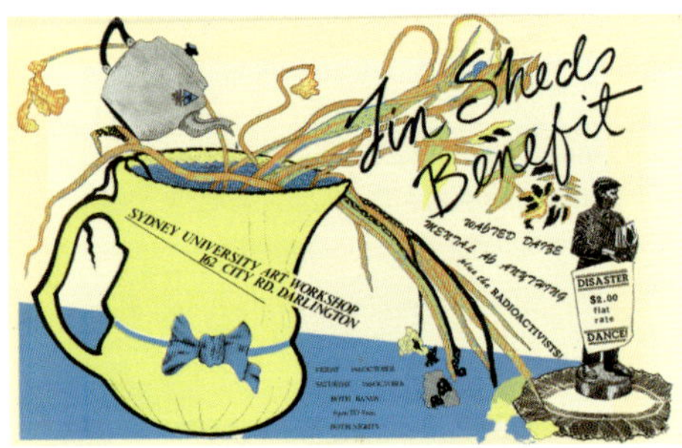


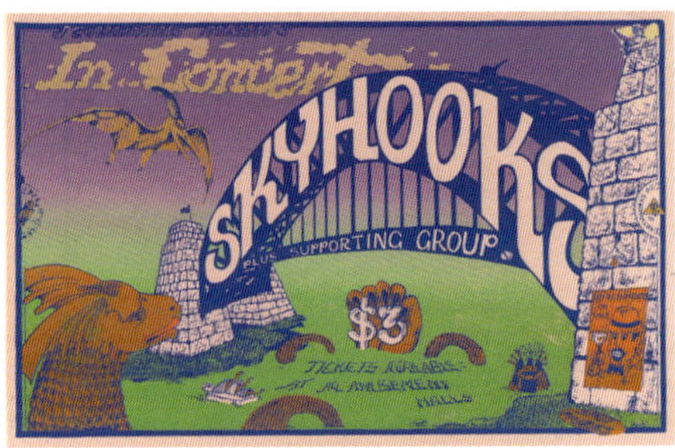


(top)
**Earthworks Poster Collective**
Australia 1972–1979
**Marie McMahon** and **Michael Callaghan**
*Tin Sheds benefit – disaster dance* 1977
screenprint, printed in colour
from five stencils
91.0 x 59.5 cm (printed image)
National Gallery of Australia, Canberra
Purchased 1982
82.992

(above)
**Earthworks Poster Collective**
Australia 1972–1979
**Mark Arbuz** born Poland 1953, Australia from 1958
*In concert – Skyhooks plus supporting group* 1975
screenprint, printed in colour,
from multiple stencils
49.0 x 76.8 cm (printed image)
National Gallery of Australia, Canberra
Purchased 1977
77.509.247

Callaghan wasn't alone. His decision to shift from a gallery practice to the streets coincided with changes in both contemporary art practice, both in Australia and overseas, and the social climate of the day. Many artists were seeking to connect with the immediate concerns of the community in a more politically direct way, and were attracted to the kinds of collaborative performance and conceptually based projects and debates happening at the Tin Sheds Art Workshops. In many respects, the political posters printed at Earthworks harnessed these two social and cultural currents. Political posters were not intended to be either precious commodities or art objects. Essentially they were pieces of ephemera, and they tapped into the shift away from an object-focused art practice. If artists sought to interrogate the social role of art, then the intense social upheaval of the late 1960s and early 1970s, a time when issues relating to the environment, gender and sexuality were being fiercely debated, provided many artists with ready subject matter.

Furthermore, Earthworks engaged with the community, not only through the message of its posters but through their process of creation. Screenprinting was by definition a communal effort, requiring several people to prepare stencils, position the paper, ink the screens and pull the squeegees and place the posters in racks to dry. This labour-intensive process was repeated two, three, sometimes up to five times depending on the number of colours used on each poster. It was not uncommon for several hundred posters to be printed. Consider the maths and you get some idea of the work involved; a poster run of 300 printed in four colours would require a squeegee to be pulled across the screen around 1200 times.

The early posters of the Earthworks Poster Collective were inspired by the psychedelic posters that emerged from Britain and San Francisco, United States, in the late 1960s. It was a style characterised by 'the deranged amalgam of brash screenprint colours, Aubrey Beardsley fantasy and typographic freakout'.[10] After the dismissal of Prime Minister Gough Whitlam in 1975, the focus on social and lifestyle issues evident in the earlier posters gave way to greater political urgency. While the early posters display a dreamy sense of whimsy, apparent in such posters as *Yellow house* 1972 and *Skyhooks* 1975, with their decorative, looping, hand-generated letterforms, the posters of the late 1970s tended to combine a single strong image with simple, striking type and represented a more forceful attitude. The posters also became technically more sophisticated. Access to better equipment improved the quality of the photostencils and increased the range of typographic options. Artists began working with photostencils, which enabled them to include photographic images from newspapers, books and magazines. This hijacking of photographic images from the mass media injected a vitality and Pop sensibility into the posters. One such poster features a close-up photograph of a policeman with protestors clashing behind him. It is screenprinted in blue and grey on a plain white background. The words 'Tomorrow's bacon', written in a child-like scrawl, hover above this scene.

Given the number of artists who printed and designed posters at Earthworks, inspiration came from diverse sources with traces of Pop art, punk, Chinese propaganda, Dada and the revolutionary graphics of the Atelier Populaire evident in many of the works. But the cutting wit common to so many Earthworks posters reflects a uniquely local vernacular, a distinctly Sydney brand of rudeness.

Earthworks prefigured not just Redback Graphix but a host of other access screenprinting workshops committed to collaborative practice around Australia. The establishment of the Whitlam Government's Community Arts Fund in 1973 enabled many alternative print media organisations to rent accommodation and purchase screenprinting equipment. Like Earthworks, some of these organisations maintained a policy of open access for untrained individuals. Others, like Redback, accepted commissioned work only. The tone and political positions adopted by the various workshops also differed between organisations. Women were particularly active in creating poster collectives around Australia. The posters produced in Adelaide by the Visual Group of the Progressive Art Movement were made by predominantly fine art trained women such as Mandy Martin, Jenny Hill and Ann Newmarch. Their posters reflected a strong feminist perspective. Comparing these posters to those from Earthworks, curator Julie Ewington described them as 'rarely light-hearted'.[11] In Brisbane – where protest rallies had become illegal in 1976 – a screenprinting facility at the University of Queensland, called Union Activities, produced numerous political posters on the pressing subject of civil liberties.

After almost ten years of poster-making and activism, Earthworks was disbanded in late 1979. A number of factors led to this decision – an application for funding was rejected and an increase in the number of screenprinting classes on offer had placed greater strain on members and equipment. However, the main problem was that the collective members were exhausted and, in some cases, ill. The dangers of working with petroleum-based inks were becoming increasingly apparent and those not made ill from the poisonous fumes were worn out from the accumulative affects of years of high adrenaline, drinking and drug-taking. Callaghan, who was one of the first to leave, said:

> We had no money and in some cases no homes ... You can't spend all your time helping others do things, maintain a workshop, do your own poster work and not become completely drained. Especially when you are living hand-to-mouth, which most of us were.[12]

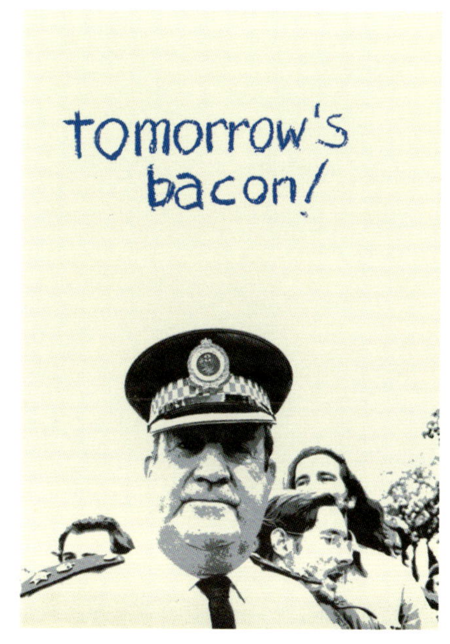


**Earthworks Poster Collective**
Australia 1972–1979
**Chips Mackinolty** born Australia 1954
*Tomorrow's bacon!* 1976
screenprint, printed in colour,
from two stencils
73.6 x 49.4 cm (printed image)
National Gallery of Australia, Canberra
Purchased 1977
77.509.256

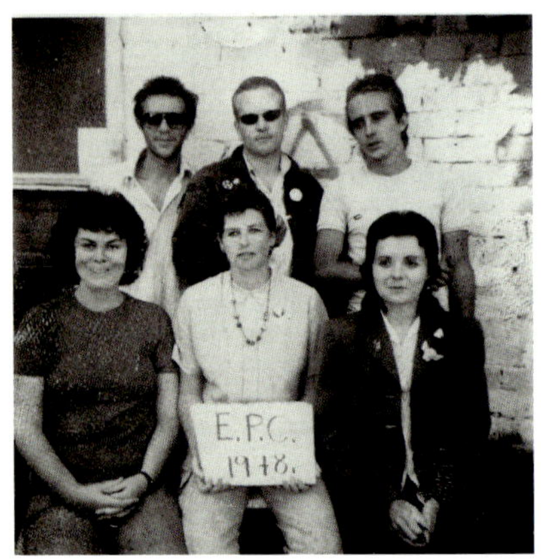


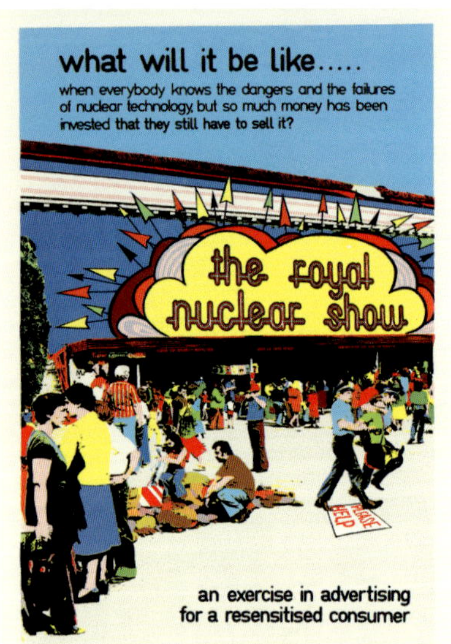


(above)
Earthworks Poster Collective 1978
(front row left to right)
Toni Robertson, Jan Mackay, Marie McMahon
(back row left to right)
Ray Young, Michael Callaghan, Chips Mackinolty

**Toni Robertson**
born Australia 1953 (designer)
*The royal nuclear show* [1] 1981
screenprint, printed in colour,
from multiple stencils
77.4 x 51.7 cm (printed image)
National Gallery of Australia, Canberra
Purchased 1982
82.1803.1

Posters continued to be produced at the Sheds after Earthworks folded, first under the name Lucifoil Poster Collective and then Tin Shed Posters, but most of the original members of the Collective dispersed around Australia to set up workshops or join existing ones. 'The poster movement', Julia Church has noted, 'was fed by intense cross-fertilization as people moved from one print workshop to another'.[13] Mackinolty formed Jalak Graphics in Katherine, Northern Territory, and later Green Ant Graphix, Robertson established Déjà Vu in Canberra; and Arbuz joined Little and Alison Alder at Megalo in Canberra. Alder and Leonie Lane from Lucifoil would join Redback Graphix some years later and become Callaghan's partners in the business once the studio moved to Sydney. McMahon and Mackay stayed in Sydney to establish 99 Designs and later Social Fabric. Young moved to Bathurst Island to print posters and fabrics for Indigenous Australian communities. Further south, in Melbourne, screenprinting groups like Another Planet and Redletter Community Workshop Posters continued to be influenced by Earthworks.[14]

From today's perspective the posters of the Earthworks Poster Collective are striking for their sheer tactility; the aesthetics of activism have changed today to accommodate the dimensions and TV-like quality of a computer screen. Web-based information or electronic documents are just as likely to announce events as printed posters. Nowadays many of the slogans from the 1970s sound naively optimistic in tone. Along with a changing world, the rhetoric of activism has altered its form.

During the 1970s, posters were predominantly pasted up around the streets to advertise rallies and protests, while leftovers were also occasionally sold for a small sum through the Collective, at select bookshops and events. The proceeds of these sales would go towards covering the cost of materials and labour. However, as the number of public protests and demonstrations petered out, posters were increasingly produced to enlighten people about domestic or workplace concerns. Speaking on the closure of Earthworks, Jan Fieldsend said, 'The need for alternative information lessened'. She noted that many of the issues raised by Earthworks posters were being addressed by the mainstream press and through government policies.

Furthermore, over the course of the decade the artists had become experts in screenprinting and were now experimenting with different techniques and increasing the number of colours used. The posters became desirable artistic entities in their own right. Unsurprisingly, people held onto them and put them up on their kitchen and living room walls. Sensing the winds of change, and in response to the cultural and social changes taking place, Redback opened its doors for business.

With the shift of posters from the outside to the inside, the poster's primary function – to provoke and persuade – inevitably shifted as well. Instead of attempting to alter existing conservative attitudes, the political poster at home expressed a belief held and a stance taken by the poster's owner. Ewington cautioned against this in 1977, when she wrote that by being displayed in homes, political posters faced a problem of 'preaching to the converted'.[15] As both agents of political action and objects of aesthetic value, screenprinted posters generated intractable questions about the significance of function and context.

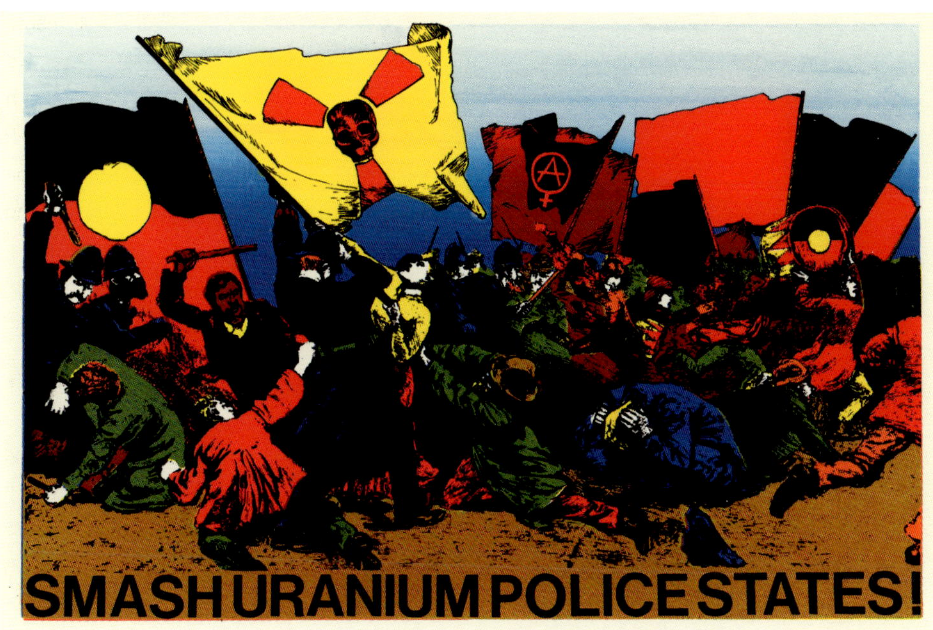


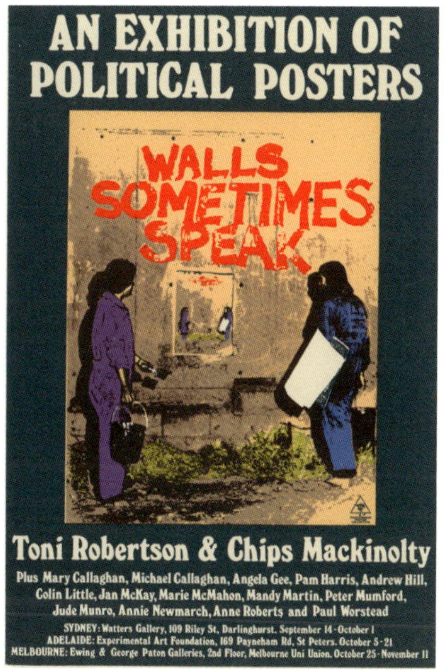


In 1977, Toni Robertson and Chips Mackinolty pushed posters into a new context of the commercial gallery with an exhibition titled *Walls sometimes speak*, which was hosted by Watters Gallery in Sydney and subsequently toured to other venues around the country. It featured screenprinted posters produced by members of Earthworks and those working in collectives in Melbourne and Adelaide. The exhibition was a great success, practically selling out before its national tour. But a piece of graffiti painted on a wall next to the gallery – 'Posters for the streets not art gallery walls' – expressed the ambivalence, if not outright hostility, felt by some. The success of the show left many of the participants with mixed feelings. On the one hand it was recognition of the work of the collective; on the other hand, it could be constructed as a sell-out. As Mackinolty said of the exhibition:

> Posters are meant for the streets. They're ephemeral things. They'll probably fall apart in ten years time. Yet at Watters, dark suited businessmen were coming in and buying them as investments. That's a complete contradiction.[16]

The following year, Callaghan and Arbuz were entrusted with archiving Earthworks posters and organising sales to institutions such as the National Gallery of Australia and the State Library of New South Wales. They devised a tiered payment system whereby institutions paid the highest price, thus providing a much needed source of income for the Collective. Though never originally intended for galleries, political posters from collectives around Australia were beginning to find their way into many state and national gallery collections. Those working in poster collectives may have rejected galleries as elitist, but in the long term for many of those committed to a screenprinting-based arts practice, the relationship with public galleries was to develop into an important one.

(left)
**Earthworks Poster Collective**
Australia 1972–1979
**Michael Callaghan**
*Smash uranium police states* c. 1978
screenprint, printed in colour, from multiple stencils
48.4 x 72.4 cm (printed image)
National Gallery of Australia, Canberra
Purchased 1982
82.986

(above)
**Earthworks Poster Collective**
Australia 1972–1979
**Toni Robertson** born Australia 1953
**Chips Mackinolty** born Australia 1954
*Walls sometimes speak* 1977
screenprint, printed in colour, from multiple stencils
72.8 x 47.8 cm (printed image)
Given in memory of Mitch Johnson, 1988
88.550

**Help! Joh!**

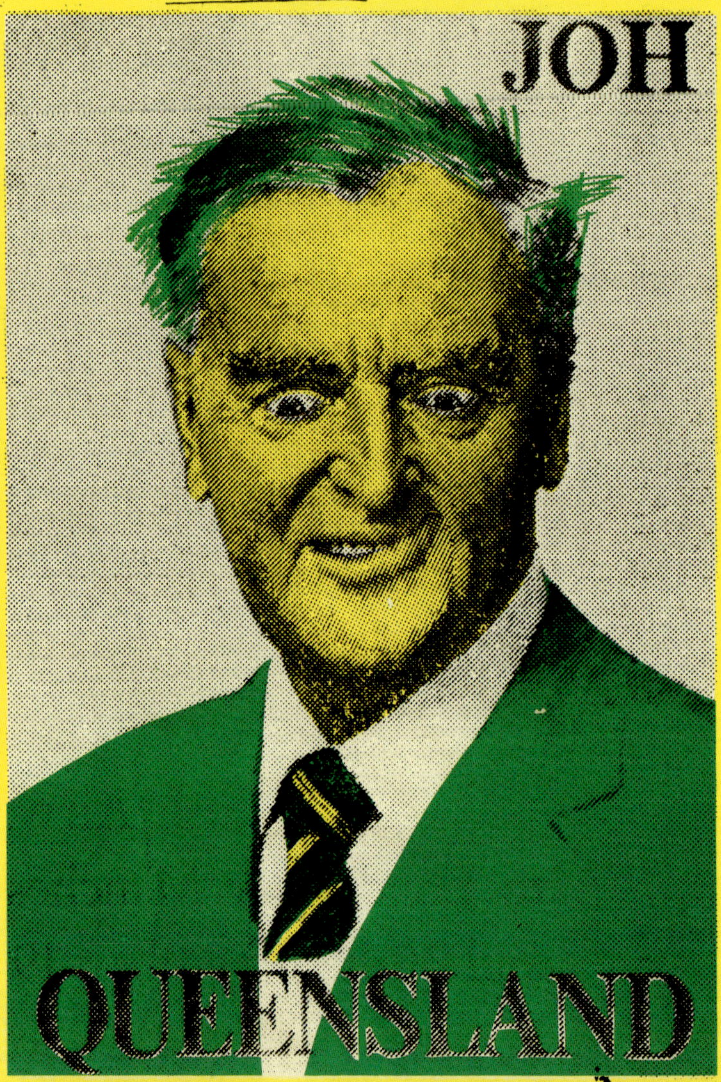


**Queensland is the greatest country on Earth. Joh helped make it that way. Now he needs your help to defend his honour.**

**For just $15 including packing and posting, you can own a brilliant 4 colour copy of the original 1983 Joh Campaign Poster. Size is 90cms × 60cms on top quality art paper ideal for framing or putting on the wall. Order yours now!**

## Brisbane

In 1974 C.F. Preseley, the founding professor of humanities at Griffith University, Queensland, visited the Tin Sheds Art Workshop on a reconnaissance mission. He planned to establish a film and drama centre at the university modelled on the Sheds.[17] It was envisaged that screenprinted posters would be a vital component of the centre. Margriet Bonnin was appointed coordinator of the Queensland Film and Drama Centre at Griffith University in 1978 and approached several Earthworks members with the offer of a paid six-month-long residency in Brisbane to help establish screenprinting facilities. Callaghan accepted the offer.

Once in Brisbane, Callaghan outfitted the new screenprinting facilities and taught students the fundamentals of screenprinting posters. Two of Callaghan's students at Griffith University, Lyn Finch and Cherie Bradshaw, later formed their own screenprinting workshop, Mantis Prints, which produced commissioned work for the Queensland trade unions on issues such as sexual harassment and health. Despite a lack of financial support, a further two political poster workshops formed in the 1980s. Graduates of Queensland College of Art formed The Black Banana collective in 1986 and Inkahoots in 1990. These organisations produced commissioned work for a range of socially concerned organisations and government departments such as the Queensland Conservation Council.[18]

In Brisbane, Callaghan was being paid a weekly wage for the first time:

> I just thought we should actually do something … about setting up a kind of workshop that did the same sort of stuff politically that was going on at the Sheds, but instituted a different culture, where you actually got paid … to develop an alternative style advertising agency for the left.[19]

Callaghan's idea – to create an advertising agency for the left – represented a significant shift away from the structure and practices of the Earthworks Poster Collective. Earthworks, along with other poster workshops, had instituted a policy of open access, which Lee-Anne Hall described as 'the practical expression of a political commitment to a democratic and participative culture'.[20] By the 1980s, however, direct participation had dwindled for a number of reasons – educational institutions had begun to offer short courses in screenprinting; petroleum-based inks had increased in price, making it an expensive option for unsubsidised users; and managing open access and maintaining the condition of facilities had become increasingly difficult. Keeping printing prices low put the workshops in a bind. While it ensured under-resourced community groups could utilise their services, the screenprinting workshops themselves remained chronically under-resourced.[21]

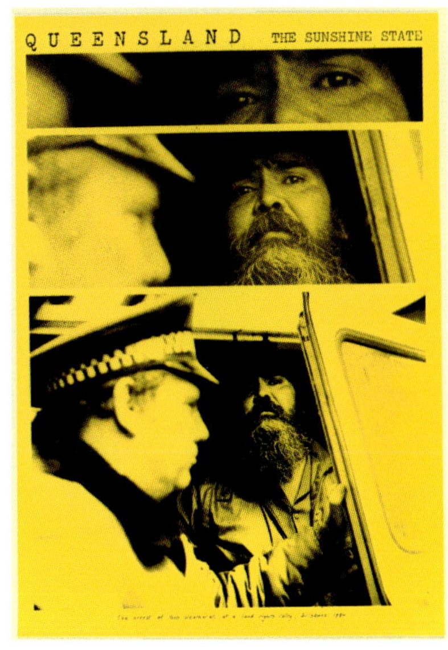


(opposite)
**Inkahoots**
Australia 1990–1993
*Help! Joh!* Newstead, Queensland 1991
screenprint, printed in colour, from three stencils
90.0 x 48.0 cm (printed image)
National Gallery of Australia, Canberra
Purchased 1993
93.587

(above)
**Black Banana Posters**
Australia 1986–1988
*Queensland – the sunshine state* Brisbane 1988
screenprint, printed in colour, from two stencils
84.1 x 57.8 cm (printed image)
The Roger Butler Fund, 1989
89.1648

Q. If the unemployed are dole bludgers,
What the fuck are the idle rich?

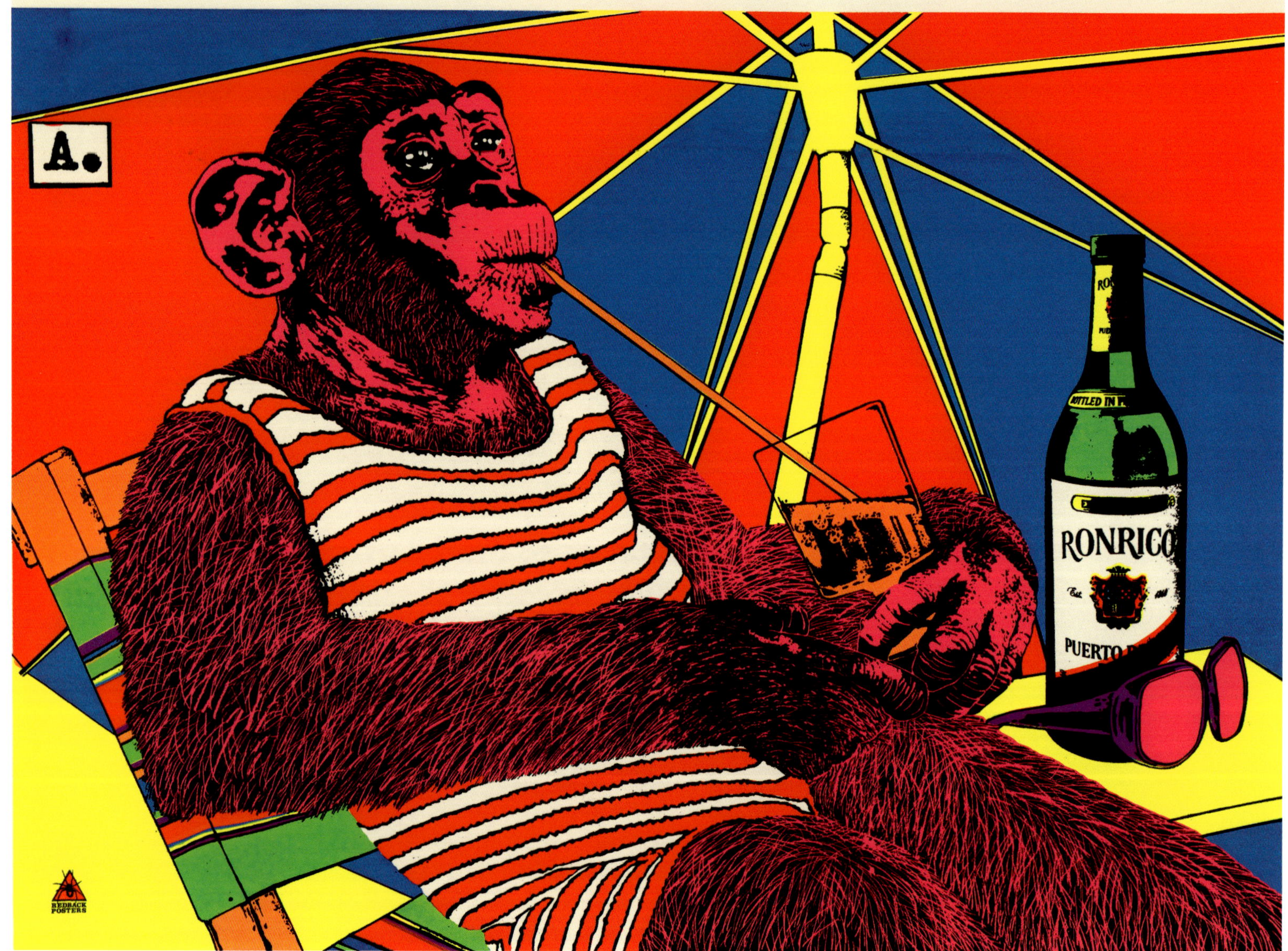

## Redback Posters

Callaghan initially named his 'advertising agency for the left' Redback Posters, and sometimes used the name 'Redblack Posters'. Its logo of a redback spider contained in a triangle with the words 'Redback Posters' written underneath echoed the triangular form of the Earthworks Posters Collective logo (in fact, several ex-Earthworks members incorporated the triangle in their new workshop logos from Mackinolty's Green Ant to Robertson's Déjà Vu) and referenced the design and colours of the anarchist's flag.

The first Redback poster printed by Callaghan was based on a genre of photographic posters popular at the time that used dressed chimpanzees arranged in human poses. Callaghan's spoof posed the rhetorical question, 'If the unemployed are dole bludgers, What the fuck are the idle rich?'. The idle rich were represented by a reclining chimp in a striped swimsuit, sipping a cocktail under a beach umbrella. Screenprinted in bright fluorescent colours, the poster was a sharp, stinging attack on society's hypocritical attitudes towards the wealthy and poor.

Callaghan produced a further three posters in Brisbane – *Onward Christian soldiers* 1979 (in collaboration with two students from a local Catholic girls high school), *What now, Mr Mao, dance?* 1979, commissioned by the Griffith University Student Union to promote a dance; *Prostitution is the rental of the body*, designed with Cherie Bradshaw and printed with Lynette Finch – and a set of fundraising postcards for the film *Greetings from Wollongong* 1982. Callaghan's disdain for the Catholic church is especially evident in *Onward Christian soldiers* and shared the sentiments of an earlier poster produced by Callaghan while still at Earthworks, *No God no master* 1977. A loose, energetic collage of photographs and paragraphs sourced primarily from the *Catholic Weekly*, *Onward Christian soldiers* depicts a group of smiling nuns as the Pope's 'Christian soldiers'. The poster's lurid colours give the nuns a maniacal quality. A combination of decorative serif and ransom note typography frames the central image of the Pope, who has his arms outstretched. In a catalogue essay on political posters, curator Clare Williamson notes Dada influences in Brisbane's punk subculture, particularly in the use of ransom-note style lettering,[22] which was popular in posters produced in Brisbane and Sydney workshops.

It became increasingly difficult for Redback to produce subversive posters once the pressures of running a self-sufficient business began to mount. The studio moved away from the openly critical stance of posters like *Onward Christian soldiers* towards a more affirmative approach.

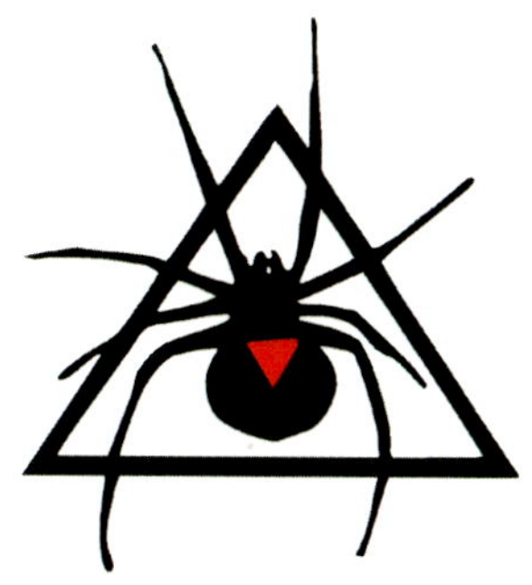

(opposite)
**Michael Callaghan** (designer and printer)
*If the unemployed are dole bludgers, what the fuck are the idle rich?* 1979

(above)
**Redback logo**

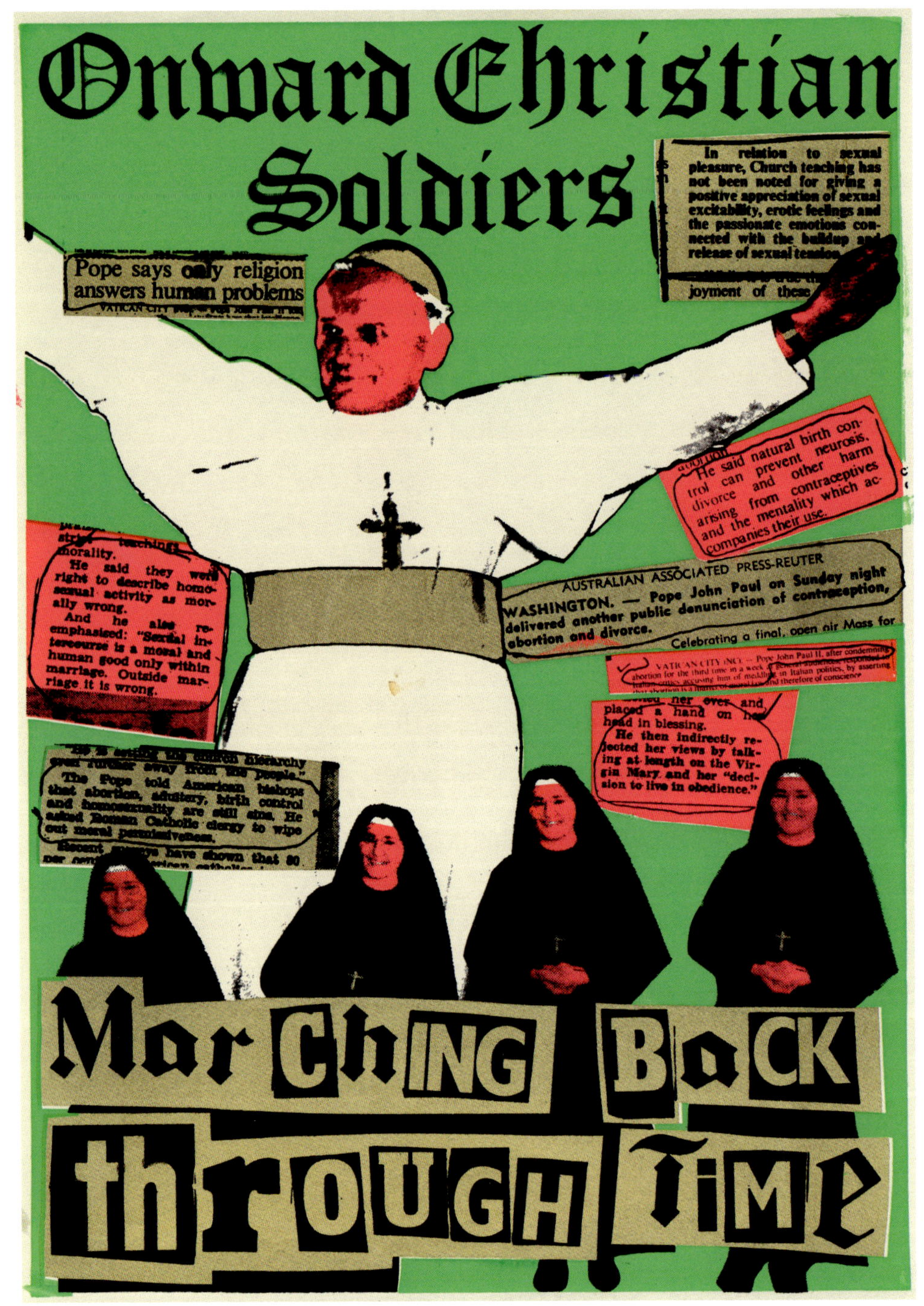

Onward Christian Soldiers
Pope says only religion answers human problems
In relation to sexual pleasure, Church teaching has not been noted for giving a positive appreciation of sexual excitability, erotic feelings and the passionate emotions connected with the buildup and release of sexual tension
joyment of these
He said natural birth control can prevent neurosis, divorce and other harm arising from contraceptives and the mentality which accompanies their use.
morality.
He said they were right to describe homosexual activity as morally wrong.
And he also emphasised: "Sexual intercourse is a moral and human good only within marriage. Outside marriage it is wrong.
AUSTRALIAN ASSOCIATED PRESS-REUTER
WASHINGTON. — Pope John Paul on Sunday night delivered another public denunciation of contraception, abortion and divorce.
Celebrating a final, open air Mass for
placed a hand on her head in blessing.
He then indirectly rejected her views by talking at length on the Virgin Mary and her "decision to live in obedience."
The Pope told American bishops that abortion, adultery, birth control and homosexuality are still sins. He asked Roman Catholic clergy to wipe out moral permissiveness.
MarChiNG BaCK throUGH TiMe

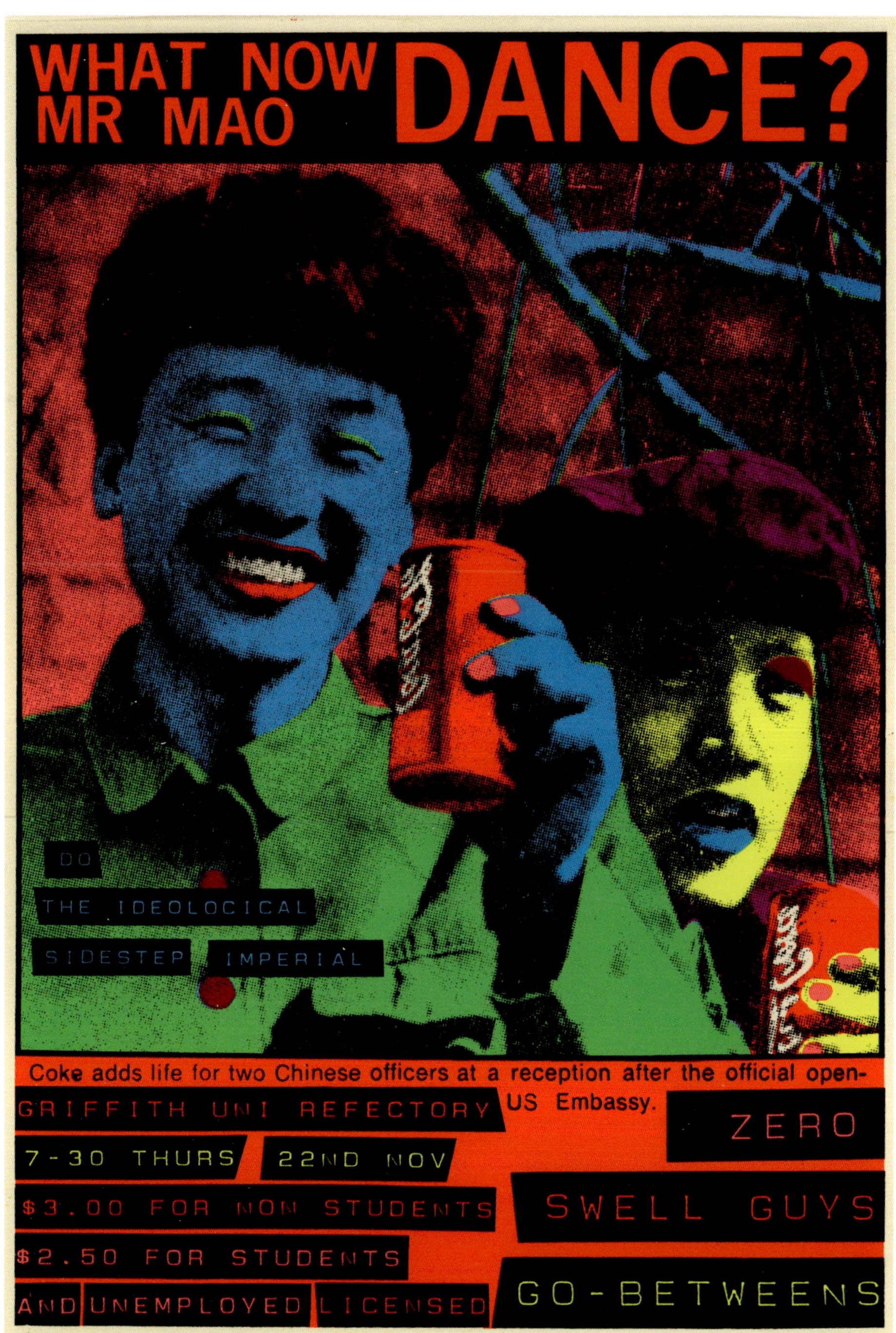


(opposite)
**Michael Callaghan and others** (designers and printers)
*Onward Christian soldiers* 1979

**Michael Callaghan** (designer and printer)
*What now, Mr Mao, dance?* 1979

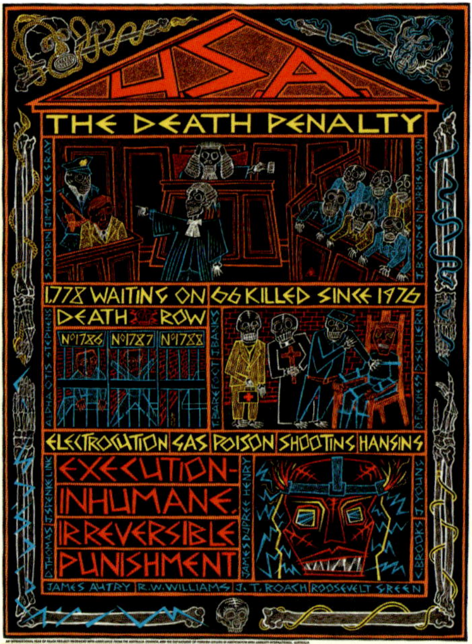


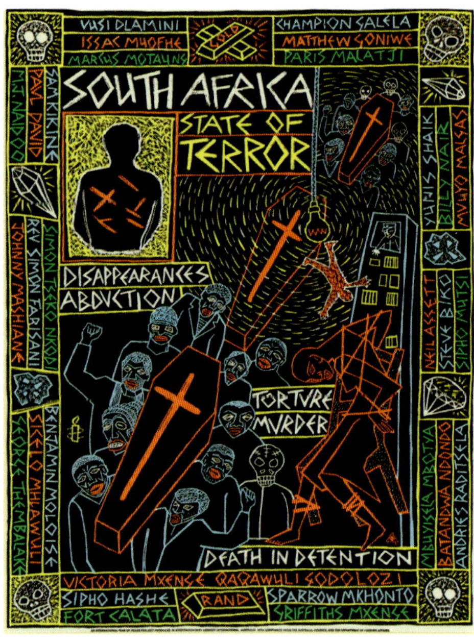


Inevitably, the radicalism that underpinned Redback's early posters diminished, but to operate a successful business for fifteen years required constant reinvention. Over time, Redback may have tempered some of its strident anger but it lost none of its compassion. In place of designing self-generated posters that were strongly oppositional, Redback sought out clients who reflected their personal views and who shared their concerns.

A series of four posters made by Redback Graphix between 1986 and 1987 to highlight human rights abuses are a case in point. Callaghan approached the Australia Council with a proposal to design and print a series of four posters for Amnesty International on the occasion of the International Year of Peace. The Australia Council awarded Redback a grant to cover the costs of materials and labour to print an edition of 500 posters from its special programs fund. Redback liaised with Amnesty International in order to formulate the subject matter for each poster. The subsequent posters – *Death penalty USA* 1988, *Amnesty / South Africa* 1986, *Chile demands justice* 1987 and *25 years Amnesty International* 1987 – were all tied in to Amnesty's forthcoming campaigns. Redback's posters for Amnesty typified the studio's initiative. It demonstrated their ability to work collaboratively with other like-minded institutions, to generate projects and also reflected Redback's negotiating skills with state funding bodies and non-profit organisations.

(above)
**Michael Callaghan** (designer)
**Alison Alder** (printer)
*Death penalty USA* 1988

(above right)
**Michael Callaghan** (designer)
**Peter Curtis** (printer)
*Amnesty / South Africa* 1986

(opposite)
**Michael Callaghan** (designer and printer)
**Alison Alder** (printer)
*Chile demands justice* 1987

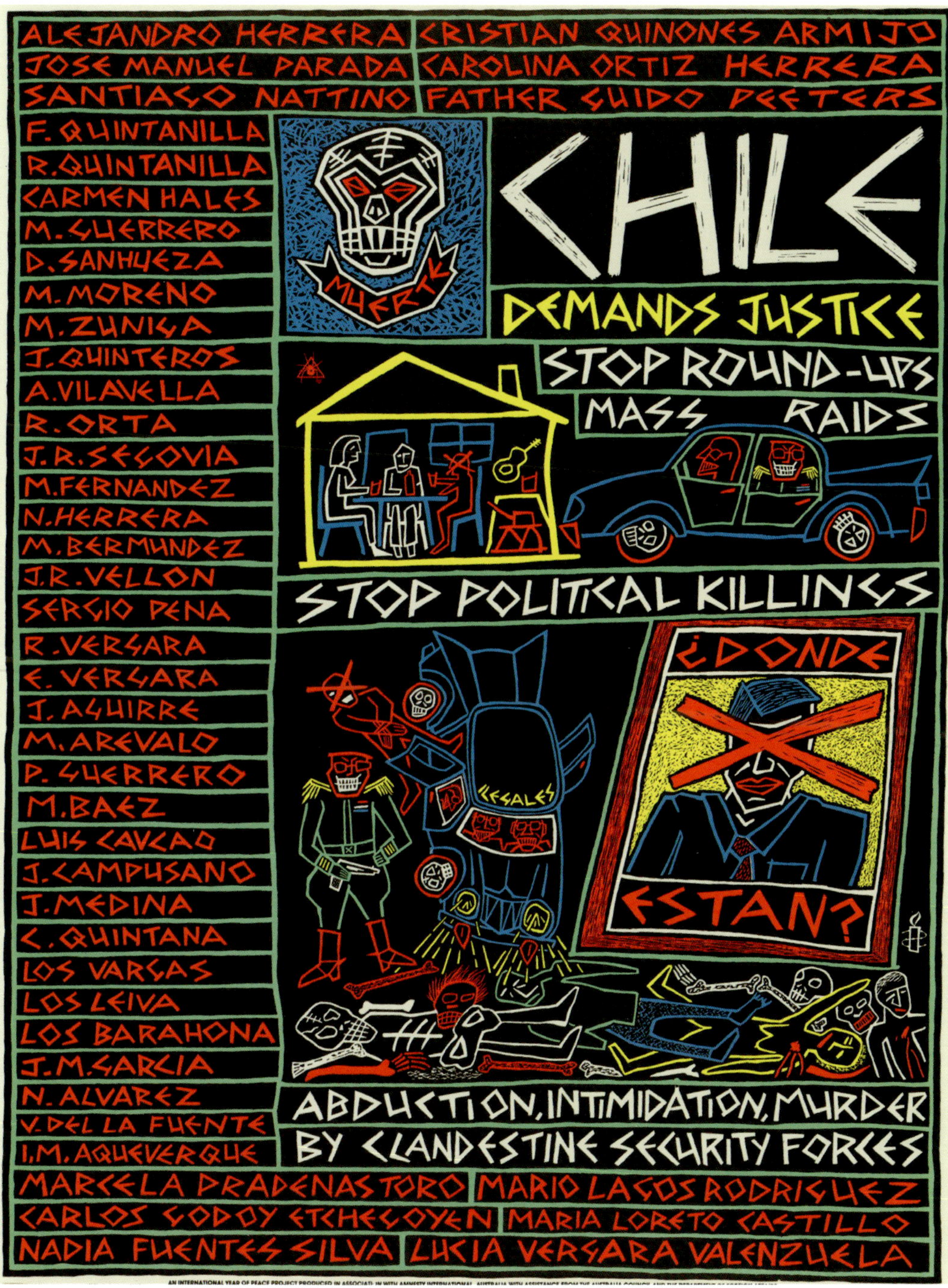
ALEJANDRO HERRERA
CRISTIAN QUINONES ARMIJO
JOSE MANUEL PARADA
CAROLINA ORTIZ HERRERA
SANTIAGO NATTINO
FATHER GUIDO PEETERS
F. QUINTANILLA
R. QUINTANILLA
CARMEN HALES
M. GUERRERO
D. SANHUEZA
M. MORENO
M. ZUNIGA
J. QUINTEROS
A. VILAVELLA
R. ORTA
J. R. SEGOVIA
M. FERNANDEZ
N. HERRERA
M. BERMUNDEZ
J. R. VELLON
SERGIO PENA
R. VERGARA
E. VERGARA
J. AGUIRRE
M. AREVALO
P. GUERRERO
M. BAEZ
LUIS CAVCAO
J. CAMPUSANO
J. MEDINA
C. QUINTANA
LOS VARGAS
LOS LEIVA
LOS BARAHONA
J. M. GARCIA
N. ALVAREZ
V. DEL LA FUENTE
I. M. AQUEVERQUE
MUERTE
CHILE
DEMANDS JUSTICE
STOP ROUND-UPS
MASS RAIDS
STOP POLITICAL KILLINGS
¿DONDE
ESTAN?
LEGALES
ABDUCTION, INTIMIDATION, MURDER
BY CLANDESTINE SECURITY FORCES
MARCELA DRADENAS TORO
MARIO LAGOS RODRIGUEZ
CARLOS GODOY ETCHEGOYEN
MARIA LORETO CASTILLO
NADIA FUENTES SILVA
LUCIA VERGARA VALENZUELA
AN INTERNATIONAL YEAR OF PEACE PROJECT PRODUCED IN ASSOCIATI IN WITH AMNESTY INTERNATIONAL

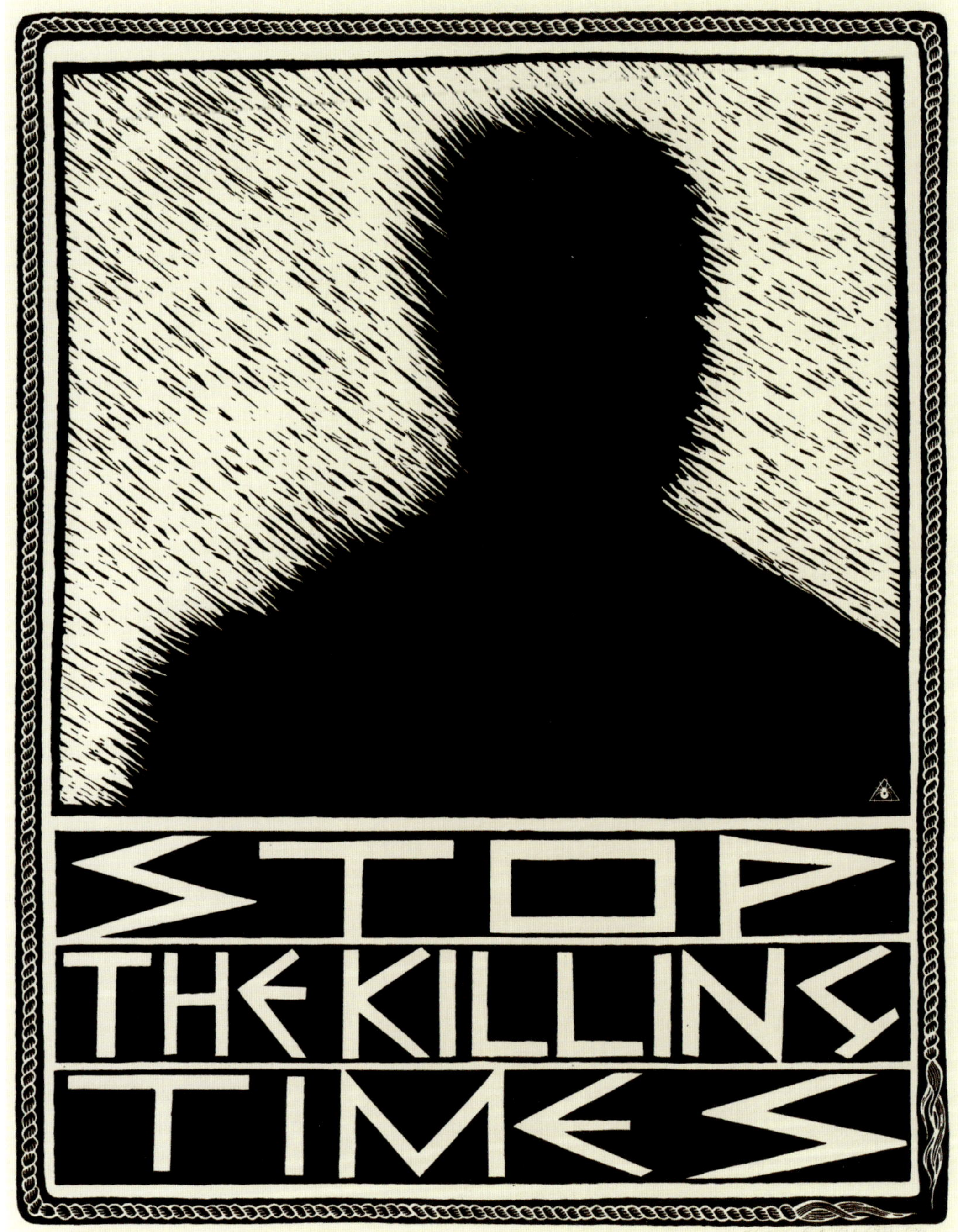
STOP
THE KILLING
TIMES

The final posters represent a remarkable and coherent body of work. Colour is reduced to its most basic symbolic properties, a powerful combination of red, black and white (except in the celebratory poster for Amnesty Anniversary which shimmers with the addition of metallic bronze, mint and blue). The *Chile*, *South Africa* and *USA* posters all feature scenes executed with simplified line work and utilise a vocabulary of simplified graphic symbols – skulls, bones, faces overlaid with a red cross, diamonds, coffins, and crucifixes. Callaghan's affinity with the work of Mexican artist José Guadalupe Posada (1851–1931) is evident in these posters, both in iconography and style. Callaghan produced the artwork for the posters using a scraperboard – a chalkboard covered with a matt black coating. The plainness of this medium suited the unadorned message of the posters themselves. Callaghan exploits the scraperboard's graphic potential by rendering the posters in simplified shapes and straight lines. The angularity of the composition is further emphasised through containment of individual words or phrases by linear rectangles.

The sense of agitated urgency is further developed through the style of illustration. Grieving faces are cross-hatched for effect in the Chile poster, while the background in the portraits of the *25 years Amnesty* poster – swirls of short, dense lines – vibrate with motion. Callaghan employs a deliberately naive illustrative style in *Chile*, *South Africa* and *USA*. The compositions are rendered in flattened out perspective to vivid effect, so that the horrifying details – mangled bodies of a crashed car, a coffin suspended upside down in a funereal procession – are tipped into full, chaotic view. In scale and paper quality, the Amnesty posters are radically different from the earlier screenprinted posters that sought to raise awareness of social and political situations around the world.

(opposite)
**Michael Callaghan** (designer)
**Peter Curtis** (printer)
*Stop the killing times* 1988

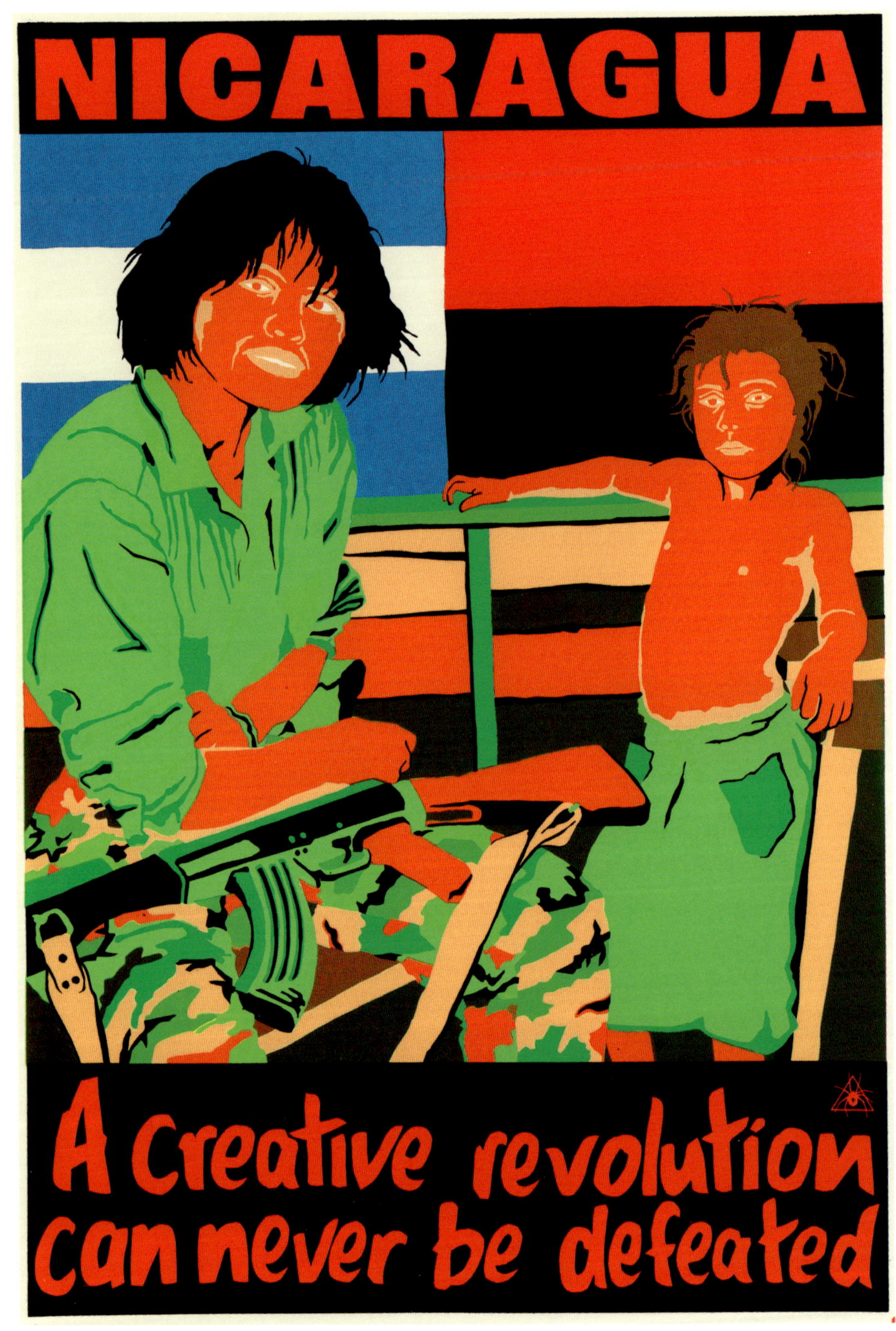
NICARAGUA
A creative revolution
can never be defeated

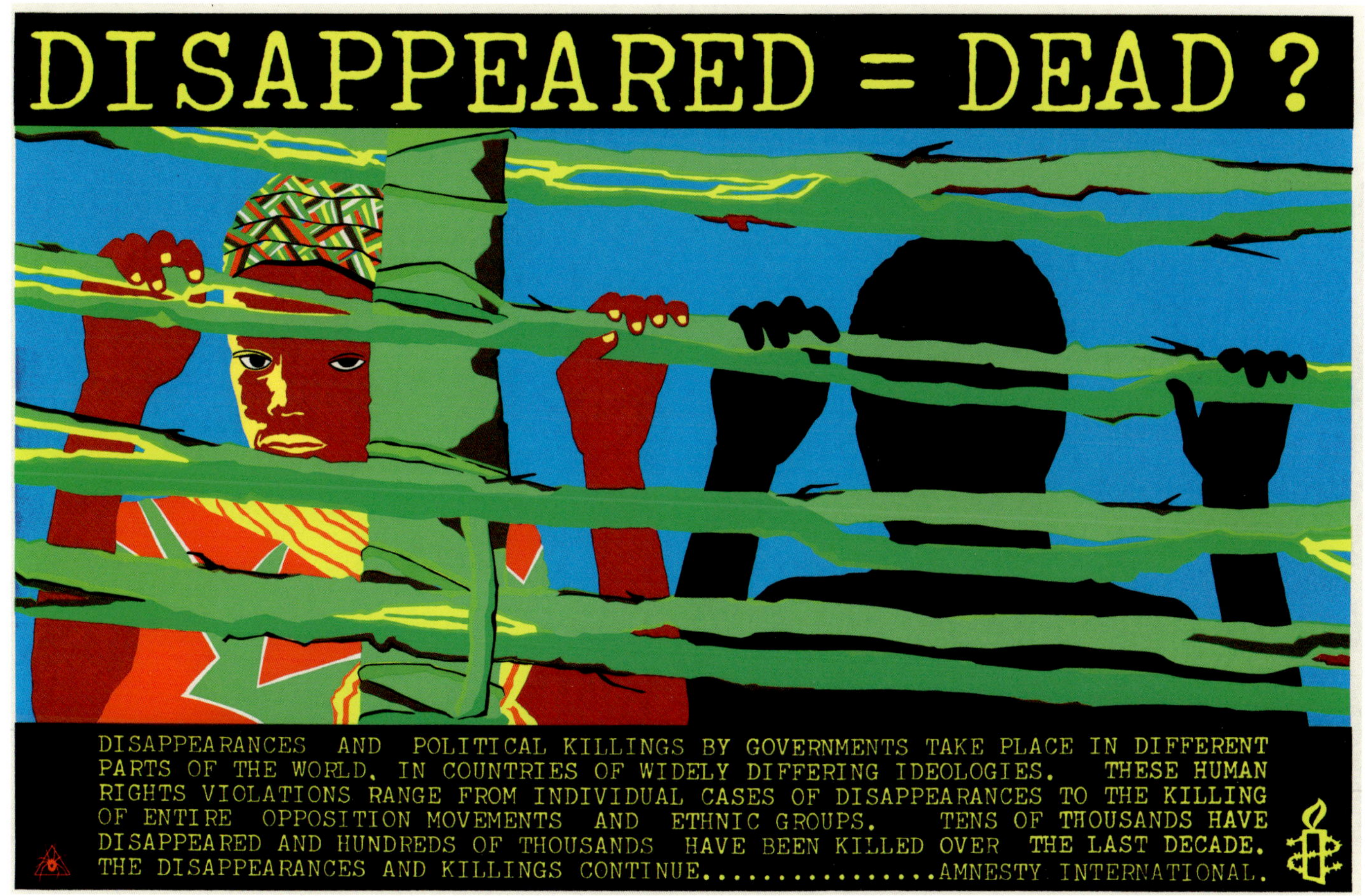


(opposite)
**Michael Callaghan** (designer and printer)
**Gregor Cullen** (designer and printer)
*Nicaragua* 1984

(above)
**Michael Callaghan** (designer and printer)
**Gregor Cullen** (designer and printer)
*Disappeared=Dead* 1983

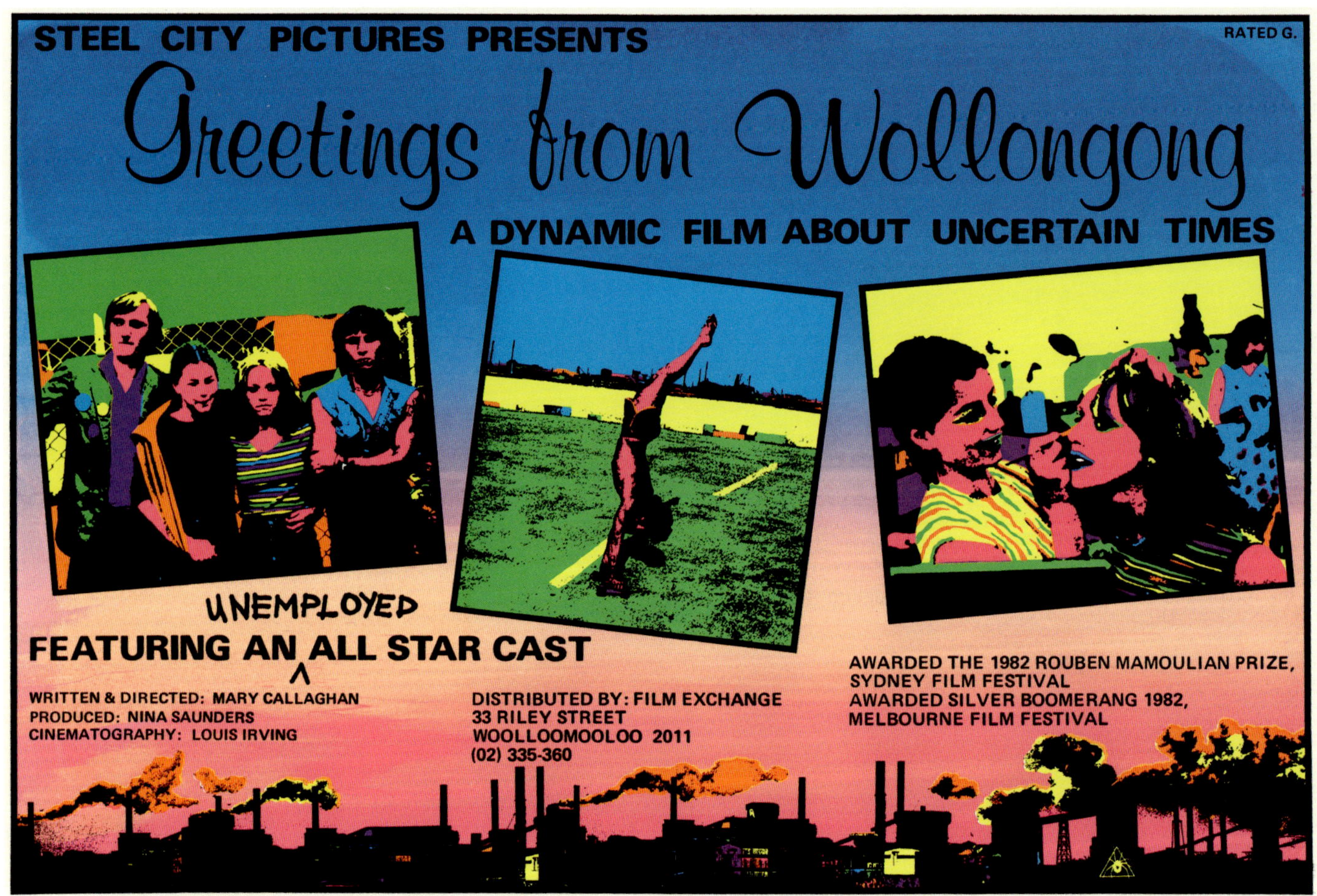

STEEL CITY PICTURES PRESENTS
RATED G.
Greetings from Wollongong
A DYNAMIC FILM ABOUT UNCERTAIN TIMES
UNEMPLOYED
FEATURING AN ALL STAR CAST
WRITTEN & DIRECTED: MARY CALLAGHAN
PRODUCED: NINA SAUNDERS
CINEMATOGRAPHY: LOUIS IRVING
DISTRIBUTED BY: FILM EXCHANGE
33 RILEY STREET
WOOLLOOMOOLOO 2011
(02) 335-360
AWARDED THE 1982 ROUBEN MAMOULIAN PRIZE,
SYDNEY FILM FESTIVAL
AWARDED SILVER BOOMERANG 1982,
MELBOURNE FILM FESTIVAL

## Greetings from Wollongong

In 1980 Callaghan's sister Mary persuaded Michael to leave Brisbane and return to their home town, the industrial city of Wollongong, to produce and art direct her short feature film, *Greetings from Wollongong* 1982.[23] Mary Callaghan, who wrote and directed the 42-minute film, shared her brother's strong social conscience. *Greetings from Wollongong* specifically addressed youth unemployment in the city. It was one of the first films to confront the social problems facing the Illawarra region. A few years later another film *Kemira* (Tom Zubrycki, 1984) and a book, *Steel City blues* (Julianne Schultz, 1985) explored similar issues.

The film's ironic title evokes a picture-perfect postcard destination, but Mary Callaghan subtly reveals the dark underbelly of the regional town. Loosely woven vignettes document the experiences of a small group of friends as they move through the city in one twenty-four-hour period in search of work and distractions. The film opens with a slow pan across Wollongong's horizon and then cuts to an aerial perspective of the flickering lights of the city. The camera circles a tall smokestack, revealing the city, harbour and surrounding suburbs below. *Greetings from Wollongong* closes with the same view of the city's horizon, simultaneously underscoring the importance of heavy industry in the region and the film's circular narrative structure.

This final evocative image of the skyline appears in Michael Callaghan's poster for the film. Along the bottom of the poster, Wollongong's billowing smokestacks and machinery rise up against a fluorescent pink sky. The pink background gradually darkens to a deep blue. On this background, the title of the film is rendered in cursive script, evoking holiday postcards. Three photographic 'snapshots' from the film – the group leaning against a fence, two girls applying make-up, a boy executing a skateboard trick – are loosely arranged below the title. Subverting the convention of many Hollywood films, the poster proclaims 'FEATURING AN ALL STAR CAST' with the word 'unemployed' inserted in a scrawl. Callaghan's film poster spoke directly to the themes of *Greetings from Wollongong*. In a catalogue essay, curator Charles Merewether wrote of this poster:

> With a clear sense of what life at the age of seventeen might mean, the images picked up on the language of this sub-culture; the world of television, clothes, dances, drinking, smoking, beat-up cars and hanging out. Gone were the text book slogans or heavy moral seriousness of the collective 'we', and no longer was design or colour subjected to a ruthless moral and ideological evaluation where black and red was o.k. 'sound' and yellow, blue or pink was 'just not on'.[24]

(opposite)
**Michael Callaghan** (designer and printer)
**Nick Southall** (printer's assistant)
*Greetings from Wollongong* 1982

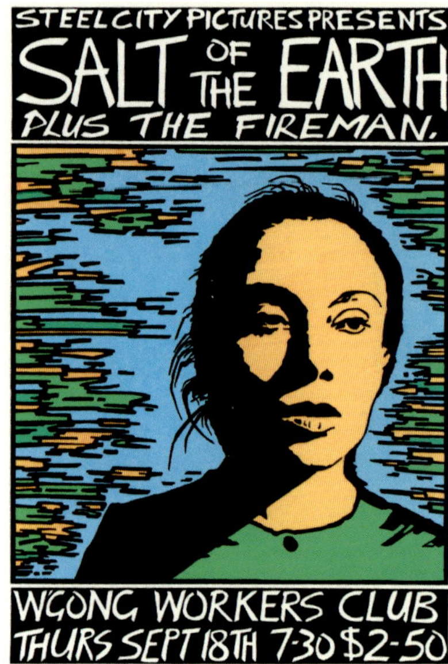


While working on the film, Michael Callaghan met Gregor Cullen. Cullen was running screenprinting workshops at the Worker's Co-op, attended by Mary Callaghan, and while Michael Callaghan and Cullen hadn't met previously, they knew of each other through shared screenprinting circles in Sydney.

By the late 1970s, Cullen had completed a degree in visual arts, majoring in painting and printmaking at the Alexander Mackie School of Art in Sydney, followed by a Diploma of Education at Sydney Teachers College. Throughout his studies he had been coming home on the weekends and working at the steelworks during the holidays. Travelling between these two very different cities prompted reflections on his art practice. Under the influence of Karl Marx's writings, Cullen began to ask questions like 'Why should I continue to belong to a practice that was gallery oriented, when … everything that surrounded me represented another life, a life of disadvantage?'[25] Michael Callaghan said of his decision to return to the city: 'It was a place that really needed some work; it was in a pretty serious crisis at the time and there was a lot of political activity going on.[26]

The two applied for funding to establish a screenprinting workshop in Wollongong, submitting a number of early Redback posters, including *Salt of the Earth* 1980 and *With babes & banners* 1980, which were designed to promote local issues and events but were printed in Sydney using the Sheds' facilities. They received an initial sum of around $24 000, which was acquired through various grants from both state and federal government arts funding agencies. The final amount was one of the largest awarded to an arts project in the Illawarra region. This sum was to support two full-time wages for one year, as well as finance the acquisition of equipment. The grants needed to be administered by an auspice organisation, so Callaghan and Cullen were consequently employed under an artists-in-residence program by the South Coast Labour Council. The agreement was that they would provide a graphic arts service for the union movement and various ethnic and community groups.

(above)
**Michael Callaghan** (designer and printer)
*Salt of the Earth* 1980

(opposite)
**Michael Callaghan** (designer and printer)
*With babes + banners* 1980

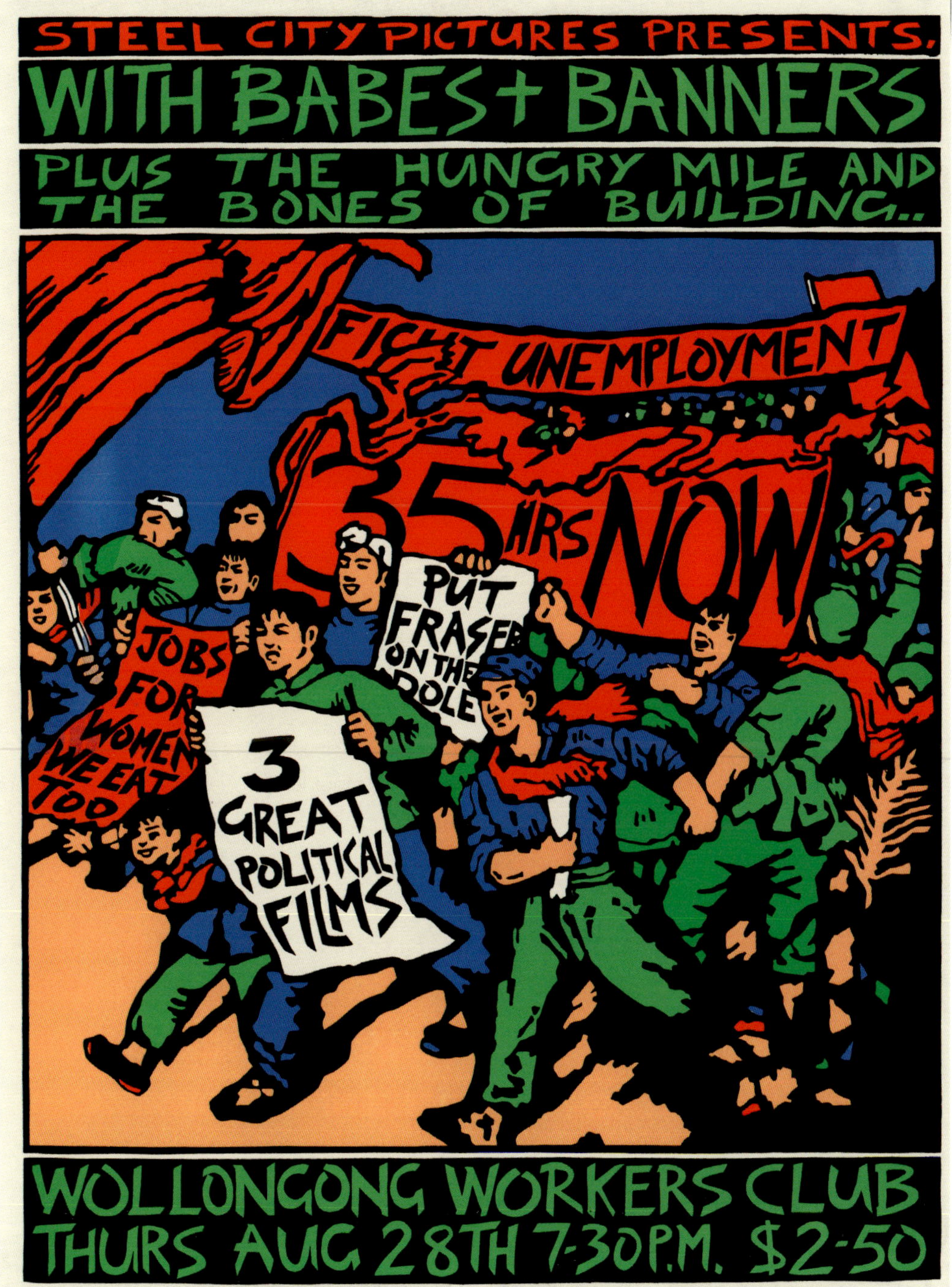
STEEL CITY PICTURES PRESENTS,
WITH BABES + BANNERS
PLUS THE HUNGRY MILE AND THE BONES OF BUILDING..
FIGHT UNEMPLOYMENT
35 HRS NOW
PUT FRASER ON THE DOLE
JOBS FOR WOMEN WE EAT TOO
3 GREAT POLITICAL FILMS
WOLLONGONG WORKERS CLUB
THURS AUG 28TH 7-30P.M. $2-50

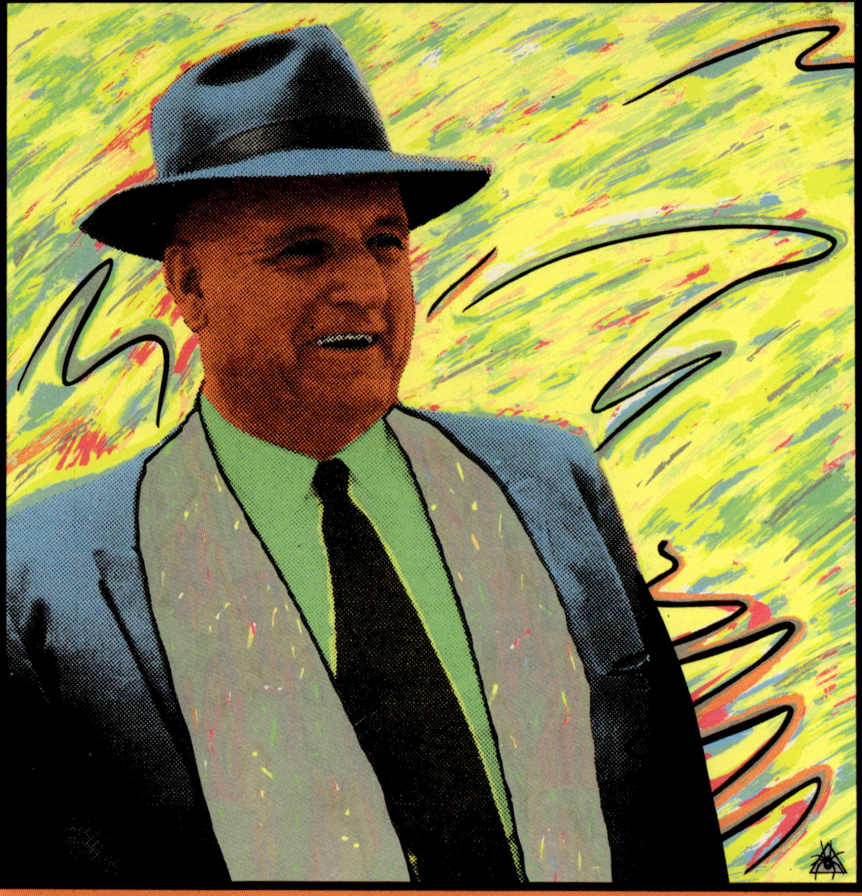


**Michael Callaghan** (designer and printer)
**Gregor Cullen** (designer and printer)
*Connor conference* 1982

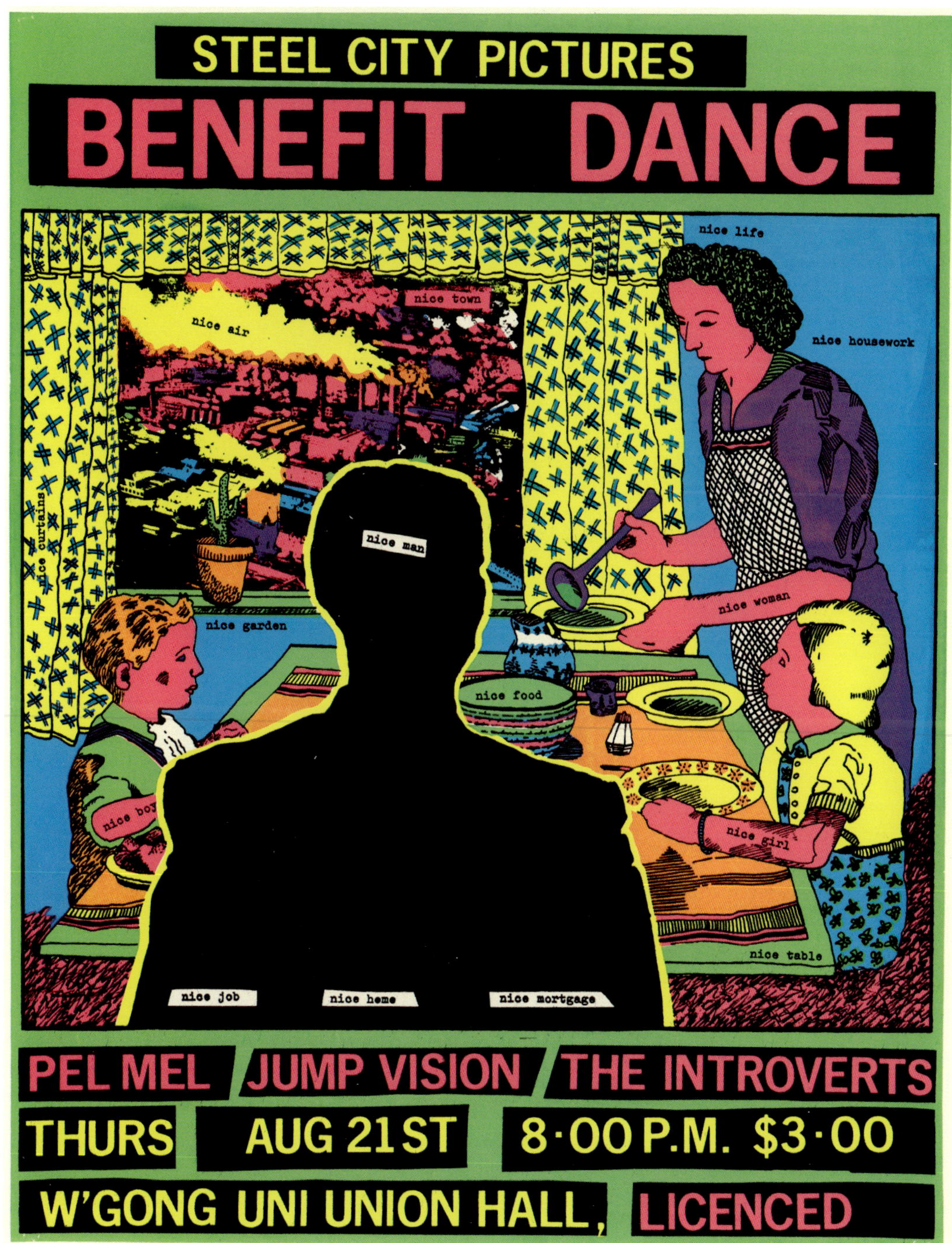


**Michael Callaghan** (designer and printer)
**Mary Callaghan** (designer)
*Nice poster* 1981

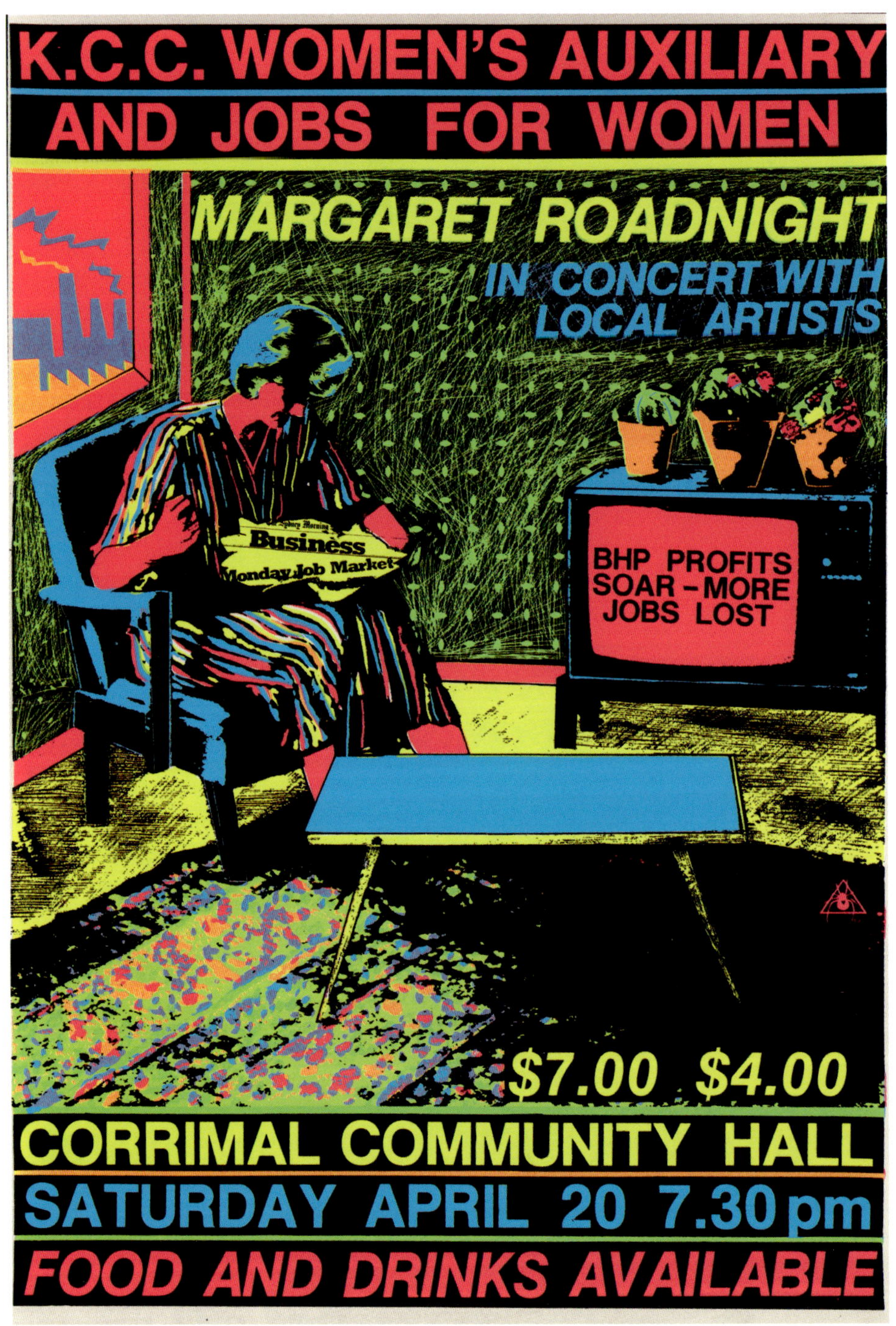
K.C.C. WOMEN'S AUXILIARY
AND JOBS FOR WOMEN
MARGARET ROADNIGHT
IN CONCERT WITH
LOCAL ARTISTS
Business
Monday Job Market
BHP PROFITS
SOAR – MORE
JOBS LOST
$7.00 $4.00
CORRIMAL COMMUNITY HALL
SATURDAY APRIL 20 7.30pm
FOOD AND DRINKS AVAILABLE

## Stuart Park

Callaghan and Cullen rented a disused kiosk in Stuart Park at a peppercorn rental from the Wollongong City Council. They renovated the building and installed an office, printing room, kitchen area and a darkroom. The studio's furniture – a large print table on wheels, a light table, layout bench, and drying racks were made by Callaghan and Cullen according to their specifications. The rudimentary facilities were still short of adequate and required the studio to develop relationships with local businesses that owned the additional equipment necessary for printing posters. Initially much of the screenprinting was done by using a combination of direct stencil, hand-cut stencil and photo stencil techniques. Some two years after opening, Redback received further funding and purchased a reprographic camera, which enabled the printing of half-tone photographic images, an exposure unit to replace the ultraviolet sunlamps and a one-armed-bandit printing table. This counterweighted screenprinting bed improved the studio's productivity and eased some of the physical discomfort of the screenprinting process.

For typesetting, Redback relied on Wollongong's local newspaper *The Illawarra Mercury*. It was an arrangement that was both expensive and time-consuming for the studio. The difficult access to typesetting facilities accounts for the typographic crudeness of some of the early Wollongong posters such as *From scratch* 1982, which was hand-rendered instead. Technological factors may also have shaped Redback's distinctive approach to composition, which often involved flanking the central image by two black bands containing type. This enabled the artists to work on the design of the image and text sections independently of one another. It was not until the mid 1980s when the studio bought its first computer that the studio ceased to outsource typesetting.

Redback secured commissions from the diverse Wollongong community. At the time more than seventy languages and dialects were spoken in the Illawarra region and Redback's early posters represent the interests of this ethnically diverse group of people. Many of the studio's commissions came out of the Wollongong Worker's Research Centre, which was part of the South Coast Labour Council. In conjunction with academics from Wollongong University, the Centre researched workplace and social issues affecting the local community, which were then developed into pamphlets and posters. Other clients included the Migrant Resource Centre, the El Salvadorian and Vietnamese communities, the Women's Auxiliary, as well as the local and national arts community and unions. Redback also produced posters for national clients such as Amnesty International Australia, Imparja, Film Australia and CAAMA. Once Redback moved to Sydney its most significant posters were designed in collaboration with Aboriginal communities addressing social and health issues.

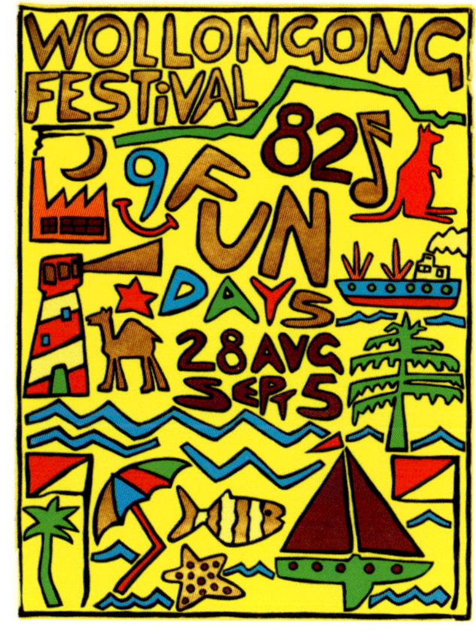


(opposite)
**Alison Alder** (designer and printer)
*Jobs for women* 1984

(above)
**Michael Callaghan** (designer and printer)
*Wollongong festival* 1982

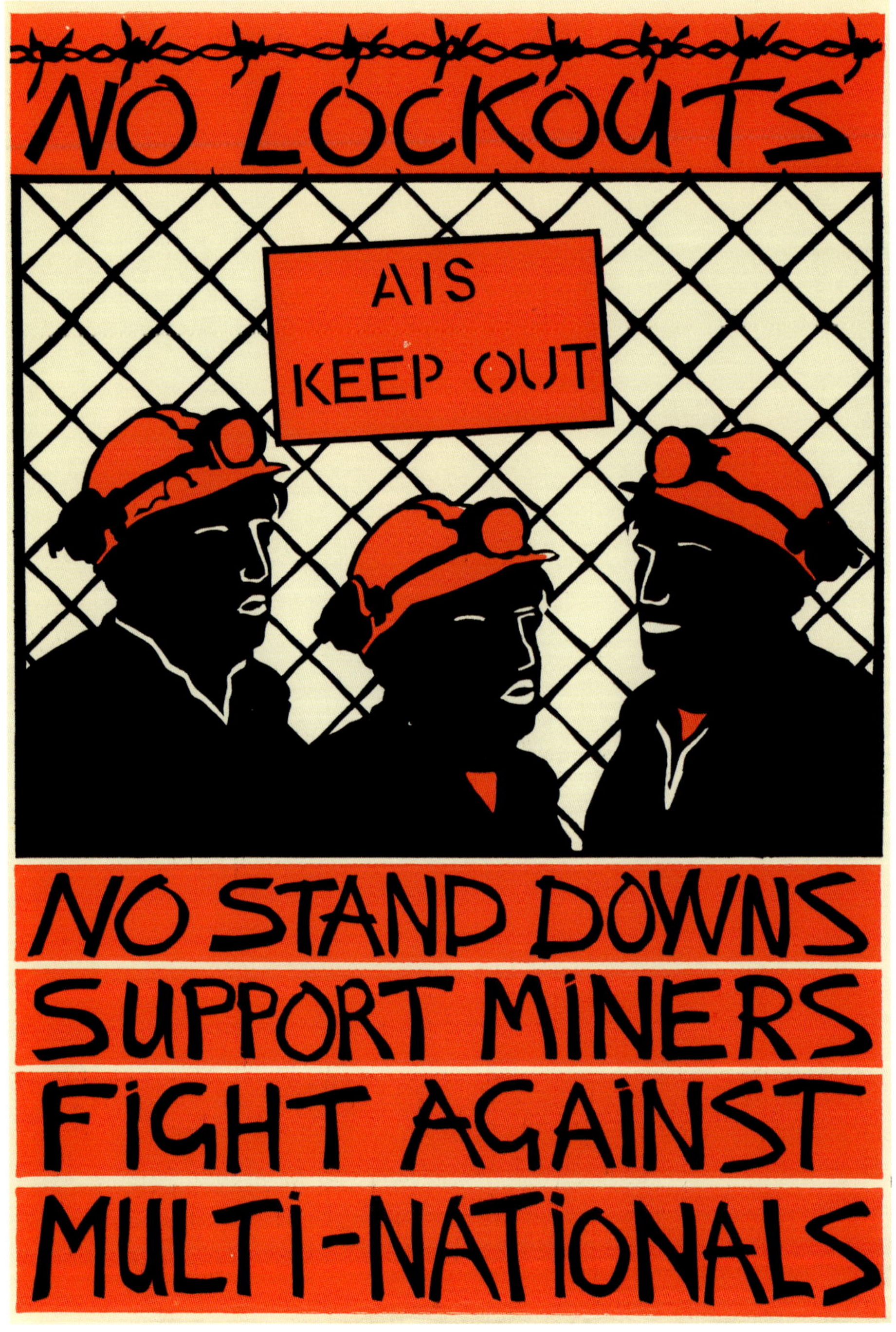
NO LOCKOUTS
AIS
KEEP OUT
NO STAND DOWNS
SUPPORT MINERS
FIGHT AGAINST
MULTI-NATIONALS

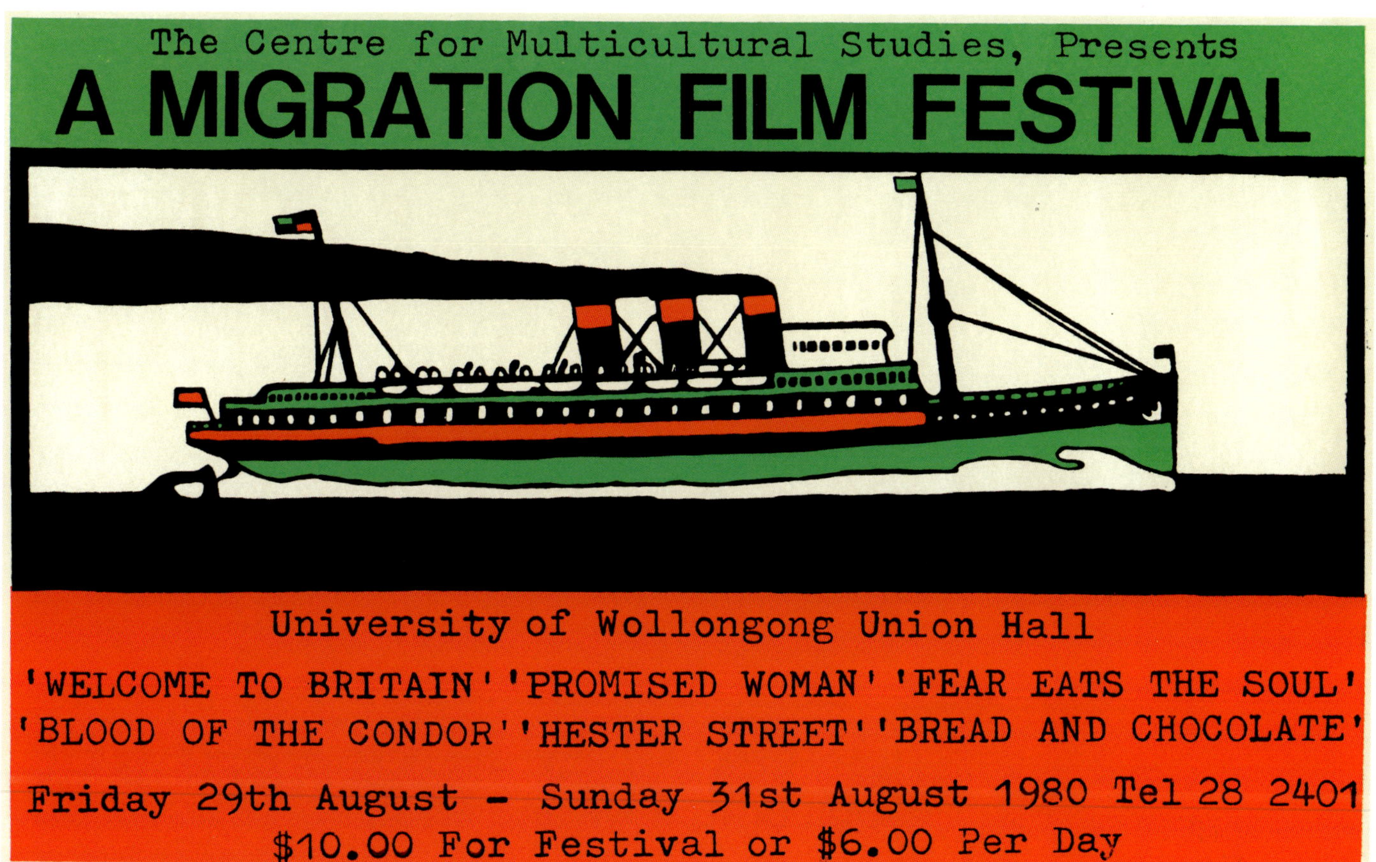


Initially design and printing fees were charged depending on the client's ability to pay. It was not unusual for clients to be unable to meet the design and production costs of jobs. When this occurred, Redback would frequently subsidise them. Callaghan explained:

> [If] you had a big department that has a large budget ... you can make enough of a profit to subsidise someone that you like to work with who had no money or just barely enough to cover the base costs.[27]

As arts funding bodies exerted pressure on the studio to achieve self-sufficiency, it became increasingly difficult for Redback to justify its fluid fee structure. The studio also assisted clients in raising funds by helping them apply for government grants directly or they negotiated with clients to donate labour and suggested ways in which they might recoup costs through the sale of posters or T-shirts. Redback's creative and flexible approach to payment options reveals their commitment to the local community. Unsurprisingly, the Stuart Park studio attracted activists and unemployed youths alike. Two of these, Sharon Pusell and Nick Southall, eventually trained as apprentices.

(opposite)
**Gregor Cullen**
(designer and printer)
*No lockouts* 1980

(above)
**Michael Callaghan**
(designer and printer)
*A migration film festival* 1981

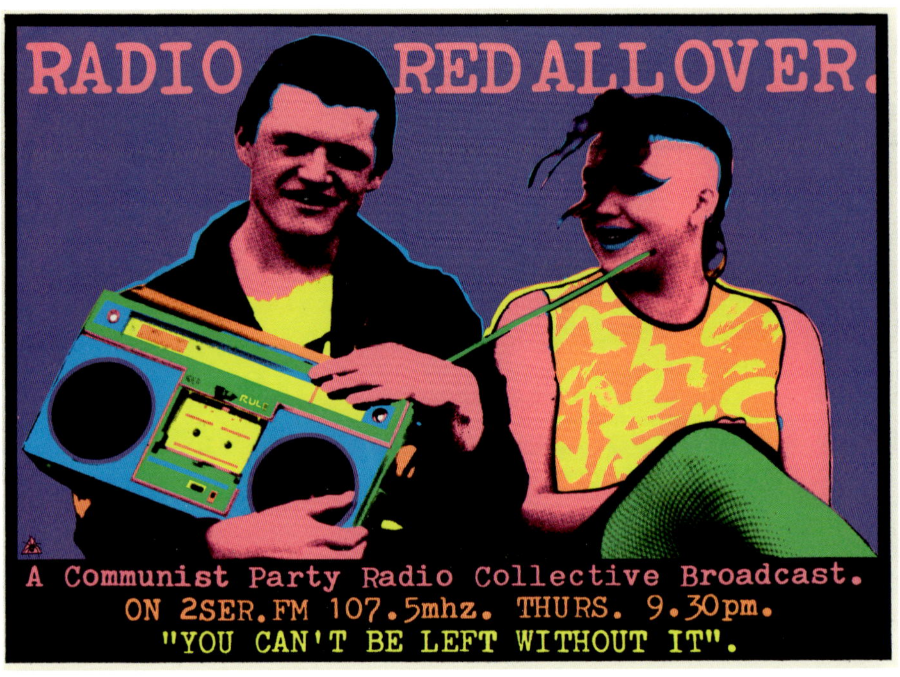


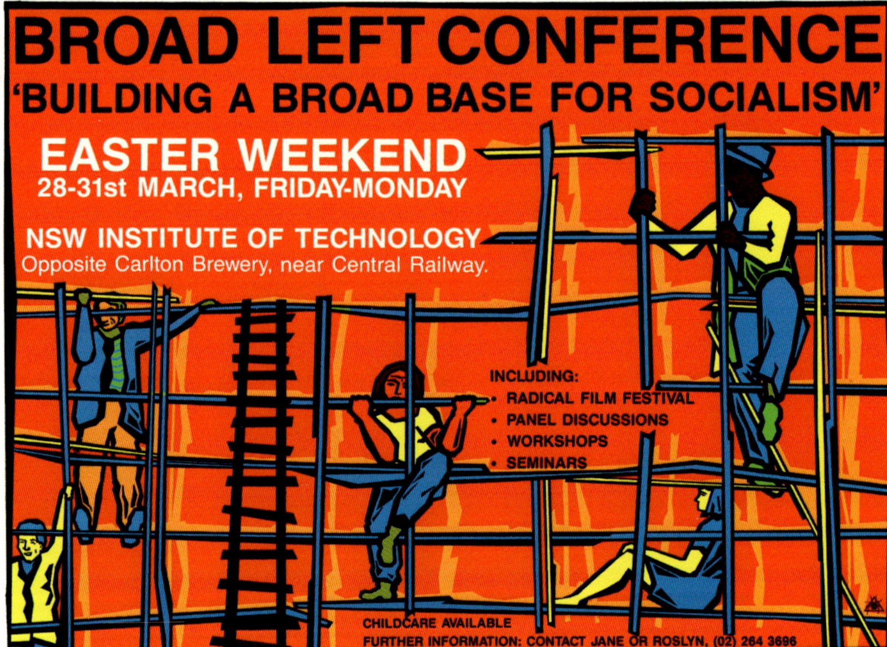


(above)
**Gregor Cullen** (designer and printer), **Nick Southall** and **Deborah Nesbitt** (printer's assistants)
*Radio red all over* 1985

(below)
**Alison Alder** (designer and printer)
*Broad left conference* 1985

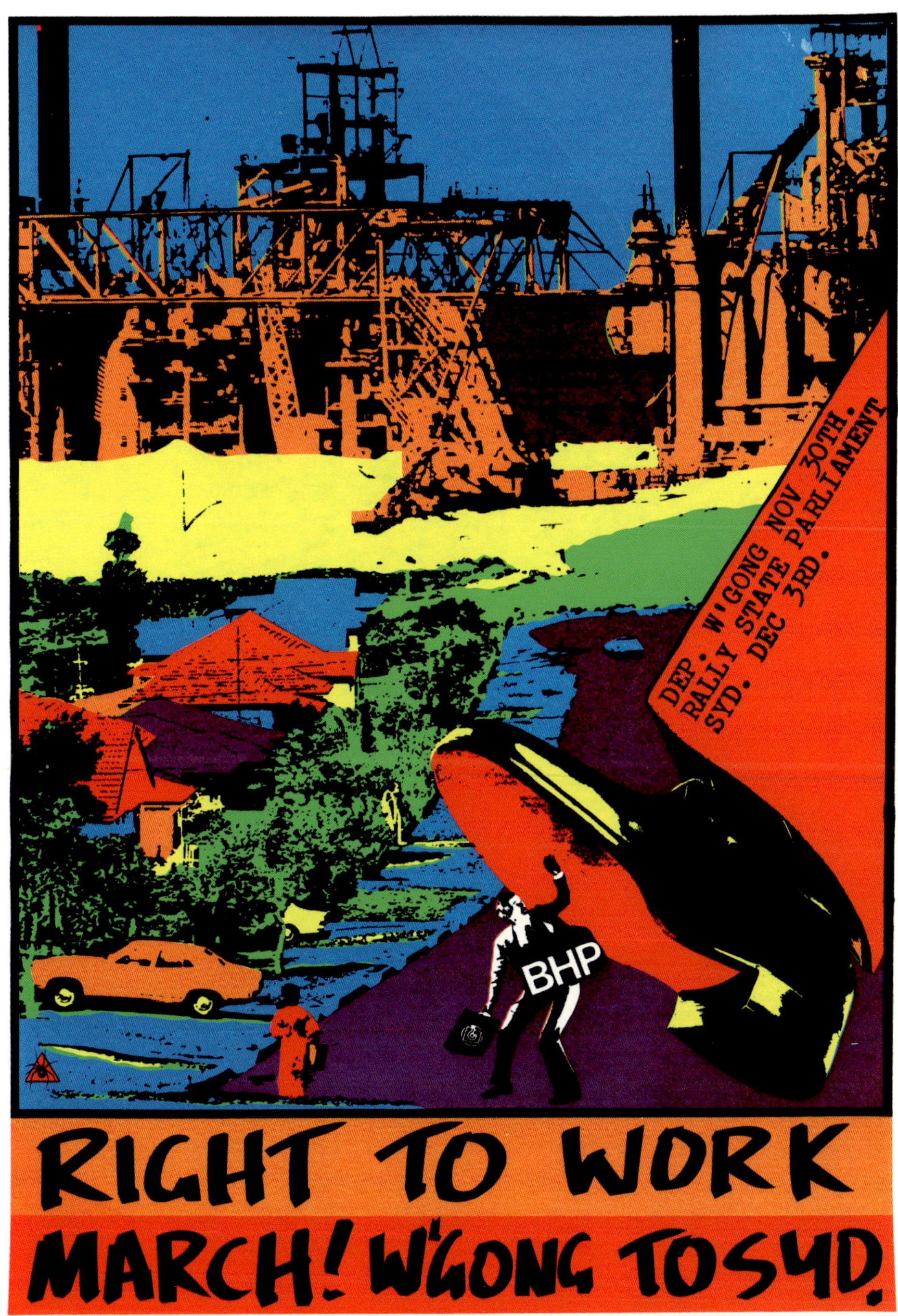


**Gregor Cullen** (designer and printer)
*Right to work march!* 1982

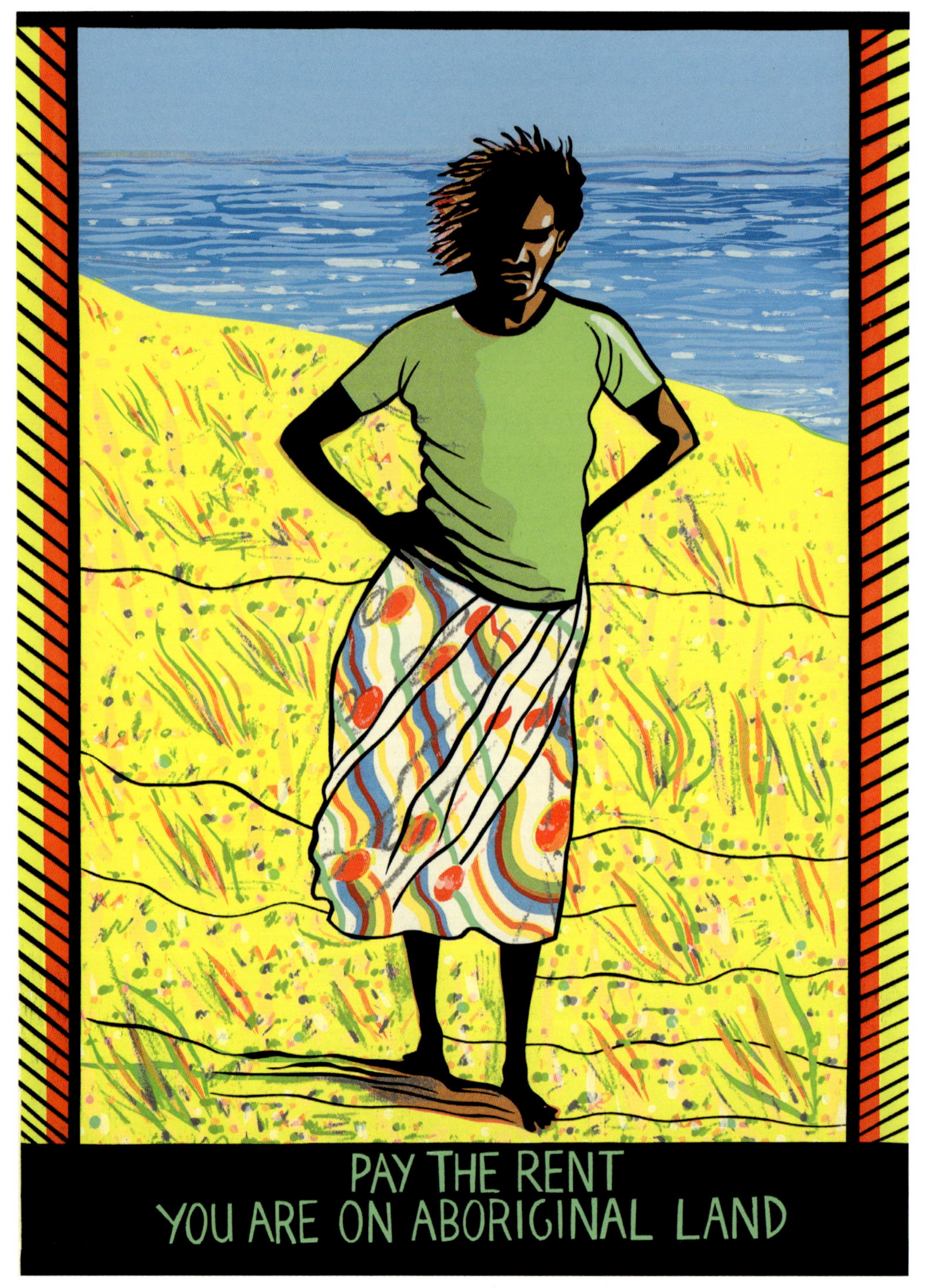
PAY THE RENT
YOU ARE ON ABORIGINAL LAND

Redback's good reputation was quickly established. The burgeoning workload meant that Cullen and Callaghan were able to hire additional people. Marie McMahon, a National Art School graduate and Tin Sheds collaborator, joined Redback in 1981 through a Wollongong City Council artist-in-residence scheme. During that year she designed two banners for a local Aboriginal organisation and another for a local Latin American group. McMahon also began to develop work originating from her time on Bathurst Island, including the first version of the now iconic poster *Pay the rent, you are on Aboriginal land* 1981. She would return to Redback in 1987 for a further year.

In 1983 Ray Young arrived at the studio as part of the Community Employment Program that encouraged businesses to hire artists. Previously Young had worked with McMahon and the local Tiwi community as Art Advisor to Tiwi Designs on Bathurst Island. The following year Leonie Lane joined Redback, having worked as a screenprinter/postermaker with Lucifoil Poster Collective at the Tin Sheds and as a freelance illustrator with community and union-based organisations. Young had experience in textiles and T-shirt screenprinting, and would stay for three years. Lane became an active partner in 1985, specialising in offset layout and design, and remained at Redback until 1990.

Alison Alder also began working at Redback in 1984. Alder had studied printmaking at the Canberra School of Art and established Megalo Screen Print in Canberra. She was living in Melbourne when the Australia Council contacted her about a printing position at Redback. Initially employed on a twelve-month contract as part of the 'Trainee Artists in the Community' program, Alder moved to Wollongong. Shortly afterwards Cullen and Callaghan travelled overseas for several months leaving the studio in the hands of Alder, Lane and Young in their absence. While Cullen was Callaghan's most important collaborator in the Wollongong years, Alder and Lane became central figures in Redback after the studio's move to Sydney the following year.

Redback posters documented the diverse social and cultural life of Wollongong in the early 1980s. Many of the events promoted or issues raised described the difficult situation the community faced. Although the sentiment behind the posters was often serious, Redback's posters were anything but dour. Printed in bright, saturated colours in contrasting hues, often 'bumped up' with fluorescent pigments, they achieved maximum impact. Images were sourced from Japanese woodblocks, Agitprop, cartoons, old *Women's Weekly* magazines, Laminex catalogues, and Pop art, producing some weird disjunctions when matched with specific causes.

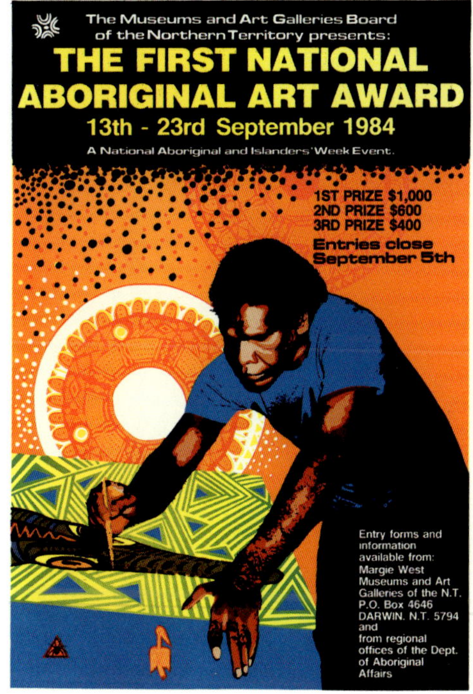


(opposite)
**Marie McMahon** (designer and printer)
*Pay the rent, you are on Aboriginal land* [1] 1981

(above)
**Ray Young** (designer and printer)
*First national Aboriginal art award* 1984

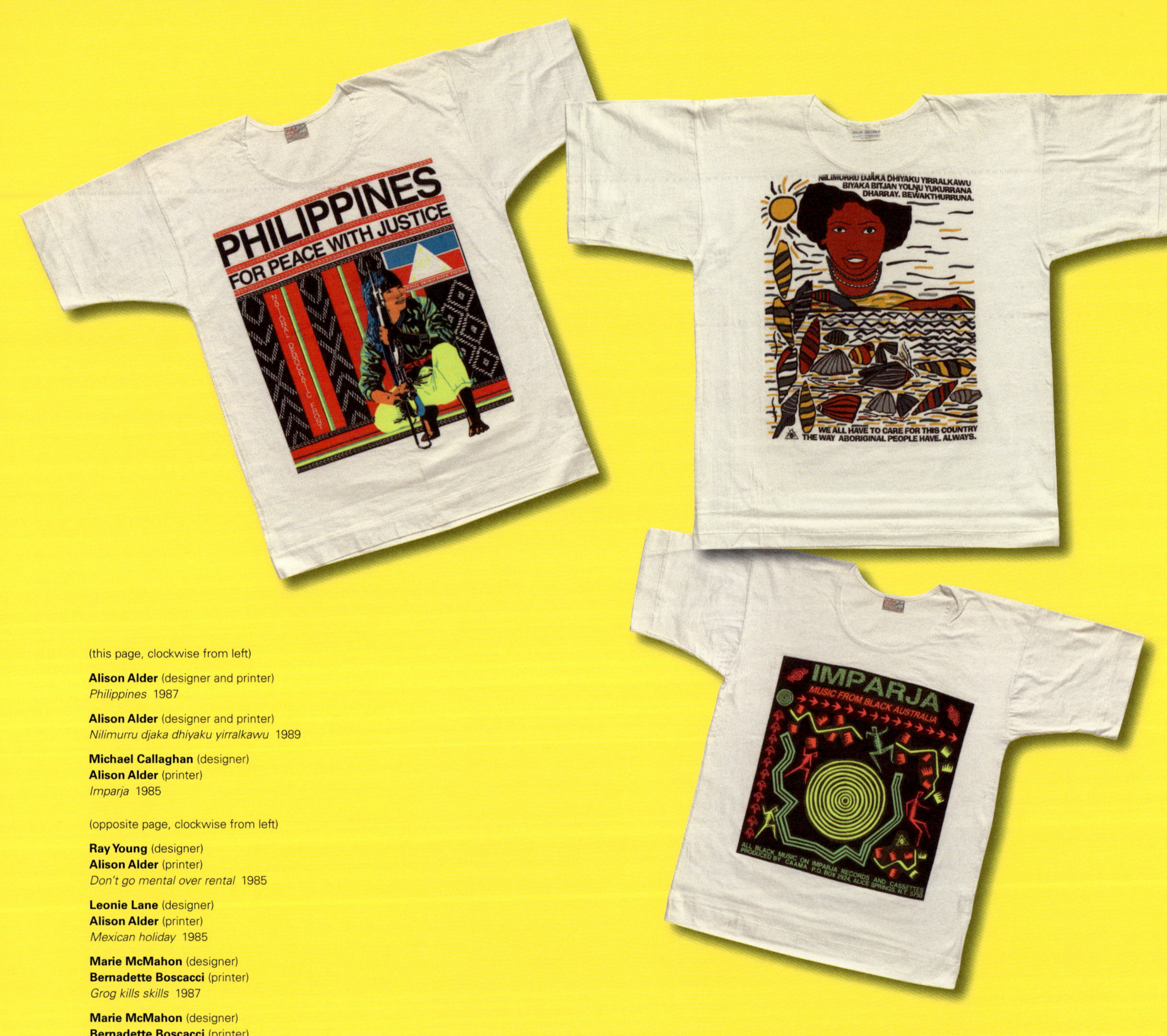


(this page, clockwise from left)

**Alison Alder** (designer and printer)
*Philippines* 1987

**Alison Alder** (designer and printer)
*Nilimurru djaka dhiyaku yirralkawu* 1989

**Michael Callaghan** (designer)
**Alison Alder** (printer)
*Imparja* 1985

(opposite page, clockwise from left)

**Ray Young** (designer)
**Alison Alder** (printer)
*Don't go mental over rental* 1985

**Leonie Lane** (designer)
**Alison Alder** (printer)
*Mexican holiday* 1985

**Marie McMahon** (designer)
**Bernadette Boscacci** (printer)
*Grog kills skills* 1987

**Marie McMahon** (designer)
**Bernadette Boscacci** (printer)
*Caring and sharing without grog* 1987

**Alison Alder** (designer and printer)
*F.P.A. Lovers Love* c. 1990

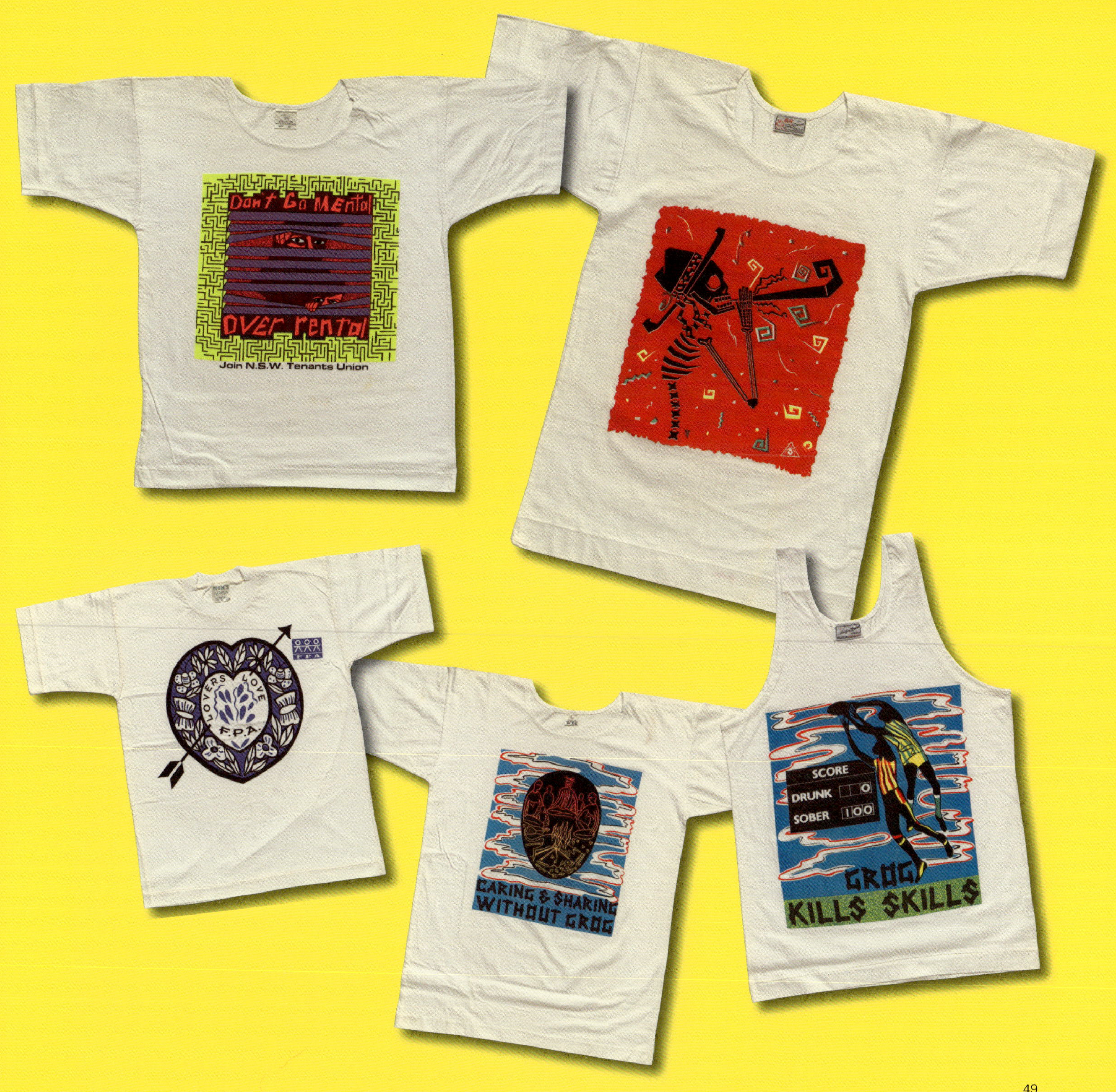
Don't Go Mental
over rental
Join N.S.W. Tenants Union
LOVERS LOVE
F.P.A.
FPA
CARING & SHARING
WITHOUT GROG
SCORE
DRUNK 0
SOBER 100
GROG
KILLS SKILLS

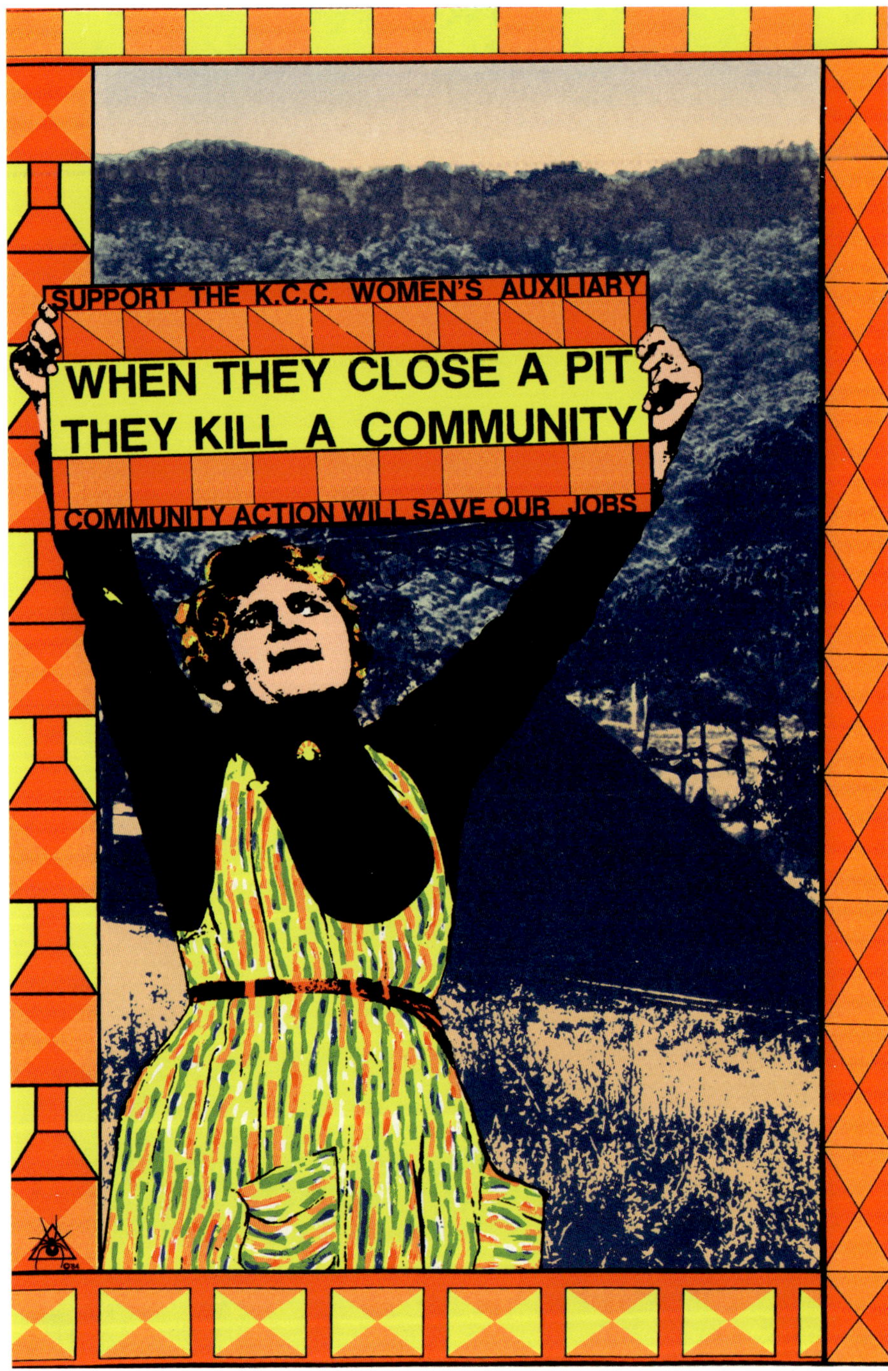


**Alison Alder** (designer and printer)
*When they close a pit they kill a community* 1984

(opposite above)
**Alison Alder** (designer and printer)
*Regional Migrant Health Centre* [1] 1984

(opposite below)
**Gregor Cullen** (designer and printer)
*Over the top* 1983

Alder's poster protesting a BP mine closure combines disparate pictorial elements of figurative illustration, photography, text and patterning. In this poster, a woman holds a sign that reads 'When they close a pit they kill a community' set against a backdrop of the Wollongong escarpment. Both the poster and the sign held by the woman are framed by bands of irregular geometric patterns. On the one hand didactic, on the other affirmative, Alder injects the poster with a quirky feminist perspective.

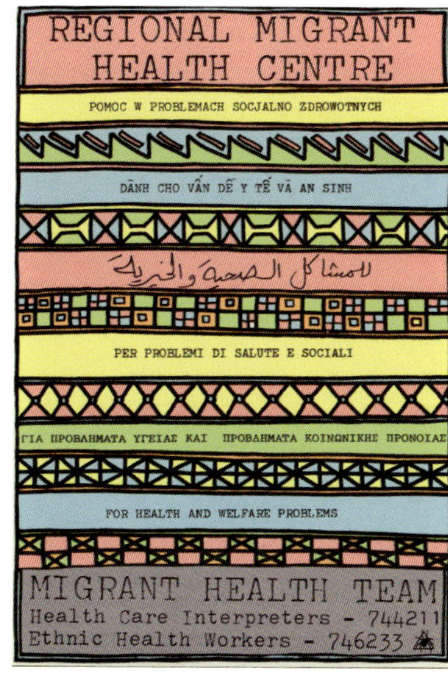


Many Redback posters incorporated patterning into the design, so it is not surprising that the studio eventually turned to designing and printing its own wrapping paper. Designs borrowed from Mexican folk art, Japanese wrapping paper, and 1960s Laminex swatches reflect both a local sensibility and the influence of travel.[28] In Alder's three posters for the Regional Migrant Health Centre, statements in different languages are inserted between variously patterned bands. Similarly, Callaghan's elegant poster *A Peña in support of El Salvador* 1983 uses the woven geometric designs, colours and technique of South American folk art to invoke a specific culture and cultural practice. In this poster, typography is hand-rendered to approximate the angular characteristic of weaving. Other times, patterns are used to sly, comic effect. In Cullen's poster for an exhibition at the Wollongong City Gallery, aptly titled *Over the top* 1983, the repetition of chainsaws form a decorative pattern against a background of gingham. The two contrasting patterns of gingham and chainsaws, simultaneously sweet and dangerous, evoke a humorous response.

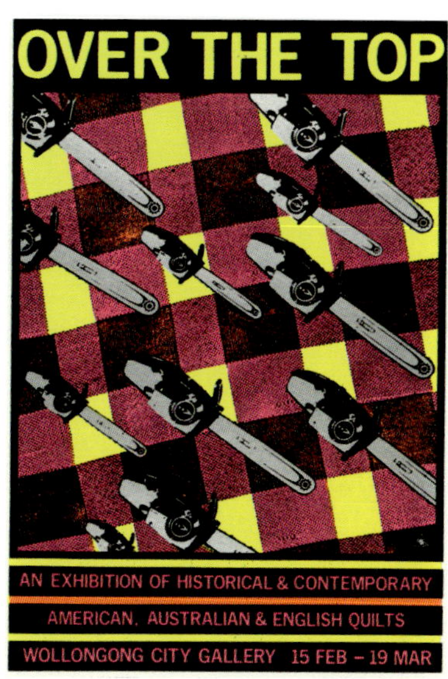


Many of the posters from this time are infused with a manic intensity. In *Raise the dole dance* 1984, a fractured, spasmodic figure 'dances' against a vertiginous mesh of patterned fragments. Both this poster and *WOW dance* 1984 have borrowed the graphic language of Japanese patterning and manga comics, and were directly influenced by Callaghan's visit to Japan. In the latter poster a businessman's head and torso are positioned centrally in the frame; blood shoots high from his head, while a stream of repeated but unintelligible characters emerge from his open mouth. In a poster to promote Heritage Week, a group of people cheer a large disembodied hand gripping a transistor radio. In *Kiama Jazz Festival* 1983, a musician plays the trumpet, his eyes closed as though in a moment of rapture, unaware of his surrounding environment, which is a bleak industrial smelter. Fragmenting, exploding, disembodied limbs, these posters describe intensely felt physical and emotional states.

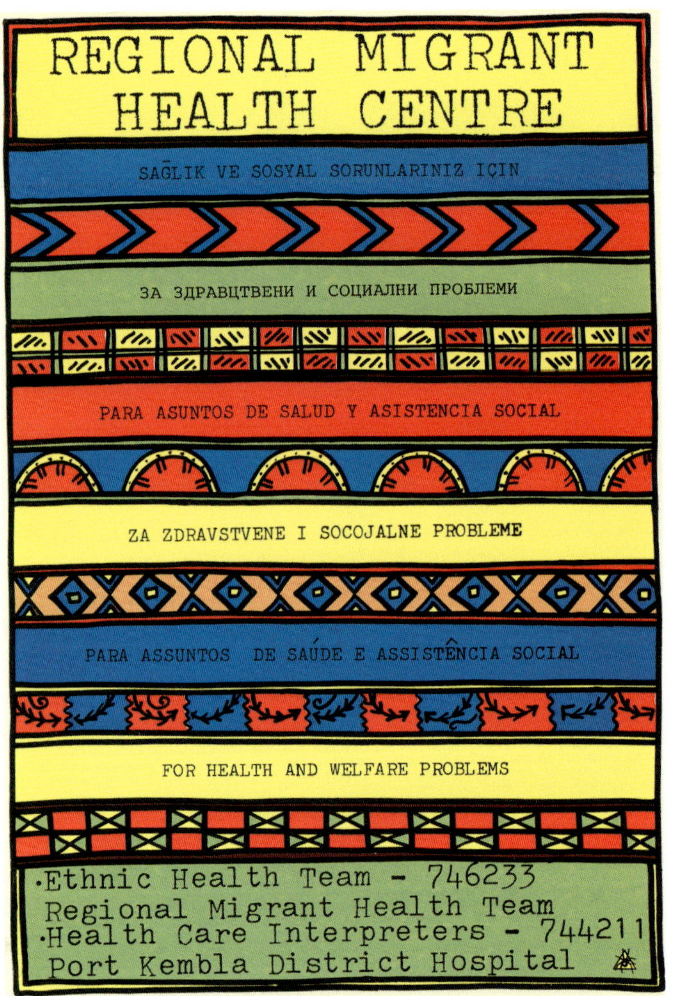


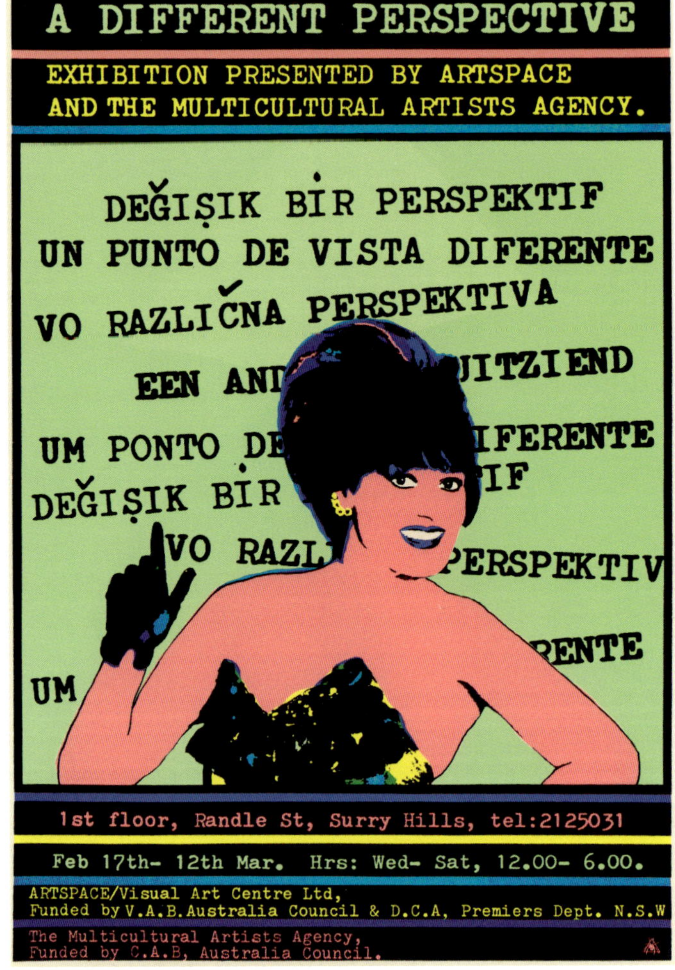


(above)
**Alison Alder** (designer and printer)
*Regional Migrant Health Centre [2]* 1984

(right)
**Gregor Cullen** (designer and printer)
*A different perspective* 1983

(opposite)
**Michael Callaghan** (designer)
*Greek tragedy* 1989

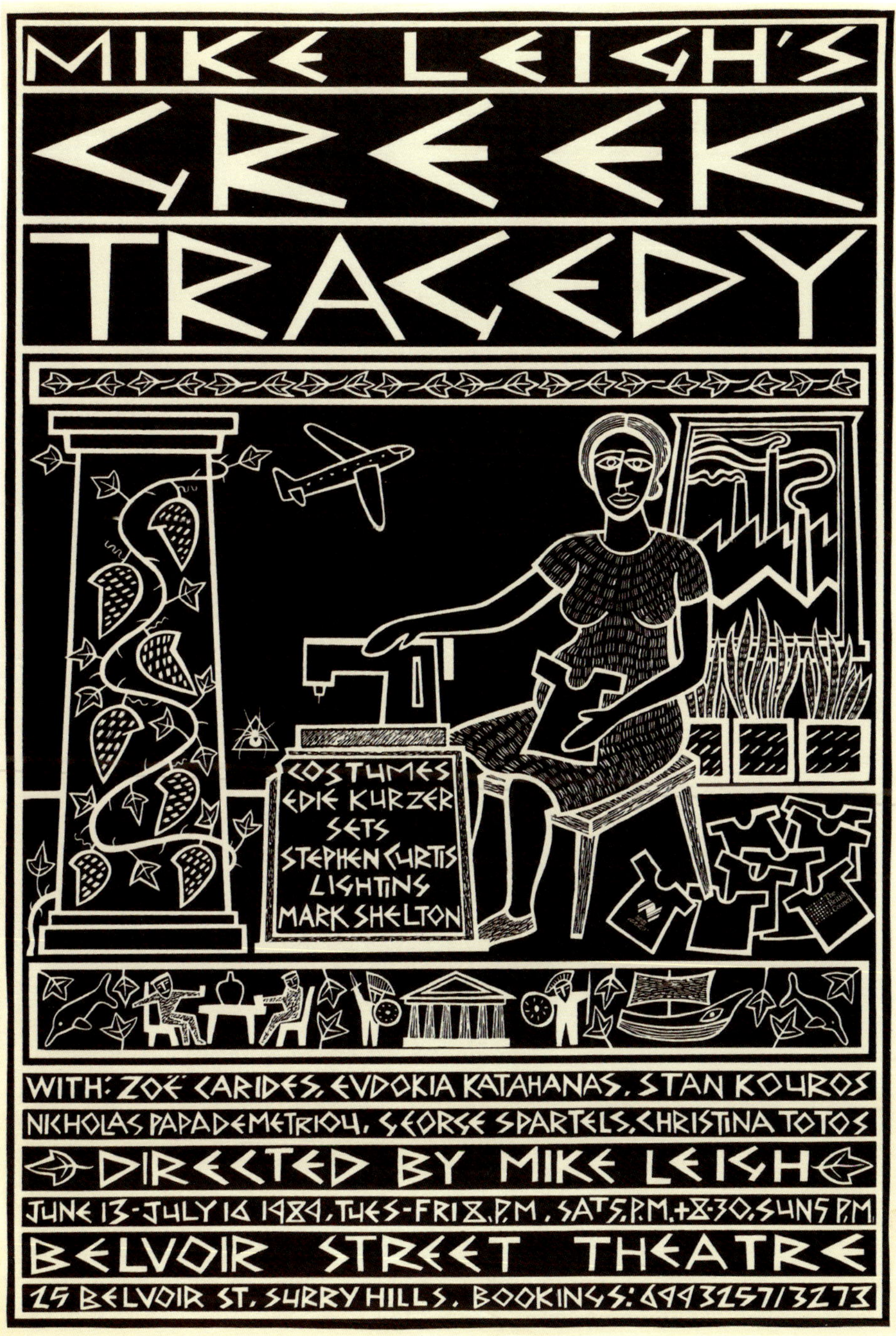
MIKE LEIGH'S
GREEK
TRAGEDY
COSTUMES
EDIE KURZER
SETS
STEPHEN CURTIS
LIGHTING
MARK SHELTON
WITH: ZOË CARIDES, EVDOKIA KATAHANAS, STAN KOUROS
NICHOLAS PAPADEMETRIOU, GEORGE SPARTELS, CHRISTINA TOTOS
DIRECTED BY MIKE LEIGH
JUNE 13 - JULY 16 1984, TUES-FRI 8.P.M., SATS 5.P.M. + 8.30, SUNS 5 P.M.
BELVOIR STREET THEATRE
25 BELVOIR ST, SURRY HILLS. BOOKINGS: 6993257/3273

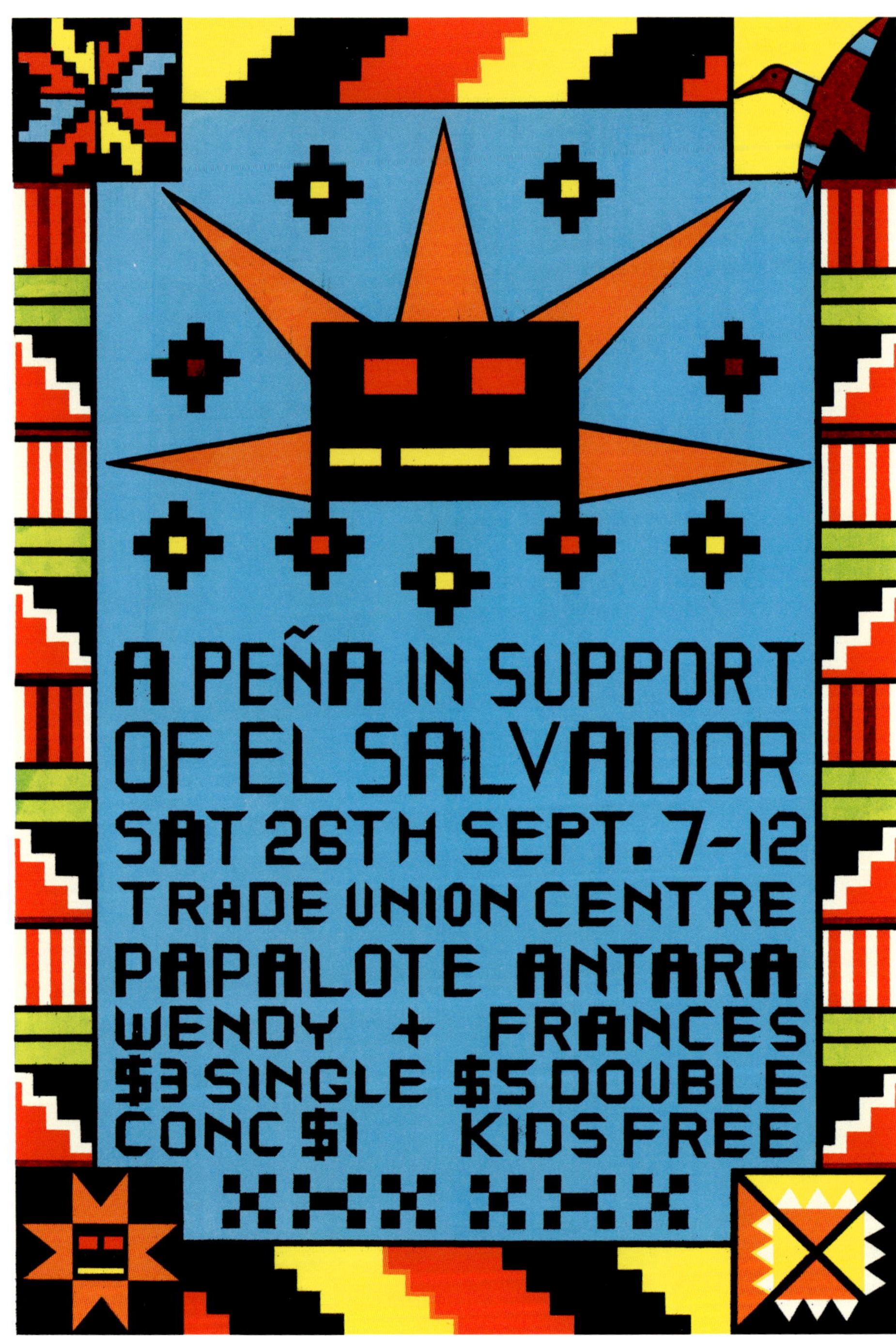


**Michael Callaghan** (designer and printer),
**Marie McMahon** (designer and printer)
*A Peña in support of El Salvador* 1981

(opposite)
**Michael Callaghan** (designer and printer),
**Alison Alder** (printer), **Sharon Pusell** (printer's assistant)
*Raise the dole dance* 1984

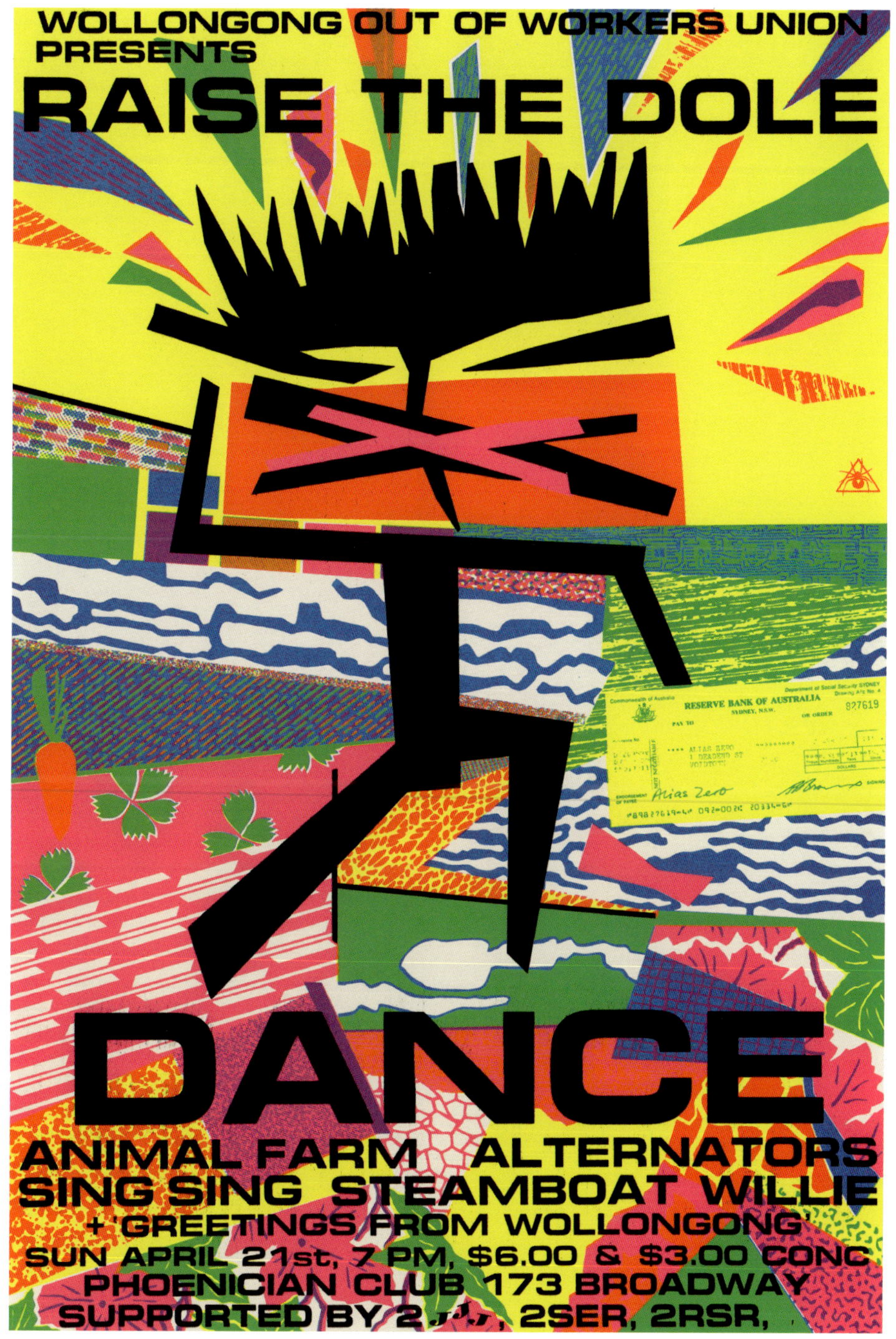
WOLLONGONG OUT OF WORKERS UNION
PRESENTS
RAISE THE DOLE
Commonwealth of Australia
RESERVE BANK OF AUSTRALIA
SYDNEY, N.S.W.
Department of Social Security SYDNEY
827619
PAY TO
OR ORDER
DOLLARS
ENDORSEMENT OF PAYEE
Alias Zero
DANCE
ANIMAL FARM ALTERNATORS
SING SING STEAMBOAT WILLIE
+ 'GREETINGS FROM WOLLONGONG'
SUN APRIL 21st, 7 PM, $6.00 & $3.00 CONC
PHOENICIAN CLUB 173 BROADWAY
SUPPORTED BY 2JJJ, 2SER, 2RSR,

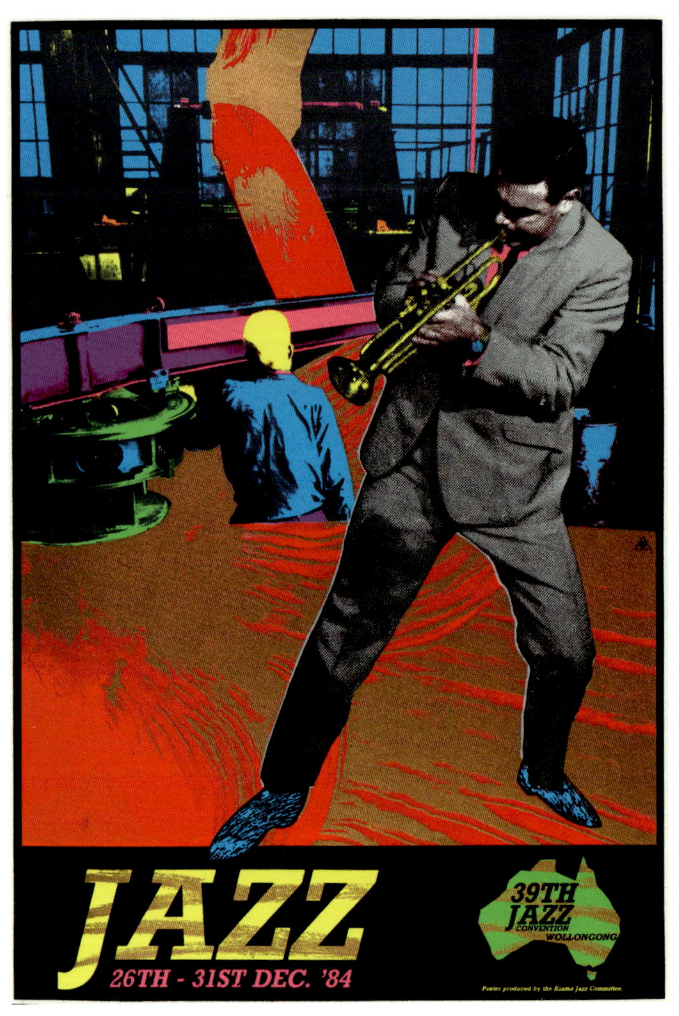
JAZZ
26TH - 31ST DEC. '84
39TH JAZZ CONVENTION WOLLONGONG
Poster produced by the Kiama Jazz Committee.

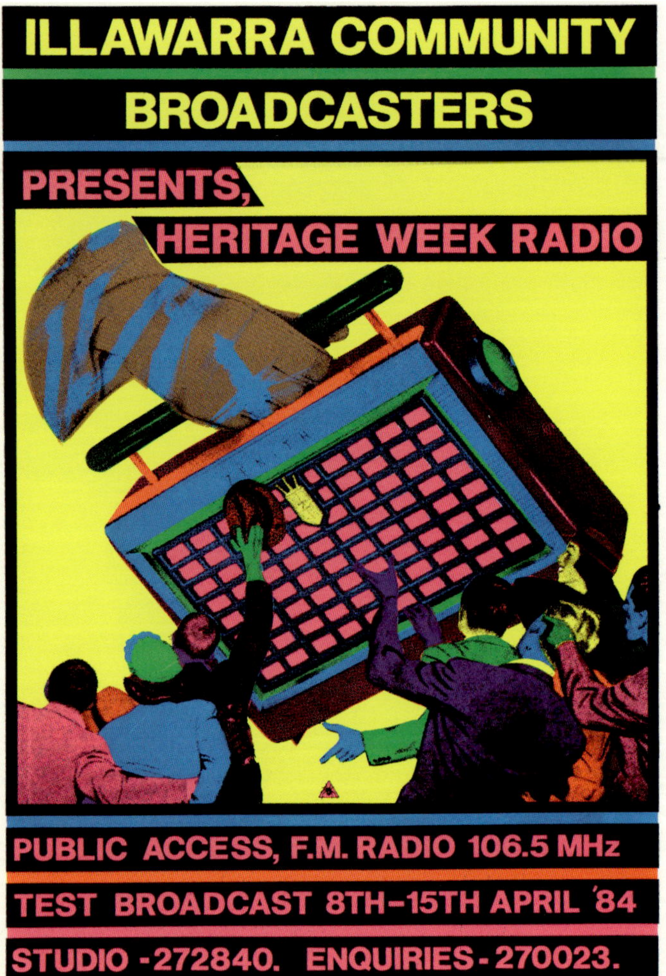
ILLAWARRA COMMUNITY
BROADCASTERS
PRESENTS,
HERITAGE WEEK RADIO
PUBLIC ACCESS, F.M. RADIO 106.5 MHz
TEST BROADCAST 8TH–15TH APRIL '84
STUDIO -272840. ENQUIRIES-270023.

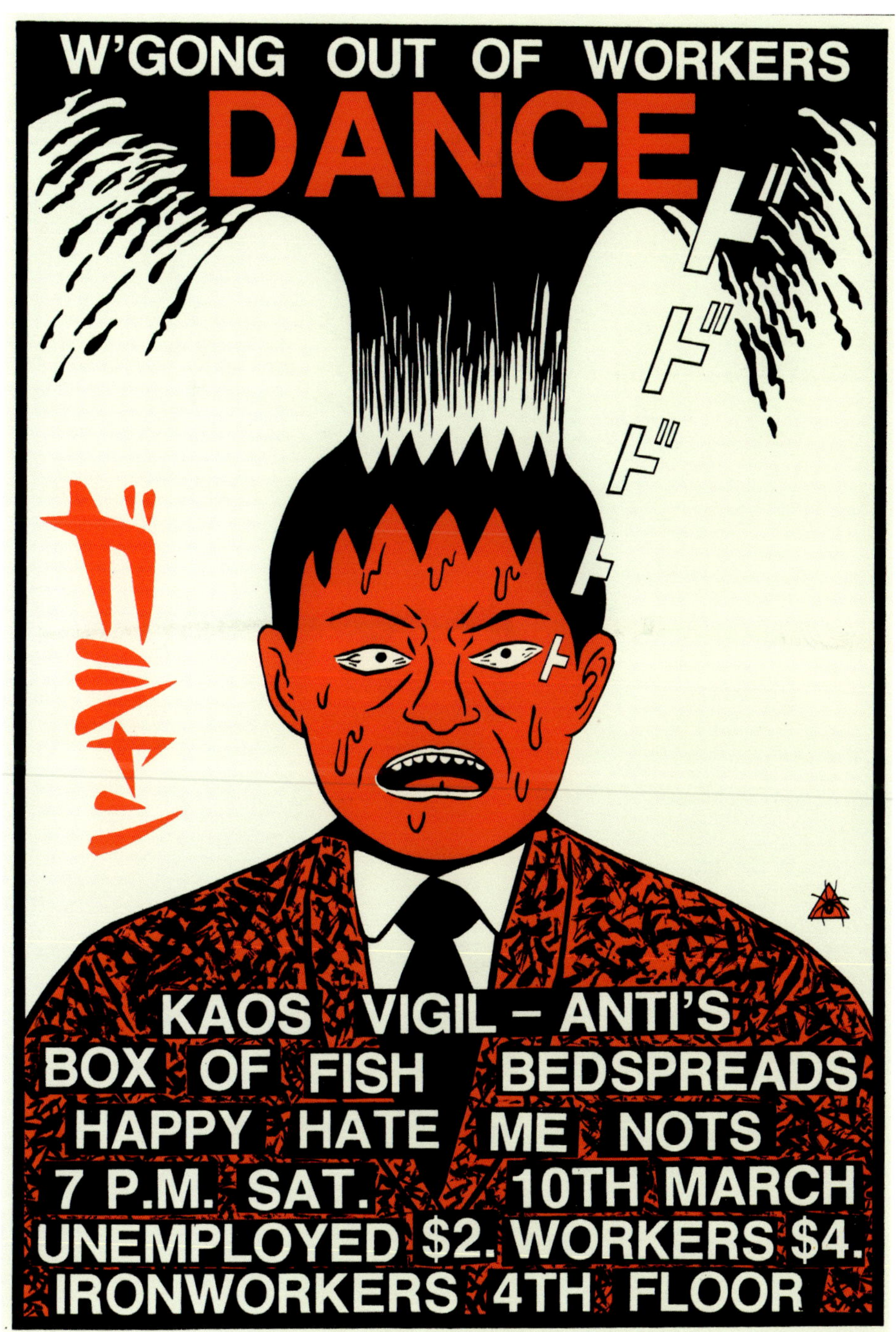


(opposite left)
**Gregor Cullen** (designer and printer)
*Kiama Jazz Festival* 1984

(opposite right)
**Michael Callaghan** (designer and printer)
**Gregor Cullen** (designer and printer)
*Illawarra Community Broadcasters* 1984

**Michael Callaghan** (designer and printer)
**Nick Southall** (printer's assistant)
*WOW dance* 1985

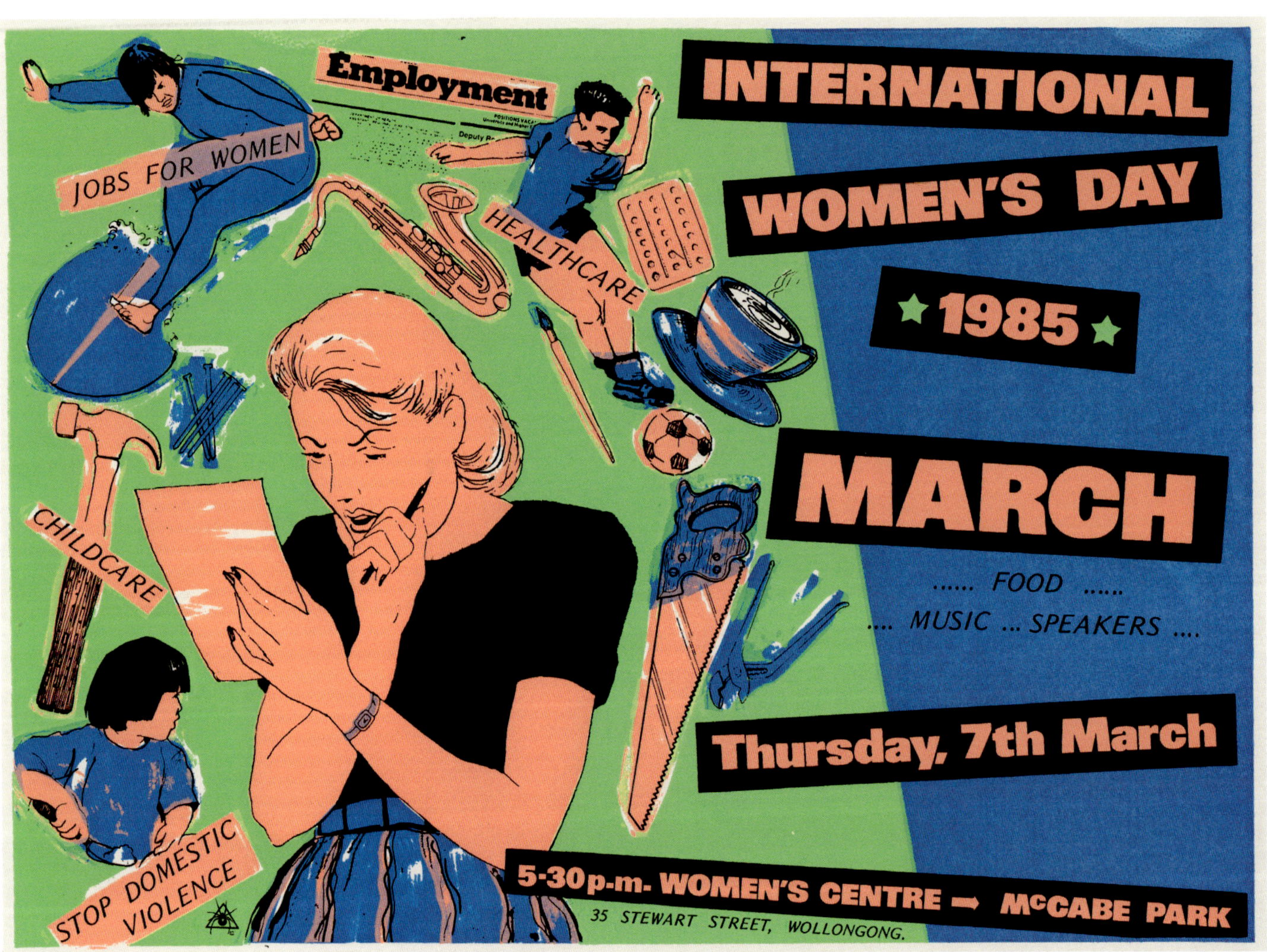
Employment
JOBS FOR WOMEN
HEALTHCARE
CHILDCARE
STOP DOMESTIC VIOLENCE
INTERNATIONAL
WOMEN'S DAY
1985
MARCH
...... FOOD ......
.... MUSIC ... SPEAKERS ....
Thursday, 7th March
5-30p.m. WOMEN'S CENTRE → McCABE PARK
35 STEWART STREET, WOLLONGONG.

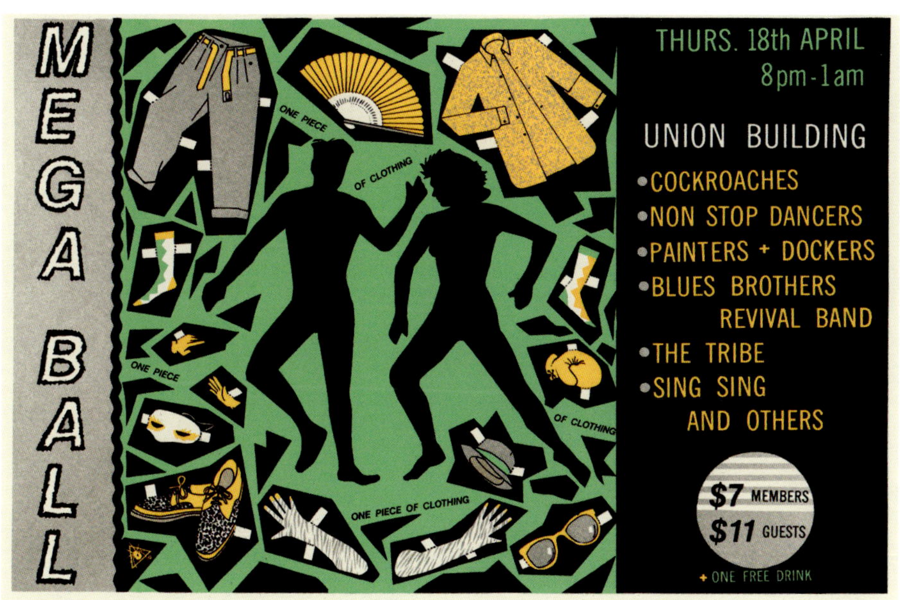


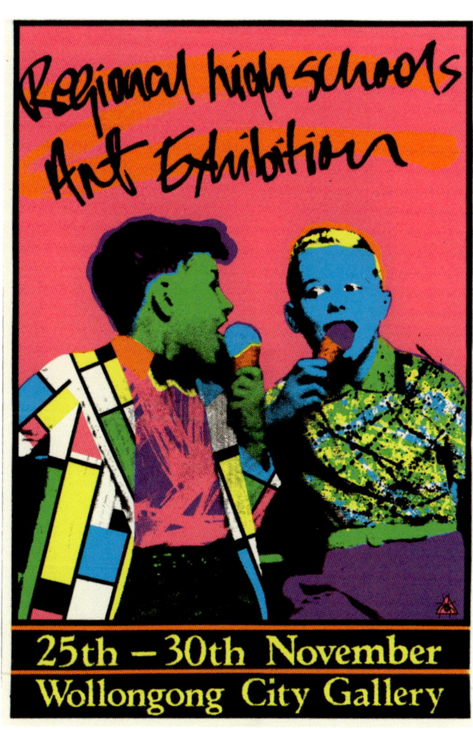


The frequent reference back to the 1950s and 1960s in Redback's posters locates this dislocated aesthetic within the context of pre-millennial tension. The fast approaching end to the twentieth century provoked a nervous response. Popular culture's fascination with visions of the future in the 1950s and 1960s had exhausted itself by the 1980s. The style of clothes, colours, décor and music in this decade manifested a fin-de-siècle nostalgia for the 1950s. Redback's posters, particularly those designed by Cullen and Lane, celebrated this retrospective moment. It is evident in the attire of the two school boys licking ice creams in Cullen's poster for the *Regional high school's art exhibition* 1984. Likewise, Cullen's poster for the Housing Information Service evokes this earlier period through both modernist architecture and illustrative style. Lane's pastel coloured wrapping paper also strongly recalls 1950s fabric design, as does the typography and illustrations in her poster *Mega ball* 1985. However, Callaghan's own incorporation of the 1950s is acerbic rather than nostalgic. A dinner table scene in a poster for a *Nice poster* 1980, in which everything, including the industrial skyline, is sarcastically labelled 'nice', openly mocks conservative postwar family values.

(opposite)
**Leonie Lane** (designer and printer)
**Alison Alder** (printer)
*International Women's Day* 1985

(above left)
**Leonie Lane** (designer and printer)
*Mega ball* 1985

(above right)
**Gregor Cullen** (designer and printer)
*Regional High Schools art exhibition* 1984

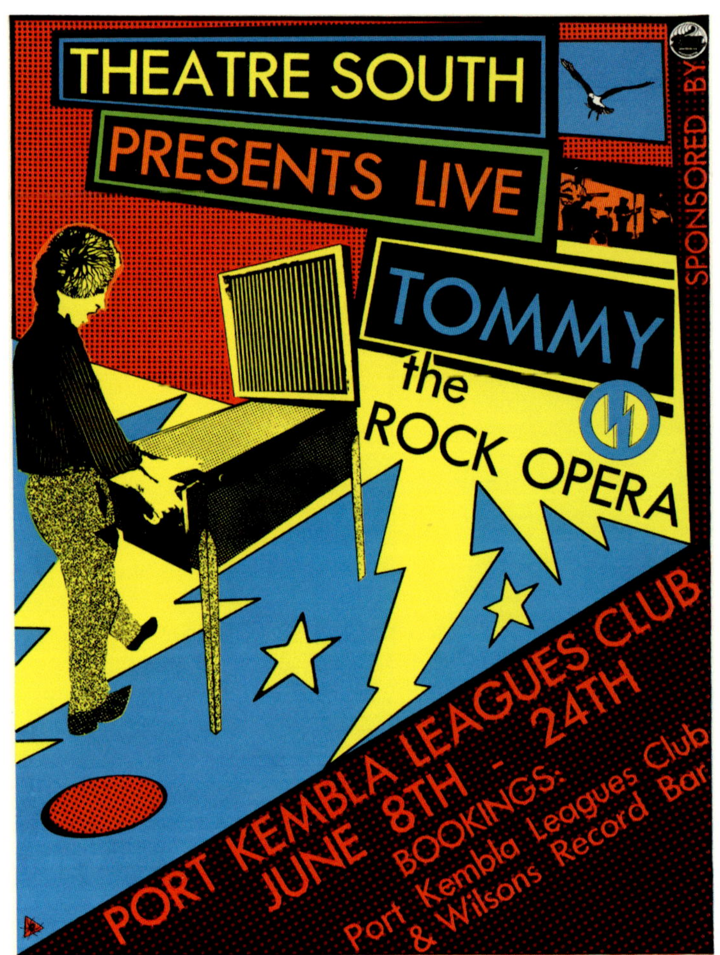


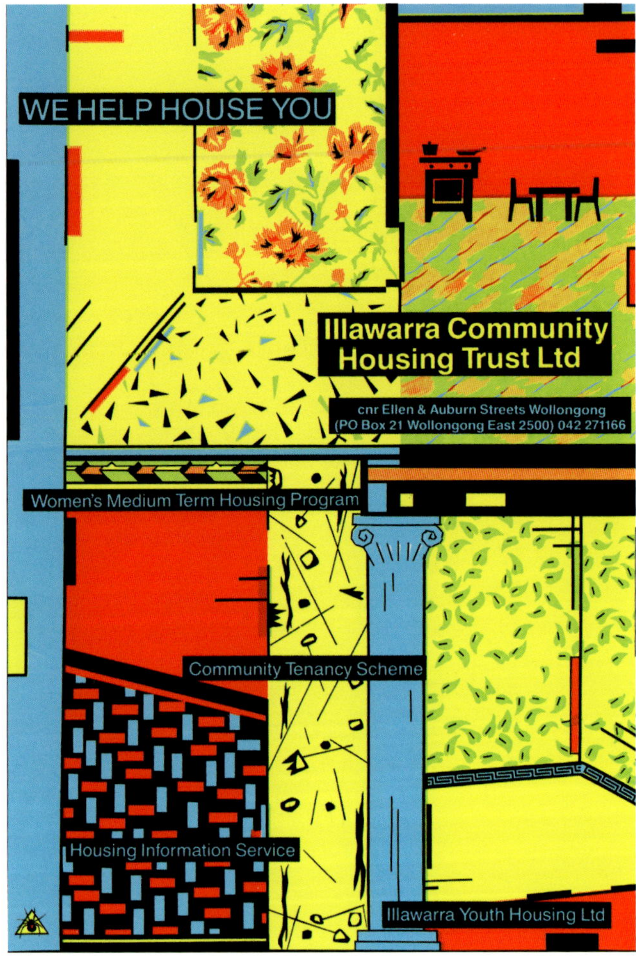


(above left)
**Ray Young** (designer and printer)
*Tommy* 1984

(above right)
**Alison Alder** (designer and printer)
*We help house you* 1984

(opposite)
**Leonie Lane** (designer and printer)
**Ray Young** (printer)
*Go blotto!* 1984

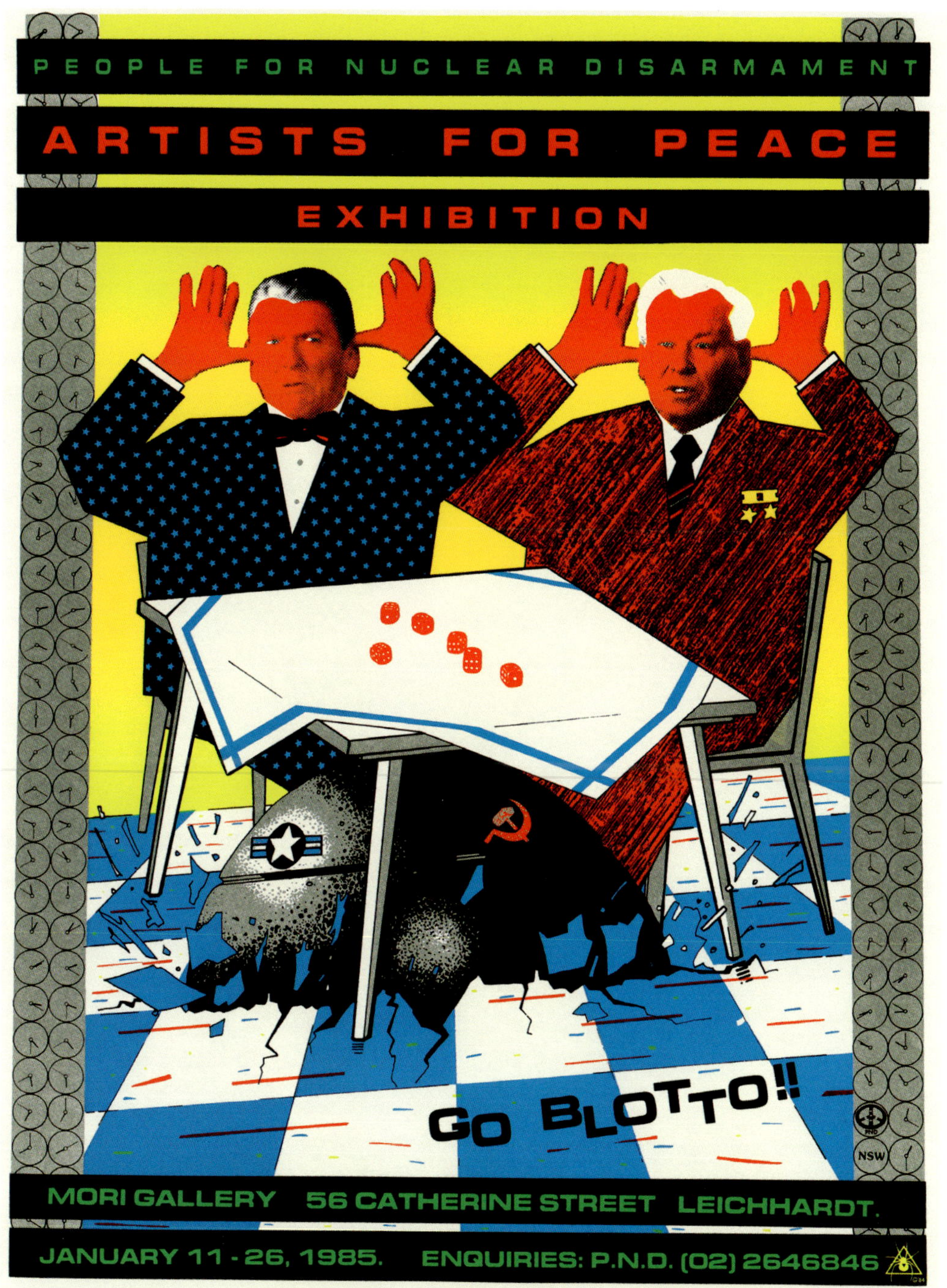
PEOPLE FOR NUCLEAR DISARMAMENT
ARTISTS FOR PEACE
EXHIBITION
GO BLOTTO!!
NSW
MORI GALLERY 56 CATHERINE STREET LEICHHARDT.
JANUARY 11 - 26, 1985. ENQUIRIES: P.N.D. (02) 2646846

## Exhibitions

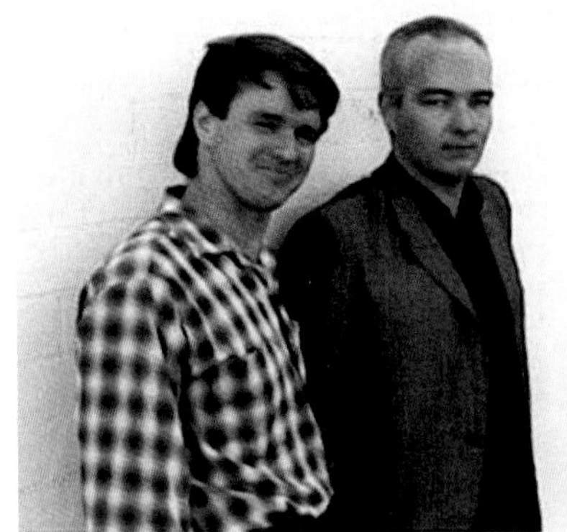

In 1984 Callaghan and Cullen flew to Los Angeles for three months to take part in the Olympic Arts Festival. Cullen's poster for Wollongong City Gallery's exhibition *Fresh blood* 1984 had impressed the festival curator on his visit to Australia. As part of the Olympics Arts Festival exhibition, Cullen and Callaghan developed posters in collaboration with a local Chicano screenprinting workshop, Self Help Graphics, on the subject of a recently passed law that offered Amnesty to illegal workers. The previous year Cullen and Callaghan, along with a group of friends that included Lane before she joined Redback, had travelled to Japan to take part in the annual peace conference held in Nagasaki. Redback's posters had been selected for inclusion in the exhibition *Continuum 83* held in Tokyo that same year. Redback's posters were also represented in *Eureka! Artists from Australia* held at the Institute for Contemporary Art in London. Both exhibitions surveyed screenprinted posters from Australian screenprinting workshops. Redback's posters were exhibited internationally again in the late 1980s when the studio took part in poster exhibitions in Japan and Russia.

The wide range of exhibitions that featured Redback posters – from commercial art shows to contemporary art spaces – both in Australia and abroad, reflects their broad appeal, even within the art world. The Olympics Arts Festival situated the studio's work firmly within a contemporary art context.[29] *Shocking diversity*, an exhibition organised by the Print Council of Australia that toured nationally in 1987, showcased printmaking practices in Sydney and featured posters from several screenprinting workshops, including Redback alongside artists such as Jeff Gibson and Elizabeth Rooney. In 1985 the Art Gallery of New South Wales curated an exhibition on art in the labour movement in the 1980s. It focused on the collaborative relationship between artists and trade unions. On display were banners and posters produced by Redback for local trade unions. Two substantial exhibitions mounted in the late 1980s, *Redback Graphix posters 1979–1985* at Wollongong City Gallery, and *Now We are 10: Redback Graphix a retrospective 1979–1989* acknowledged Redback's contribution to art, politics and design.

However, it was the anti-Bicentennial exhibition *Right here right now: Australia 1988*, that proved locally political posters still had bite. Curated by Lee-Ann Hall of Co-Media, this touring exhibition sought to present an alternative view of the Bicentennial celebrations and featured the work of over thirty artists from screenprinting workshops around Australia. Co-Media commissioned posters on the subject of the bicentennial. Among the artists represented were Ann Newmarch,

(above)
Gregor Cullen and Michael Callaghan in 1983

(opposite)
**Gregor Cullen** (designer and printer)
*Fresh blood* 1983

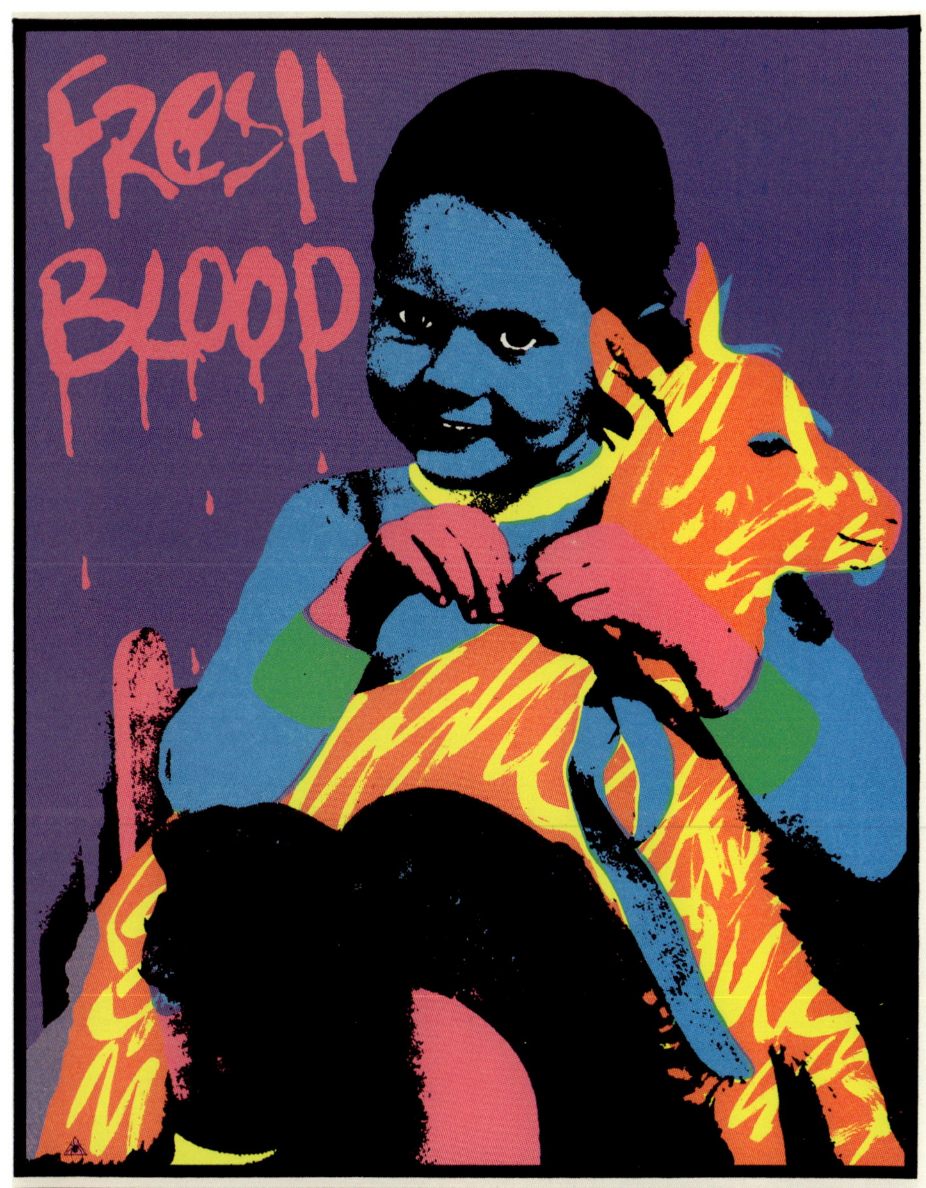
FRESH
BLOOD
FRESH BLOOD EXHIBITION 14TH DEC - 18TH JAN.
WOLLONGONG CITY GALLERY.

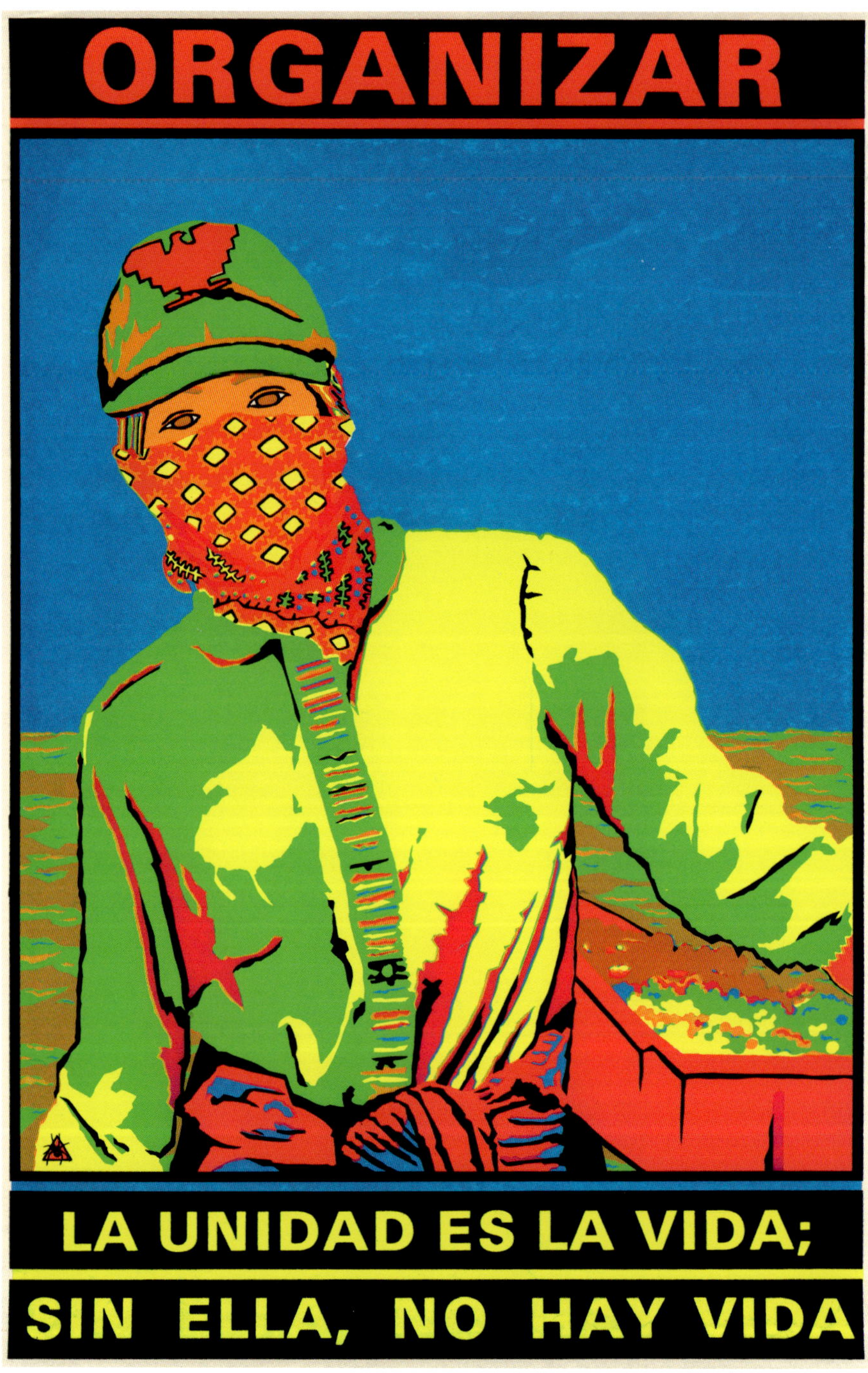


**Michael Callaghan** (designer and printer)
**Gregor Cullen** (designer and printer)
*Organizar* 1984

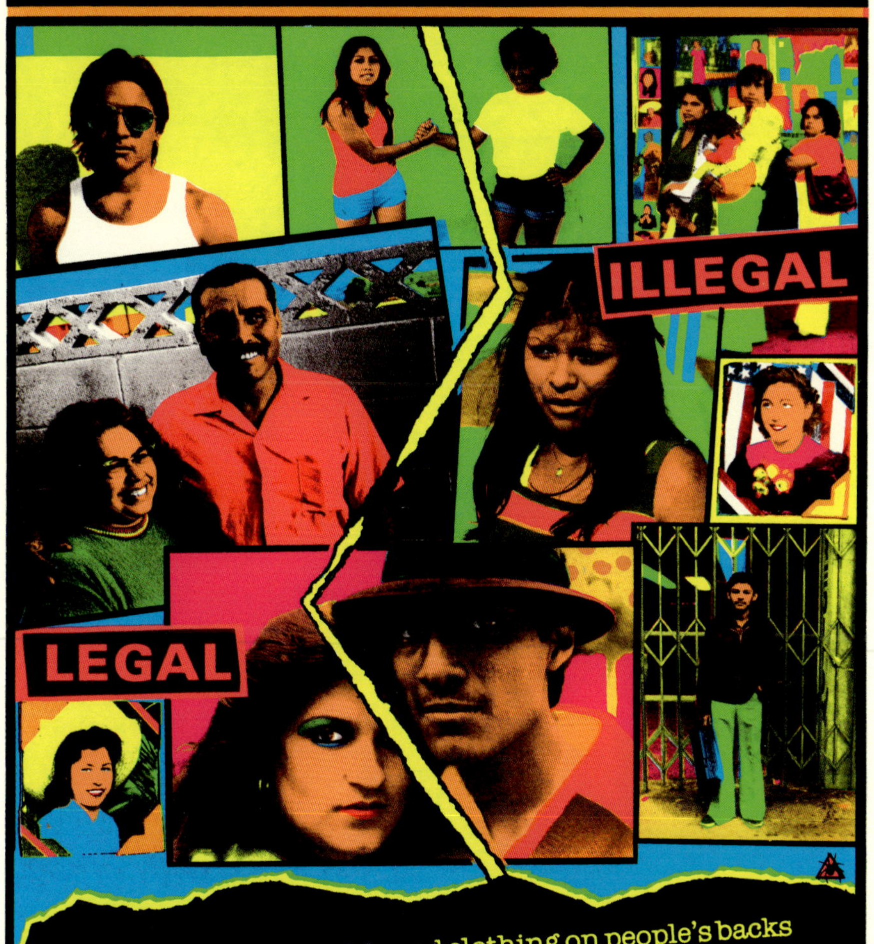


**Michael Callaghan** (designer and printer)
**Gregor Cullen** (designer and printer)
*Illegal/Legal* 1984

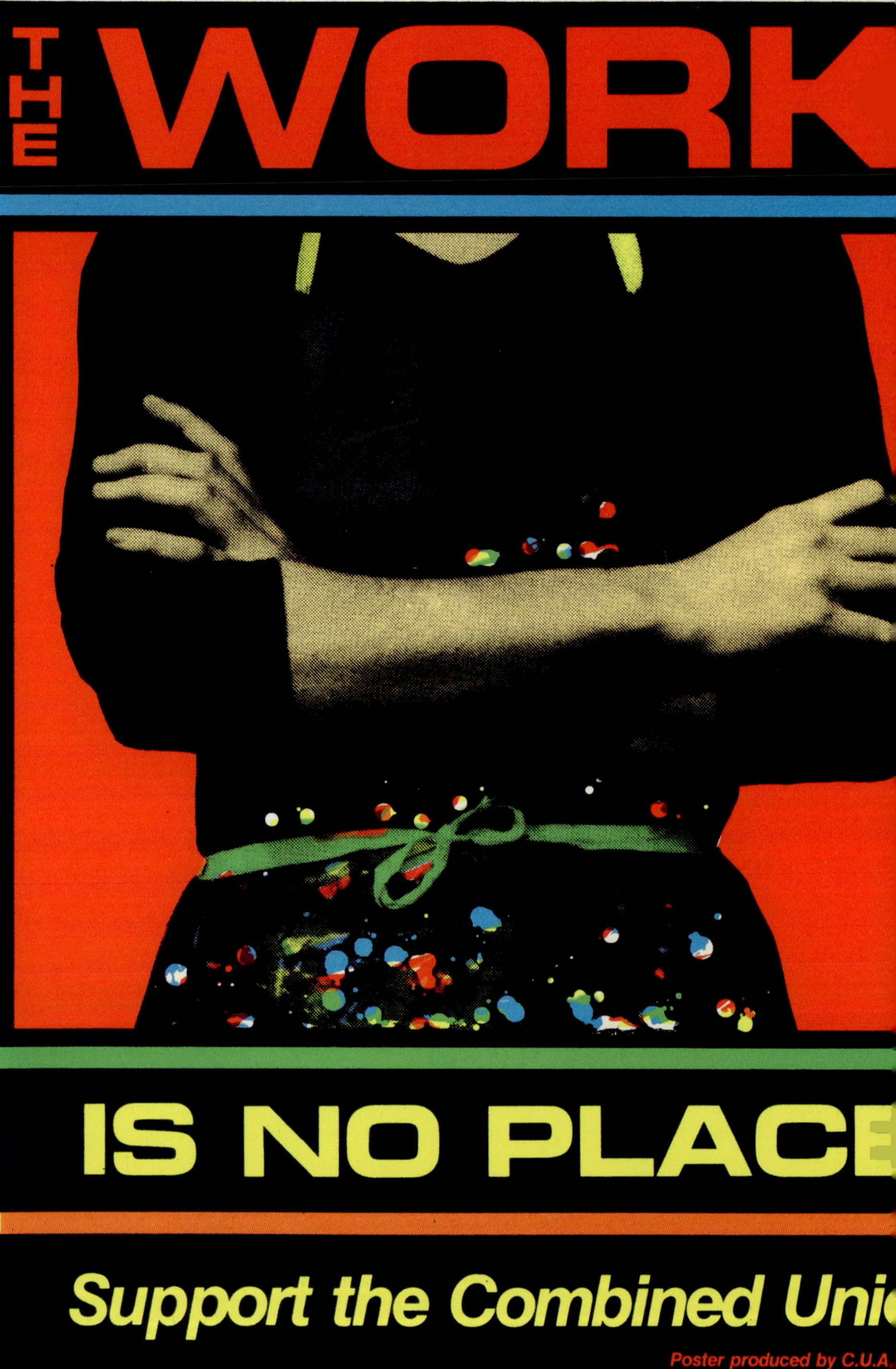
THE
WORK
IS NO PLACE
Support the Combined Uni
Poster produced by C.U.A.

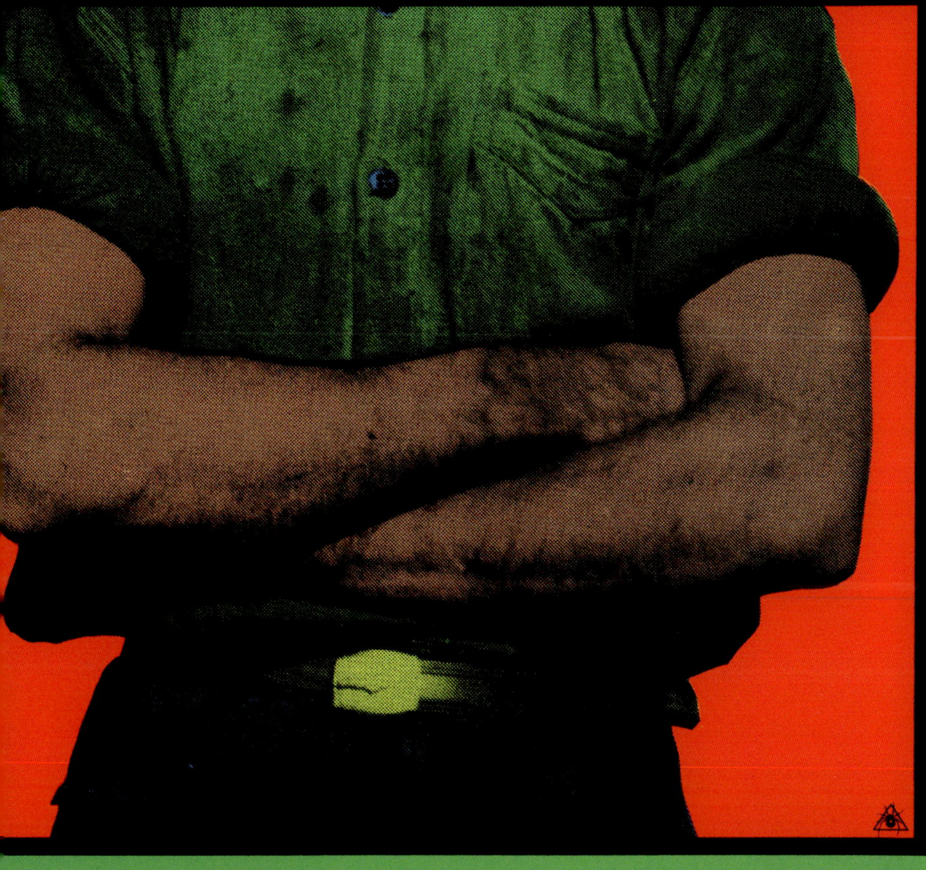


**Gregor Cullen** (designer and printer)
*The workplace is no place for racism* 1985

Chips Mackinolty, Jan Fieldsend, Julia Church, Toni Robertson, Paul Worstead and Ray Young, whose affiliation with screenprinting workshops extended as far back as the mid 1970s. Not since that decade, when posters possessed a real sense of political urgency, did a single issue generate such a powerful response. In her catalogue essay, Julie Ewington wrote:

> *Right here right now* counters revisionist nationalism with a new stock of images and motifs, some time-honored others recently emerged and some born of historical circumstances.[30]

The inventive visual language apparent in these posters – the Aboriginal flag, rainbow serpent, Captain Cook, Sydney Harbour Bridge, weapons, bones and land, along with slogans such as 'We have survived' addressed a range of issues from land rights to contact history.

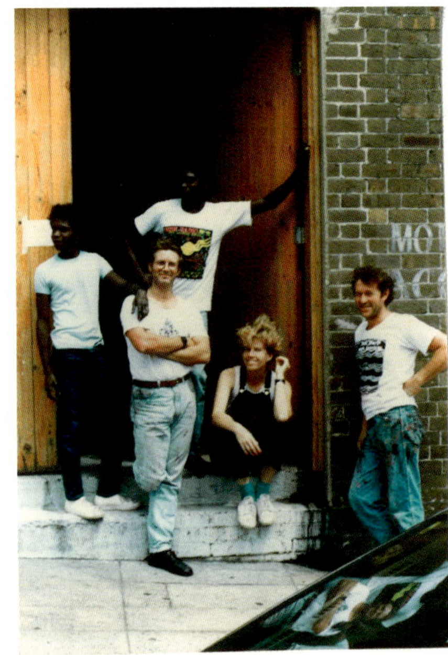

(above)
(From left) Neville Namarnyilk, Peter Curtis, Osmond Kantilla, Alison Alder, Ray Young outside Redback Graphix, Annandale in 1986. Photograph courtesy of Leonie Lane

**Michael Callaghan** (designer and printer)
**Ray Young** (printer)
*Tokyo hit beat* 1984

## 180 km north

When the lease expired on the Stuart Park studio in 1985 it coincided with a deepening local recession which had affected Redback's commissions. Callaghan and Cullen had always discussed the possibility of relocating to Sydney as a measure of their success, but Cullen's sense of commitment to Wollongong remained stronger than Callaghan's. He recalls: 'I hoped it would never happen … my roots were here 120 per cent'. Callaghan, on the other hand, had become increasingly frustrated with life in Wollongong and wanted to return to Sydney to expand the business. In addition, there were pockets of resistance within the council to renewing the lease. In the end, Cullen stayed in Wollongong and Callaghan relocated to Sydney with Alder and Lane. Of their relationship, Cullen has said: 'We performed like a rock and roll band. We had a fairly good partnership for five intense years and then like rock and roll bands do, we split up.'[31] Cullen still lives in Wollongong and continues to work in the area of design at the University of Wollongong, where he holds a teaching position.

Alder, Lane and Callaghan went into partnership in Sydney, and with financial backing bought a two-storey warehouse in Annandale. As with the Stuart Park studio, Callaghan and a friend customised the entire warehouse, separating out the printing and design areas over two levels. It took six months to refurbish the space. Alder recalls: 'We sunk a fair bit of money into it, trying to get a good ventilation system … By the time we finished we had a really beautiful workshop.'[32]

At Annandale the business grew to become a large, vibrant studio employing ten staff at its peak. As well as designers and printers, Redback employed a bookkeeper and several young apprentices. As the business expanded they also engaged an accountant to sort out contracts.

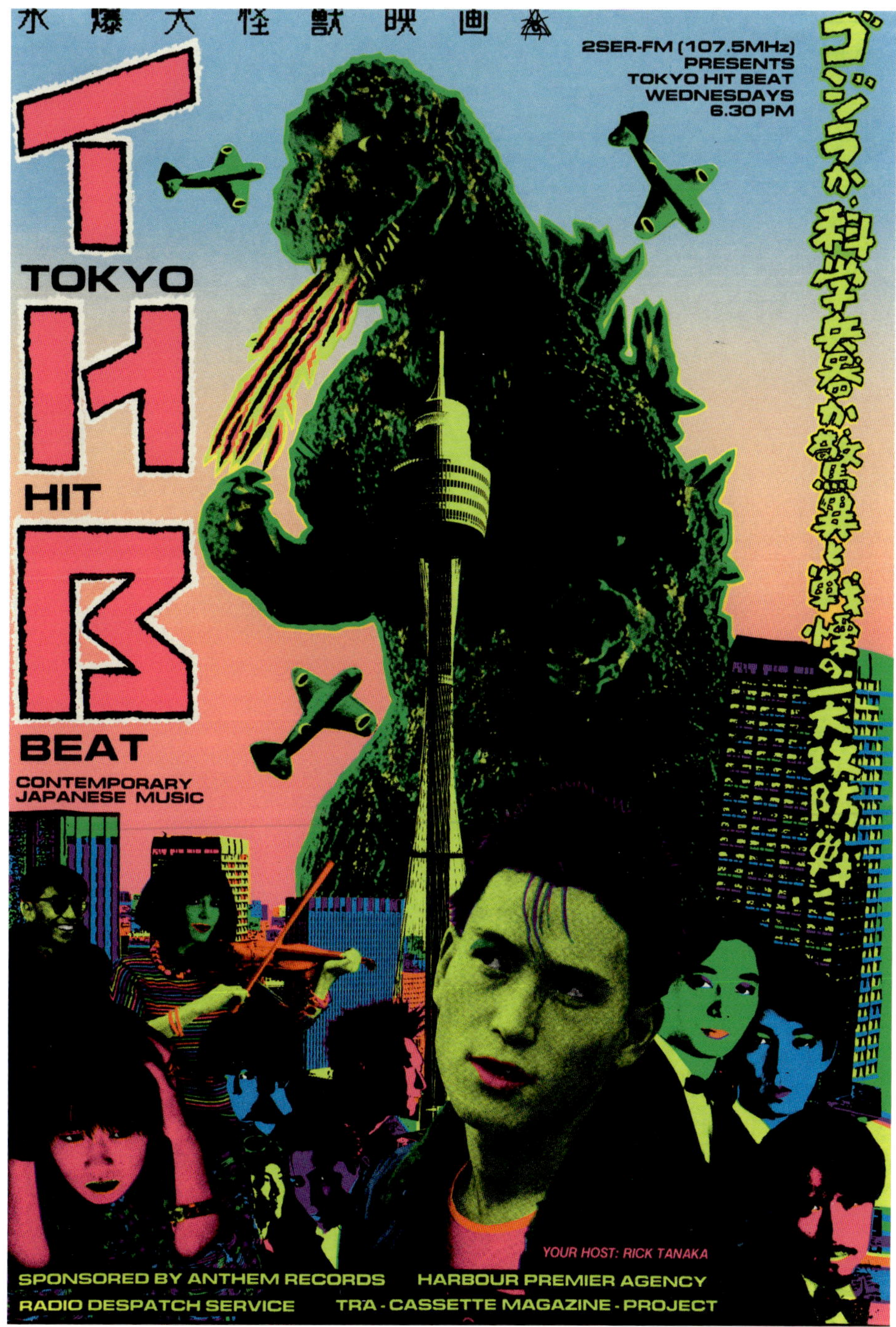

水爆大怪獣映画
2SER-FM (107.5MHz)
PRESENTS
TOKYO HIT BEAT
WEDNESDAYS
6.30 PM
ゴジラか、科学兵器か、驚異と戦慄の一大攻防戦！
TOKYO
HIT
BEAT
CONTEMPORARY
JAPANESE MUSIC
YOUR HOST: RICK TANAKA
SPONSORED BY ANTHEM RECORDS
HARBOUR PREMIER AGENCY
RADIO DESPATCH SERVICE
TRA - CASSETTE MAGAZINE - PROJECT

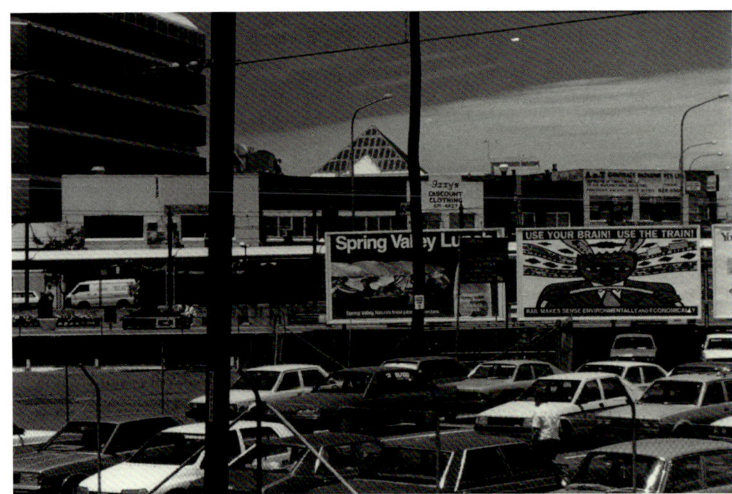

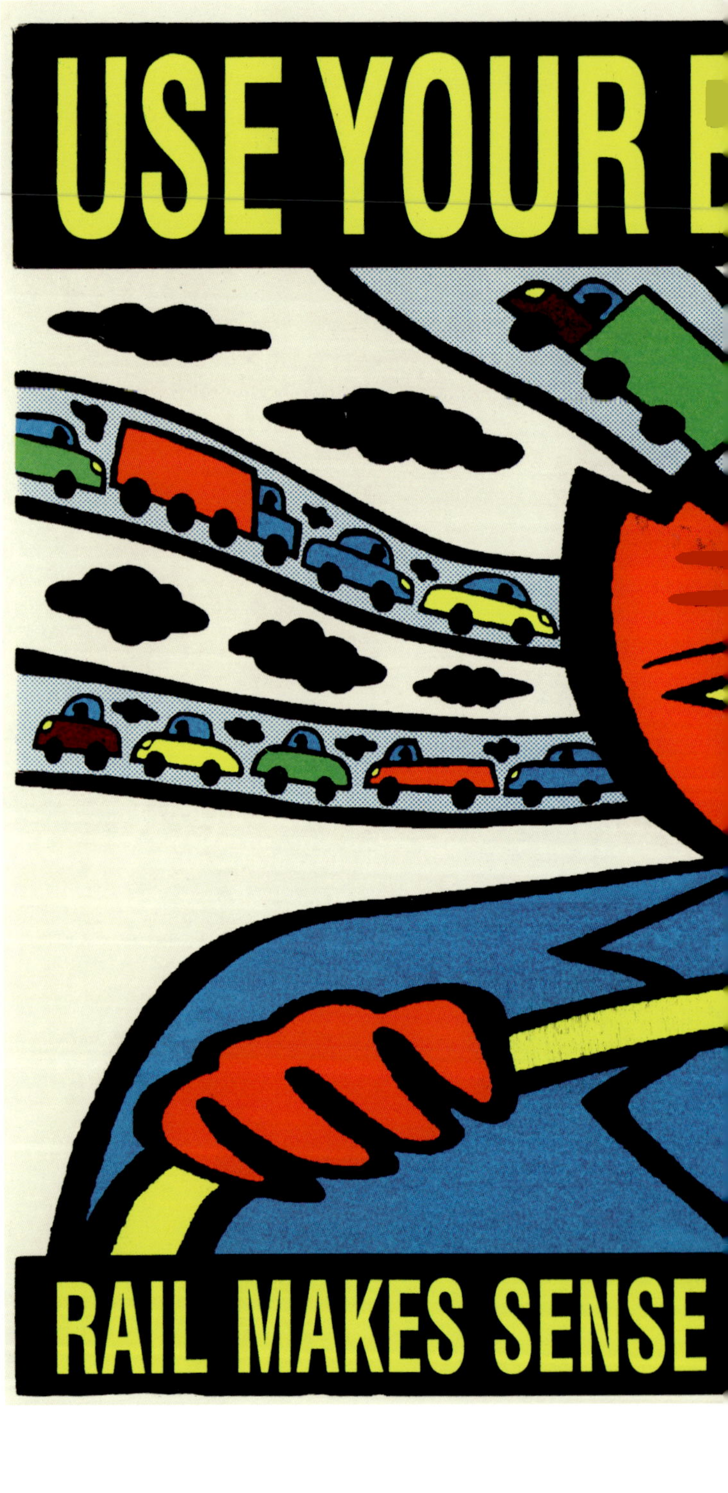

(above)
Installation photo of billboard at Blacktown, Sydney

(right)
**Michael Callaghan** (designer)
**Paul Cockram** (film planner)
*Use your brain, use the train* [billboard] 1990

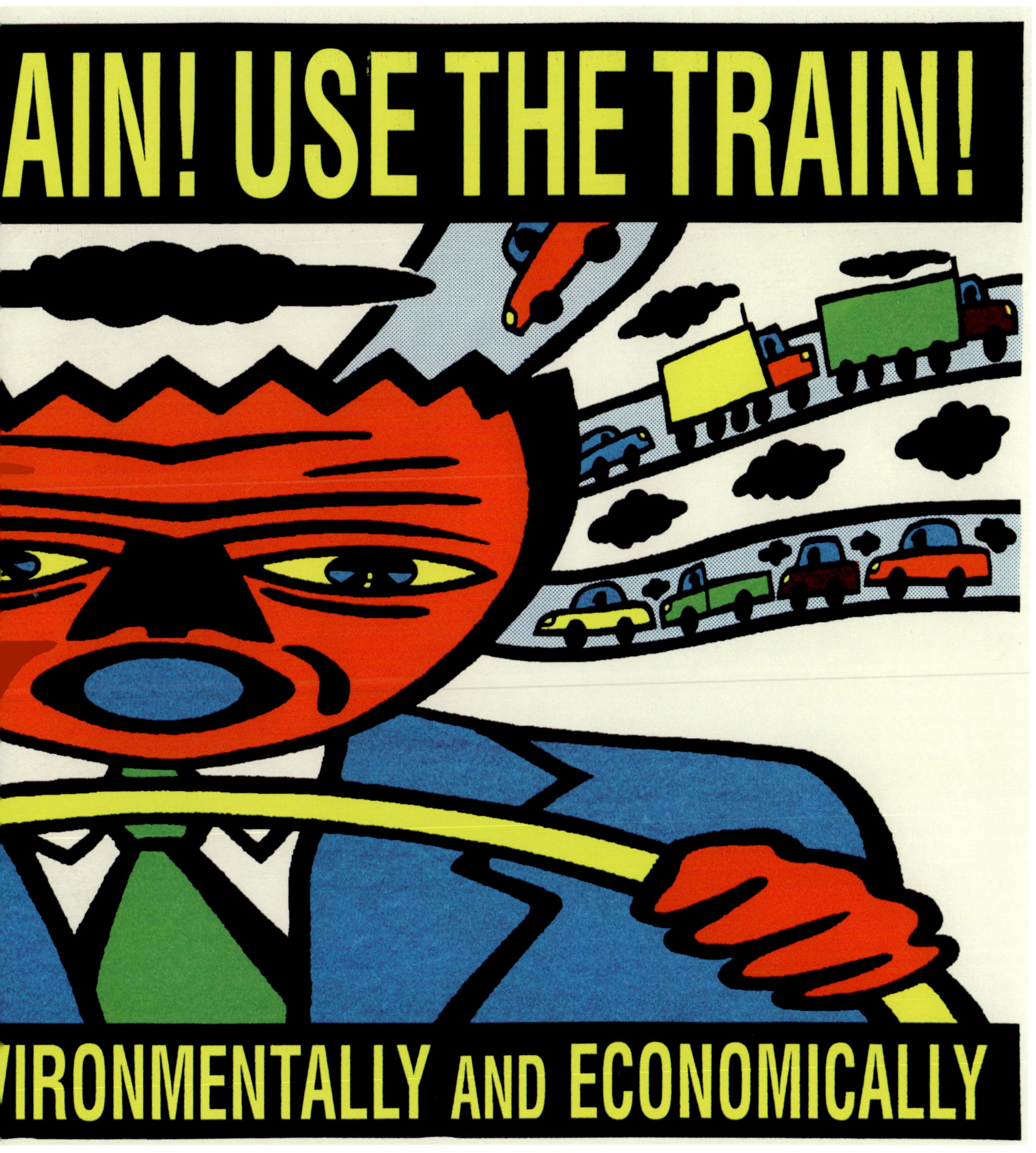
AIN! USE THE TRAIN!
IRONMENTALLY AND ECONOMICALLY

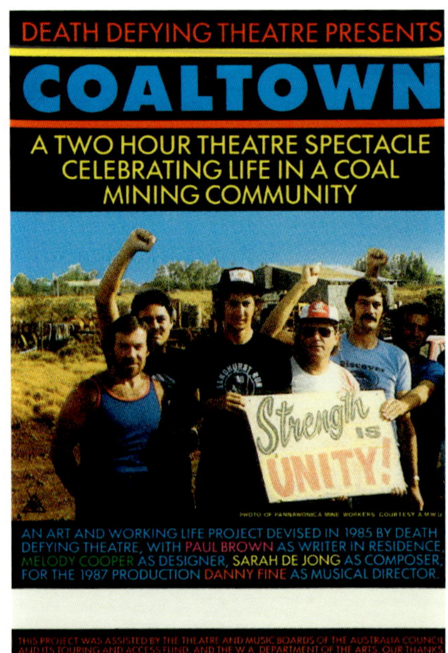


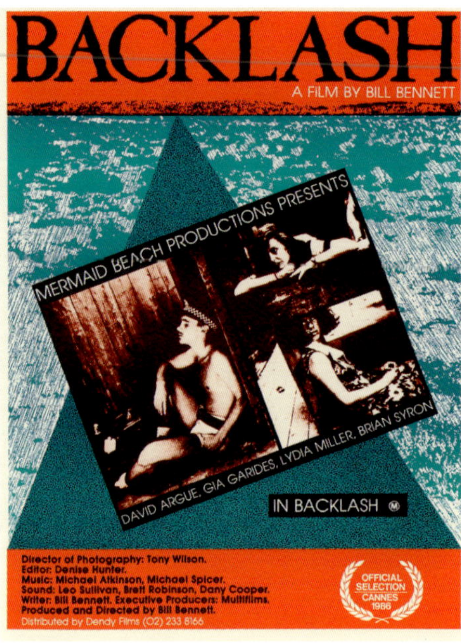


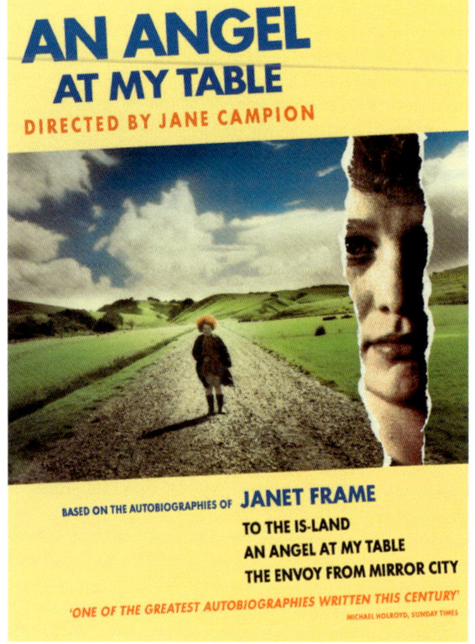


(above left)
**Alison Alder** (designer and printer)
*Coaltown* 1987

(above middle)
**Ray Young** (designer)
*Backlash* 1986

(above right)
**Leonie Lane** (designer)
*Leaflet: An angel at my table* c. 1990

(opposite)
**Michael Callaghan** (designer)
Tender hooks 1989

Callaghan and Alder managed the invoicing and workload, while individual jobs were distributed by consensus with each artist liaising directly with clients. The line between friendship and business was deliberately blurred, with many of Redback's clients coming from their broad social network. Friends and clients would drop by for boisterous lunches and regular Friday night drinks.

In Sydney the studio continued its relationship with national clients like Amnesty International and CAAMA and forged new ones. Film Australia commissioned Redback to produce a series of video covers and film posters for documentary and fiction feature films.

The Federal Labor Government provided Redback Graphix with a diverse range of work through its various departments. The Annandale studio produced posters for several national campaigns initiated by the Commonwealth Department of Health: 'Beat the Grog', HIV/AIDS awareness, nutrition and health awareness; and the Electoral Commission commissioned Redback to raise awareness of voting issues in Indigenous Australian communities. It was the technical virtuosity and remarkable graphics of these federally funded projects that defined the posters from the Annandale studio.

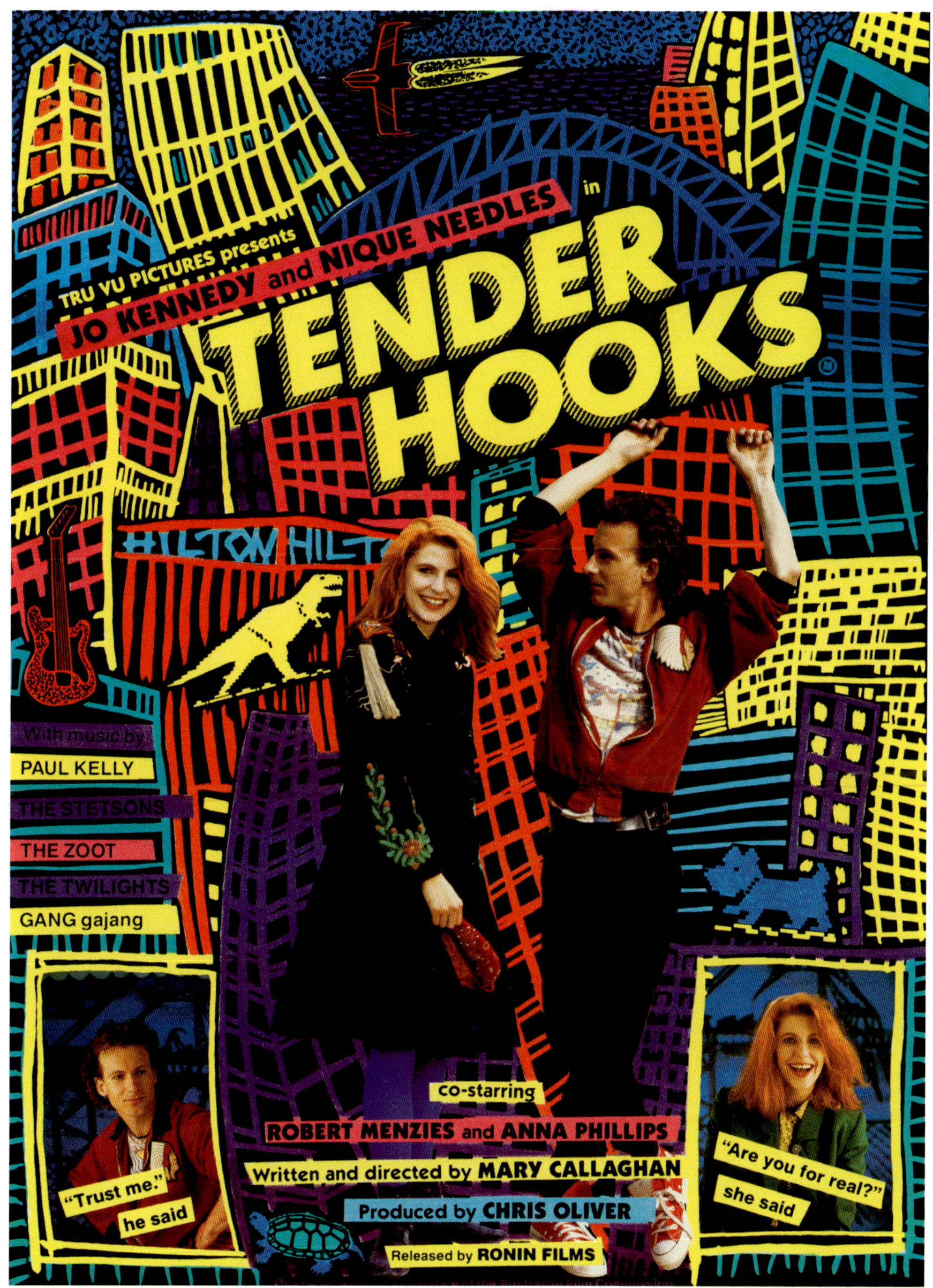
TRU VU PICTURES presents
JO KENNEDY and NIQUE NEEDLES
in
TENDER HOOKS
With music by
PAUL KELLY
THE STETSONS
THE ZOOT
THE TWILIGHTS
GANG gajang
co-starring
ROBERT MENZIES and ANNA PHILLIPS
Written and directed by MARY CALLAGHAN
Produced by CHRIS OLIVER
Released by RONIN FILMS
"Trust me."
he said
"Are you for real?"
she said

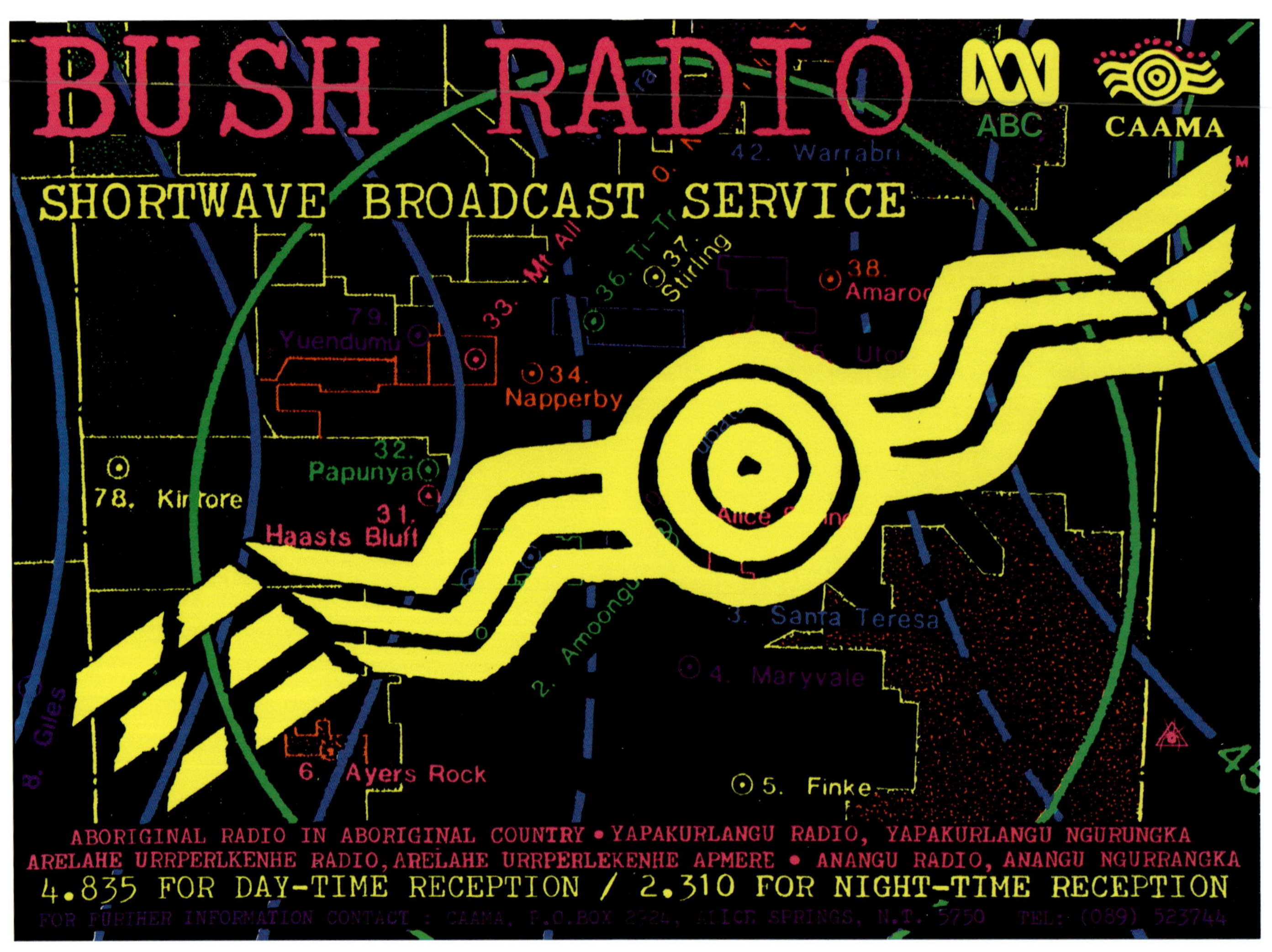


**Michael Callaghan** (designer and printer)
**Ray Young** (printer)
*Bush radio* 1985

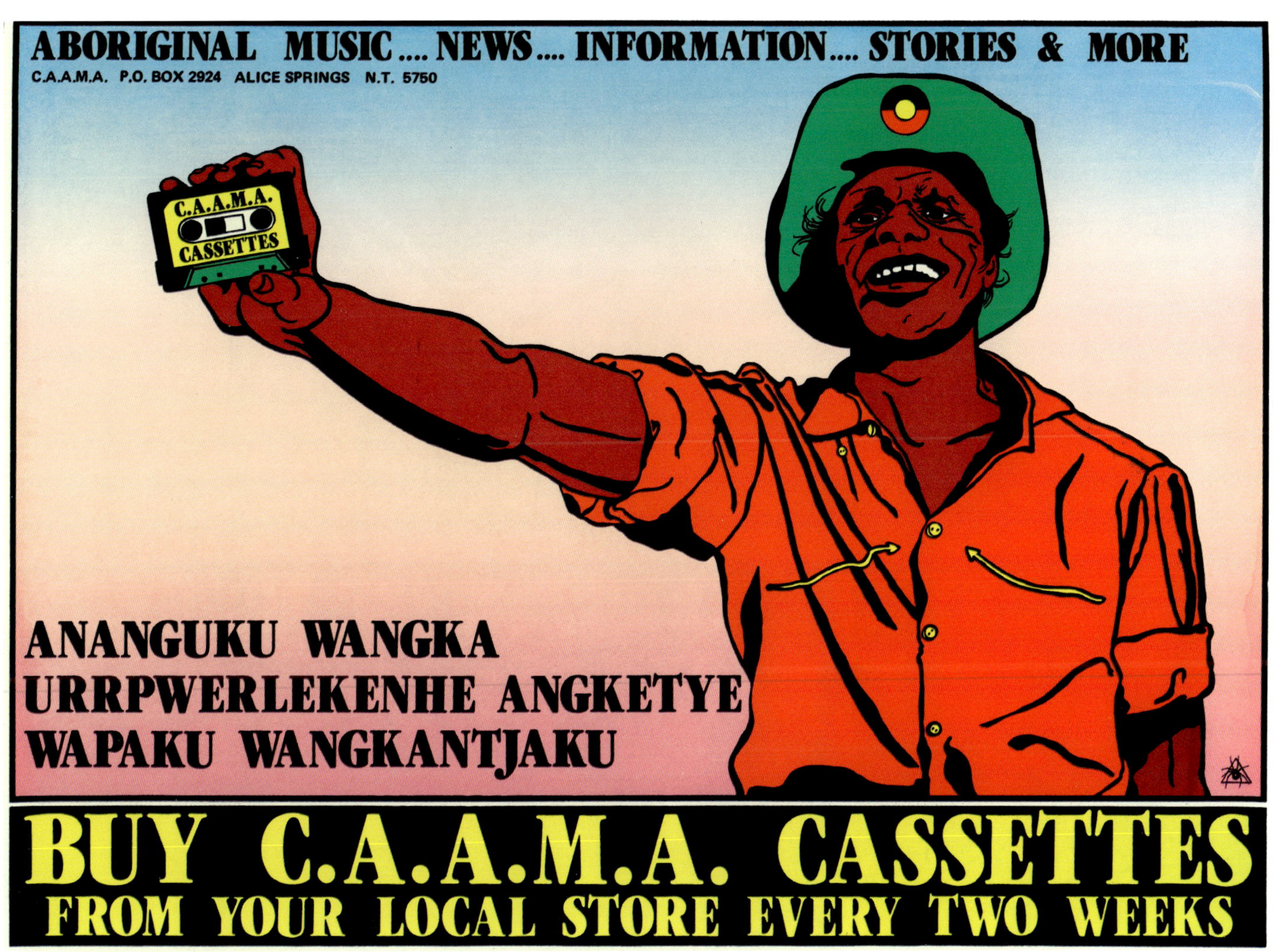


**Michael Callaghan** (designer and printer)
**Jeff Stewart** (illustrator)
*Buy CAAMA cassettes* 1984

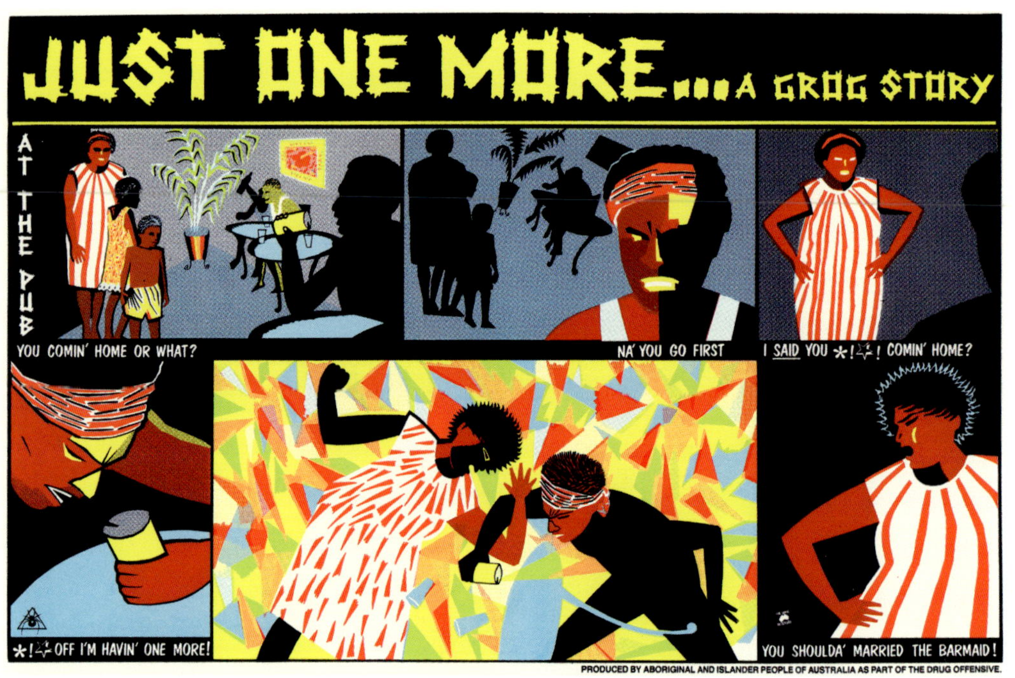
JUST ONE MORE... A GROG STORY
AT THE PUB
YOU COMIN' HOME OR WHAT?
NA' YOU GO FIRST
I SAID YOU *!*! COMIN' HOME?
*!* OFF I'M HAVIN' ONE MORE!
YOU SHOULDA' MARRIED THE BARMAID!
PRODUCED BY ABORIGINAL AND ISLANDER PEOPLE OF AUSTRALIA AS PART OF THE DRUG OFFENSIVE.

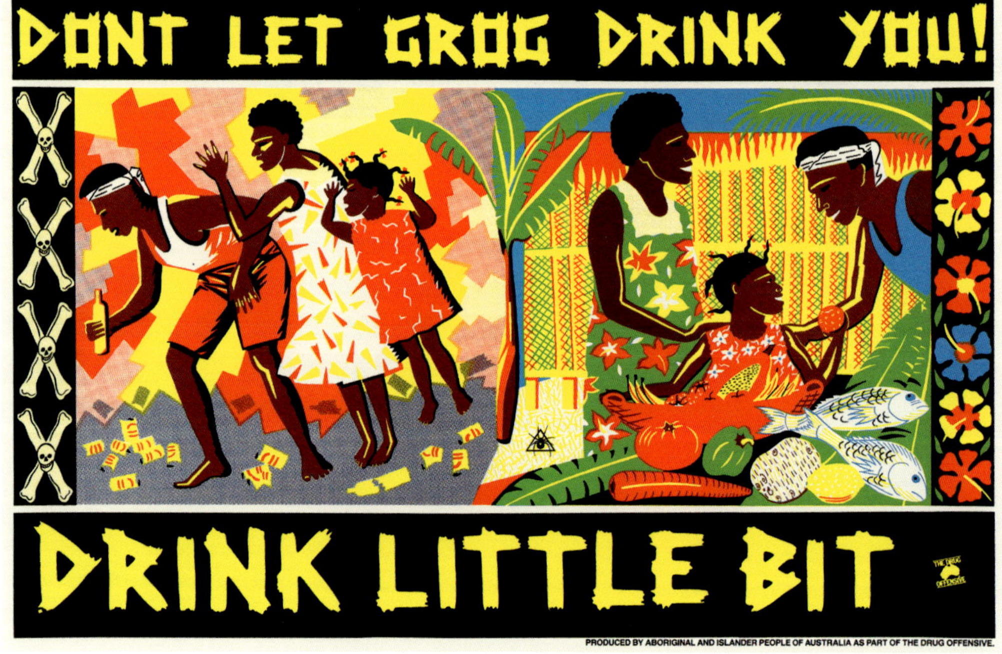
DONT LET GROG DRINK YOU!
DRINK LITTLE BIT
THE DRUG OFFENSIVE
PRODUCED BY ABORIGINAL AND ISLANDER PEOPLE OF AUSTRALIA AS PART OF THE DRUG OFFENSIVE.

Marie McMahon returned to Redback in 1987 and worked on several of these federally funded government posters, initially for the Electoral Commission and later a Department of Health initiative to address alcohol abuse in Aboriginal communities. Paul Cockram had arrived at the studio the previous year. His experience in offset printing and graphic design enabled the studio to experiment with offset techniques, using four screens: cyan, magenta, yellow and black, to reproduce multiple colours using a dot screen. He was instrumental in producing the technically complex, large-scale poster series *May day* 1986, *Eight hour day* 1987 and *Women and work* 1988.

While the visual material may have been largely sourced from McMahon's own archive, the concepts for the posters were developed in close consultation with Aboriginal communities. This was the case for all of the federally funded campaigns that Callaghan, Alder, Stephen Lees, Young and Cockram worked on as well. Government health workers would meet with communities to discuss ideas for campaigns and isolate particular issues.

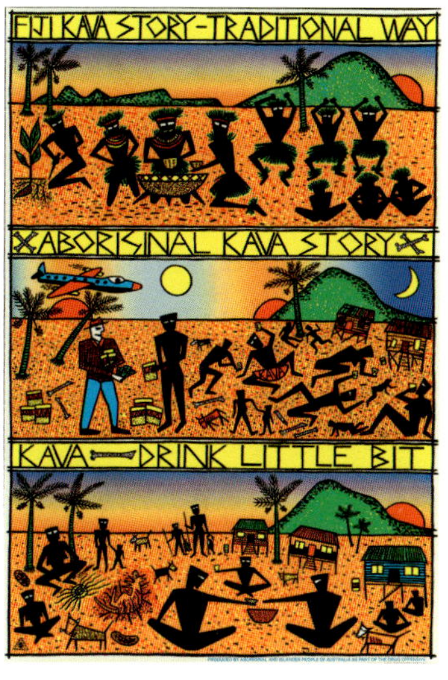


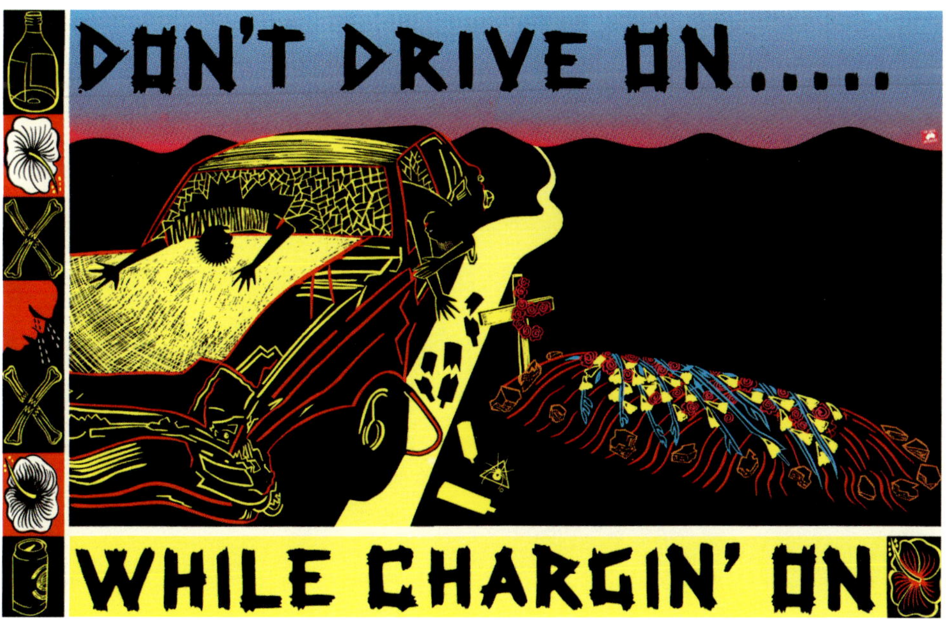


(opposite above)
**Marie McMahon** (designer and printer)
**Peter Curtis** (printer)
*Just one more* 1988

(opposite below)
**Marie McMahon** (designer and printer)
**Peter Curtis** (printer)
*Drink little bit* 1987

(left)
**Marie McMahon** (designer) and
**Peter Curtis** (printer)
*Don't drive on* 1987

(above)
**Michael Callaghan** (designer) and
**Alison Alder** (printer)
*Kava story* 1988

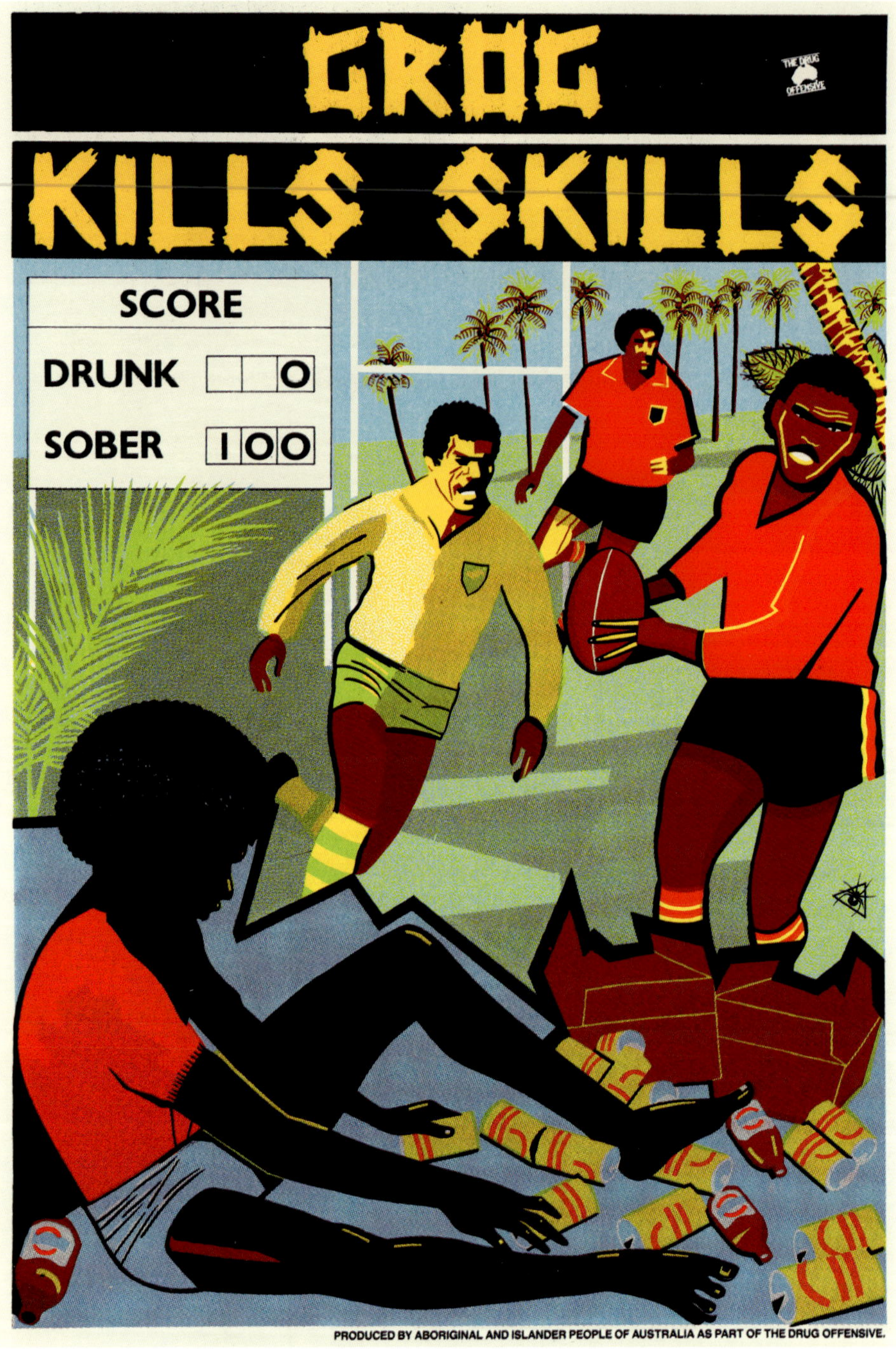


**Marie McMahon** (designer)
**Peter Curtis** (printer)
*Grog kills skills* [football] 1988

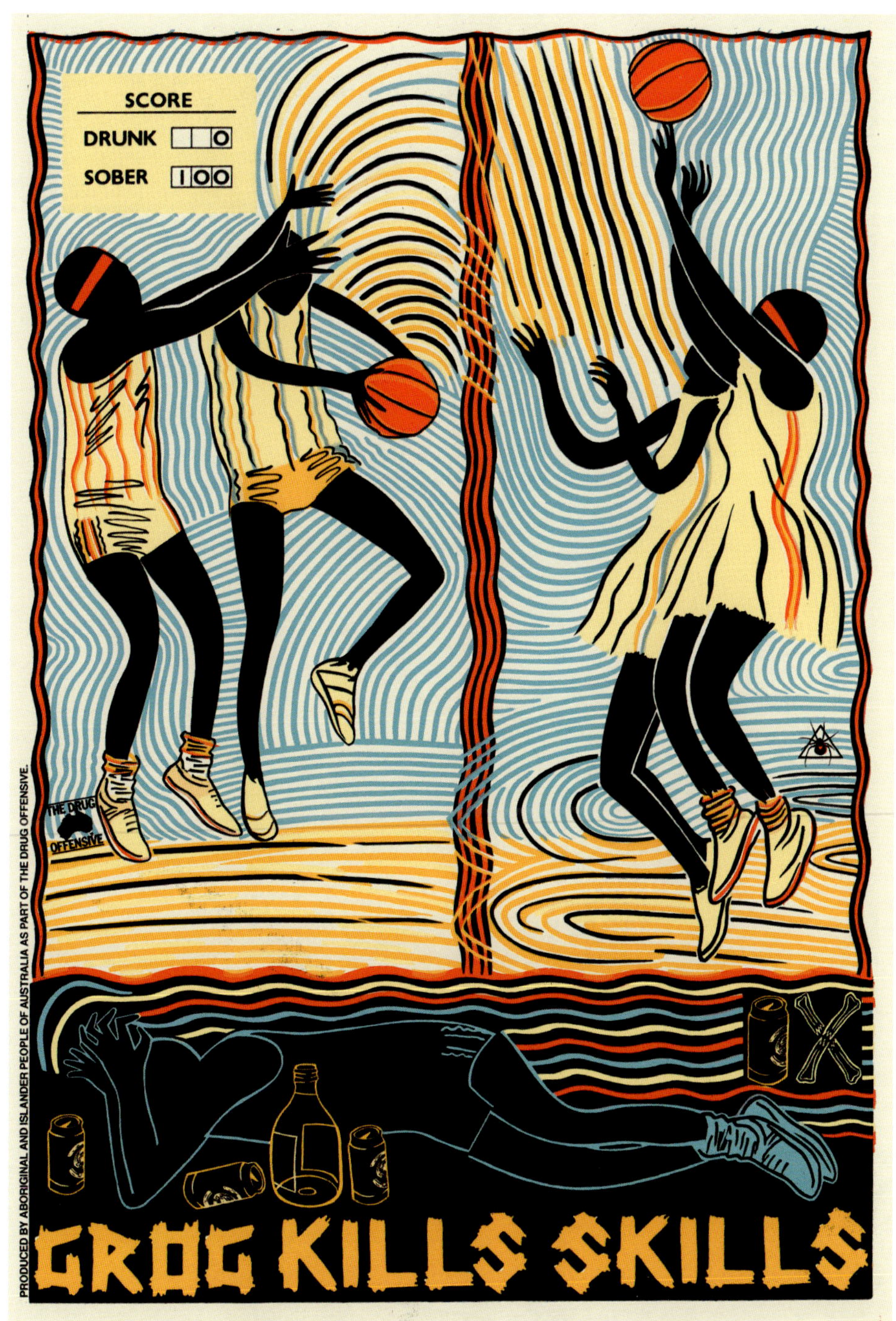


**Marie McMahon** (designer)
**Peter Curtis** (printer)
*Grog kills skills* [basketball] 1986

In these sessions text would often be finalised and accompanied by rough thumbnail sketches. Based on these sketches, McMahon would produce small versions of the poster, which would then be relayed back to the communities for comment. Once the design was finalised, McMahon would reproduce the illustration on drafting film using film correction paint. Ultimately McMahon was ambivalent about the effectiveness of the posters that she felt had been 'designed by committee'.[33]

McMahon's first poster was for the Drug Offensive campaign. *Grog kills skills* 1988 depicts a rugby match with a scoreboard that features team names changed to read 'drunk' and 'sober'. Utilising the yellow, red and black of the Aboriginal flag, as well as blue and brown, this five-stencil poster combines illustrative techniques that are representational and semi-abstract within the one composition. Symbolic elements are frequently embedded in McMahon's posters. In *Empty kids* 1987, a skeleton stands beside a petrol pump, his leg entangled in the hose that pumps petrol into a coffin. The cross on the coffin's lid directs the viewer towards some floating figures. McMahon drew on her personal experience living in Aboriginal communities in establishing the night-time setting. She remembered sniffers being described as 'spooks of the night', so fashioned them as ghostly figures.[34] Rather than taking a moralistic position, the poster attempted to promote a more compassionate approach. Many of McMahon's illustrations were based on her own personal photographs taken while living in Aboriginal communities and reproduced in composite form.

In the course of this collaborative work practice, a distinctive visual language emerged that combined elements of Aboriginal and non-Aboriginal style, symbolism, historical and artistic references.[35] For a federally funded AIDS prevention program, Callaghan and Cockram designed a poster in collaboration with Torres Strait Islander communities that was based on the *Phantom*, a DC comic popular with the locals. The resulting poster, *Condoman* 1988, features a black, condom-wielding superhero who urges people to 'use Frenchies!'. Its broad appeal prompted the government to re-order and distribute the poster within the Australian Navy. Several more AIDS prevention posters were commissioned by the Government to address the Torres Strait Islander communities – *You don't have to be a queenie to get AIDS* 1988 and *No condom – no way* 1988. Like *Condoman*, they were set against a recognisable background of palm trees and beaches and rendered in a graphic style of comic books.

(opposite)
**Marie McMahon** (designer)
**Peter Curtis** (printer)
*Empty kids* 1987

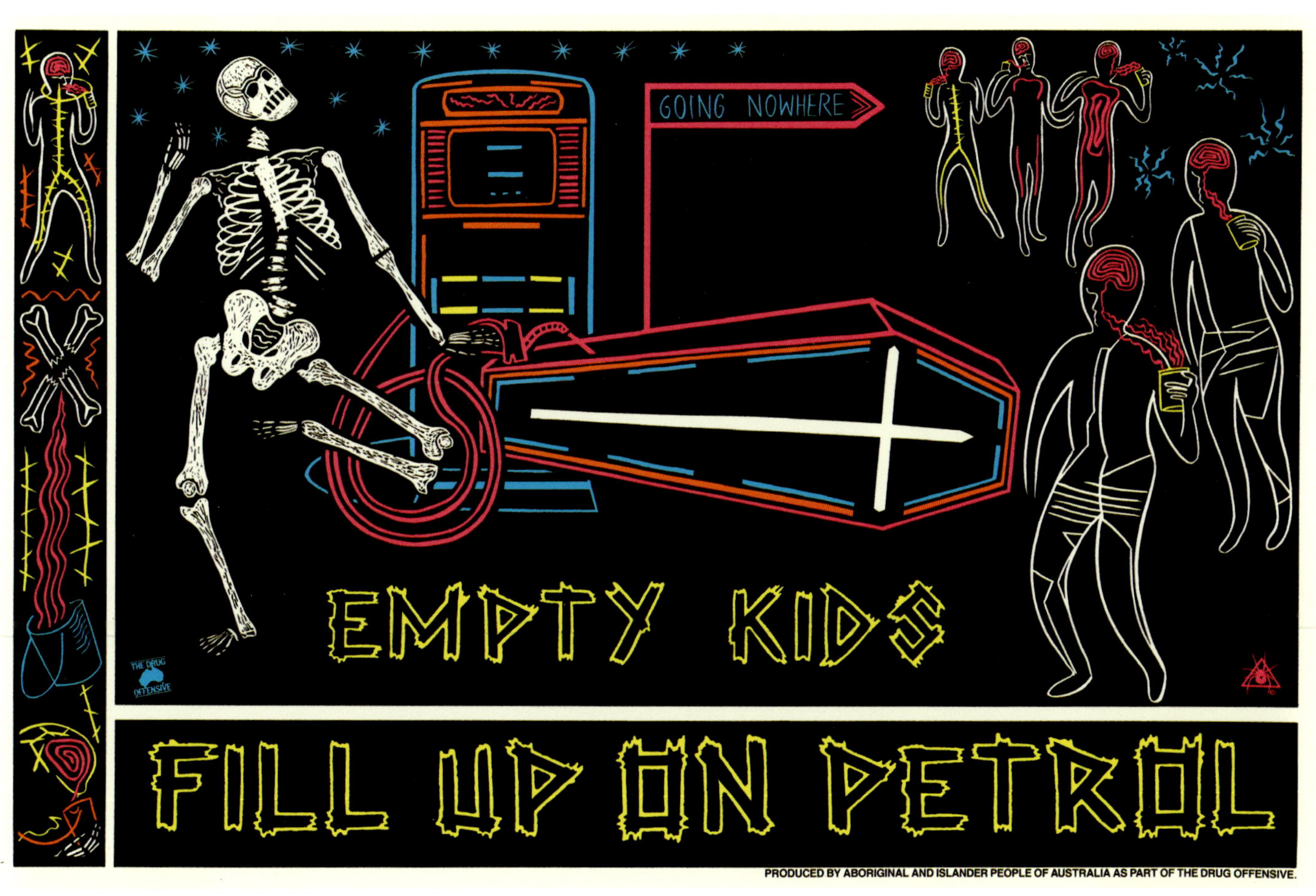
GOING NOWHERE
EMPTY KIDS
THE DRUG OFFENSIVE
FILL UP ON PETROL
PRODUCED BY ABORIGINAL AND ISLANDER PEOPLE OF AUSTRALIA AS PART OF THE DRUG OFFENSIVE.

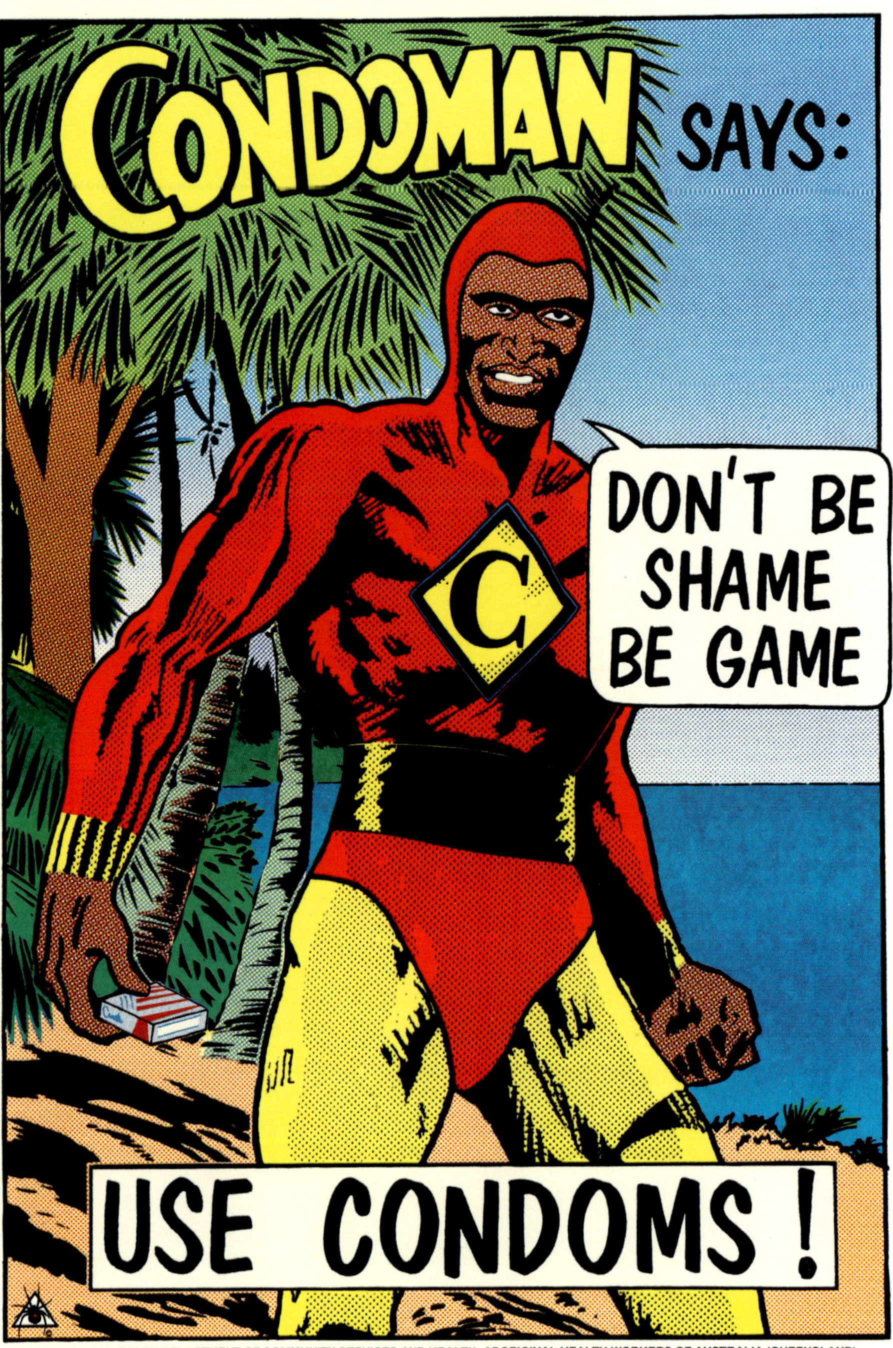


**Michael Callaghan** (designer)
**Marie McMahon** (illustrator)
**Paul Cockram** (film planner)
*Condoman says: Use condoms!* 1988

(opposite)
**Stephen Lees** (designer)
**Paul Cockram** (film planner)
**Alison Alder** (printer)
*No condom – no way!* 1988

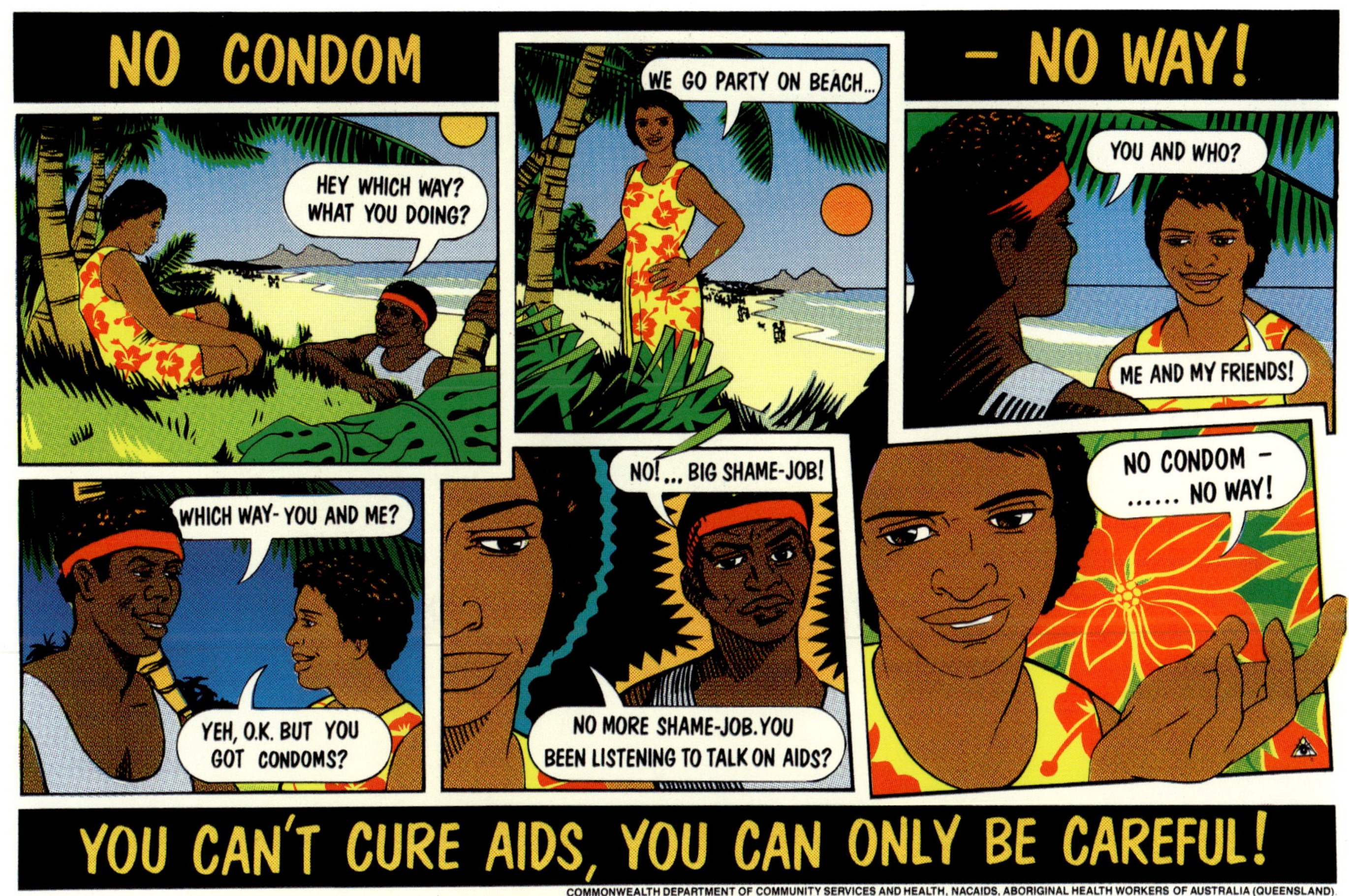
NO CONDOM – NO WAY!
HEY WHICH WAY? WHAT YOU DOING?
WE GO PARTY ON BEACH...
YOU AND WHO?
ME AND MY FRIENDS!
WHICH WAY- YOU AND ME?
YEH, O.K. BUT YOU GOT CONDOMS?
NO! ... BIG SHAME-JOB!
NO MORE SHAME-JOB. YOU BEEN LISTENING TO TALK ON AIDS?
NO CONDOM – ...... NO WAY!
YOU CAN'T CURE AIDS, YOU CAN ONLY BE CAREFUL!
COMMONWEALTH DEPARTMENT OF COMMUNITY SERVICES AND HEALTH, NACAIDS, ABORIGINAL HEALTH WORKERS OF AUSTRALIA (QUEENSLAND)

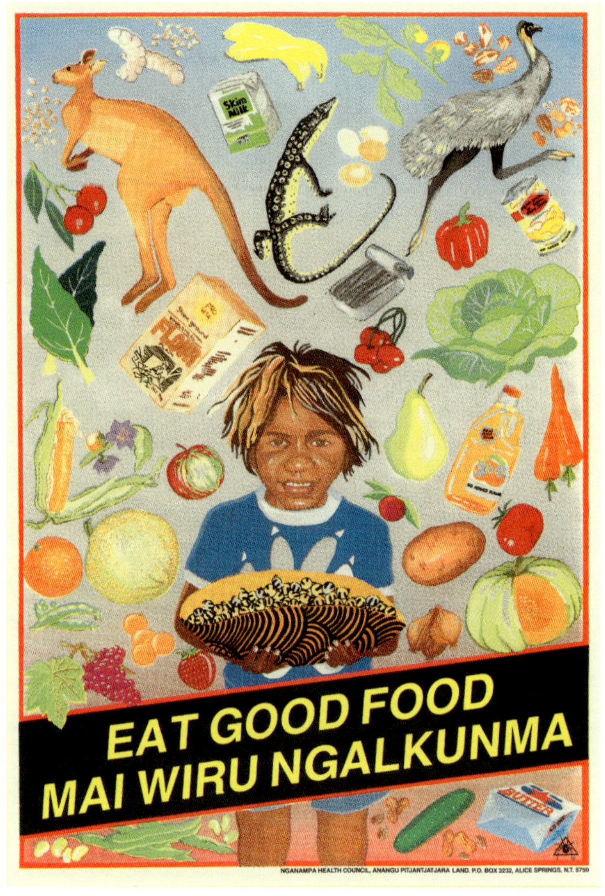


While Condoman appropriated images from US popular culture, other posters designed by Redback adopted the motifs and designs of Aboriginal art and craft. McMahon's series on the subject of alcohol abuse, *Pregnancy* 1988, *Grog kills skills – basketball* 1988 borrow the 'X-ray' technique and fine line work of paintings from Western Arnhem Land; *Caring and sharing without grog* 1987, makes use of the carved emu eggs of the Lower Murray River region; *Enrol and vote* 1987 draws on the decorative fabrics of the Torres Strait. By combining Indigenous and non-Indigenous elements, the posters are invested with a particularly intense quality. This effect of excess is evident, for example, in the repeated line marks that surround an illustration of a basketball player in *Grog kills skills – basketball*. It references both the style of paintings from Arnhem Land as well as the conventions of comic books, in which a series of lines signify movement. The very proliferation of lines in McMahon's poster is fantastically disconcerting.

**Leonie Lane** (designer and printer)
**Peter Curtis** (printer)
*Eat good food* 1987

(opposite)
**Marie McMahon** (designer)
**Alison Alder** (printer)
*Pregnancy* 1988

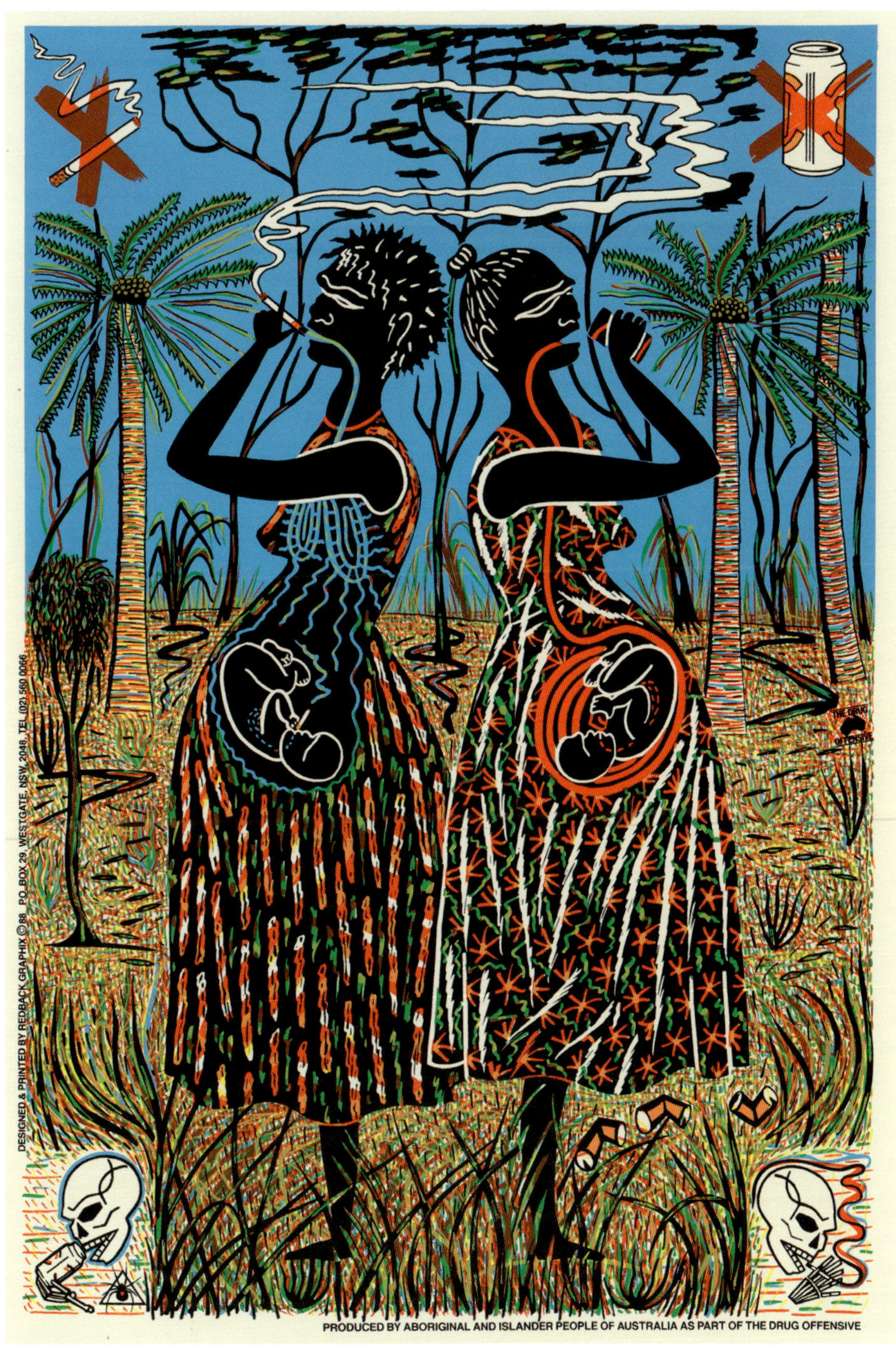
DESIGNED & PRINTED BY REDBACK GRAPHIX © 88 P.O. BOX 29, WESTGATE, NSW 2048. TEL (02) 560 0096
THE DRUG OFFENSIVE
PRODUCED BY ABORIGINAL AND ISLANDER PEOPLE OF AUSTRALIA AS PART OF THE DRUG OFFENSIVE

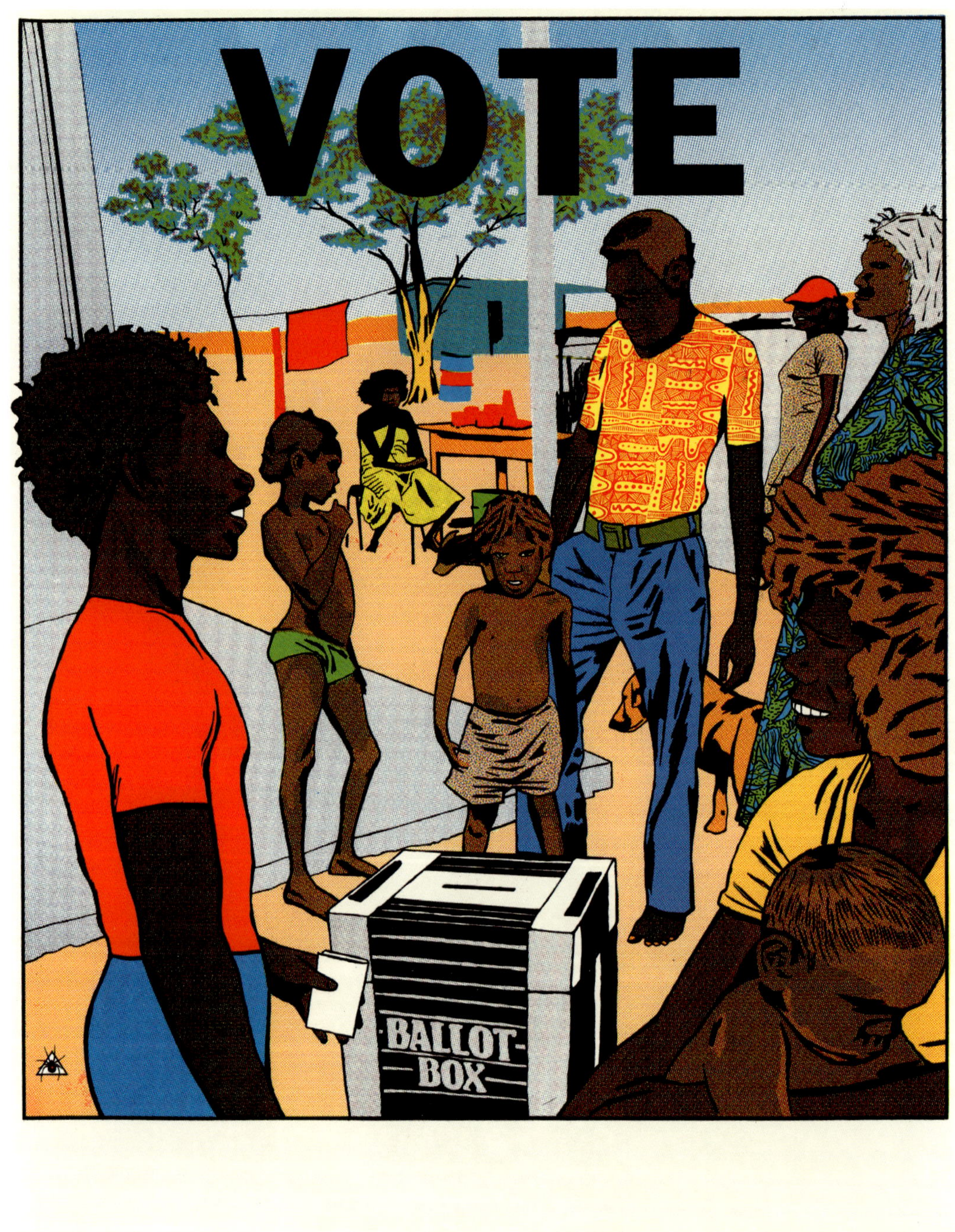
VOTE
BALLOT-
BOX

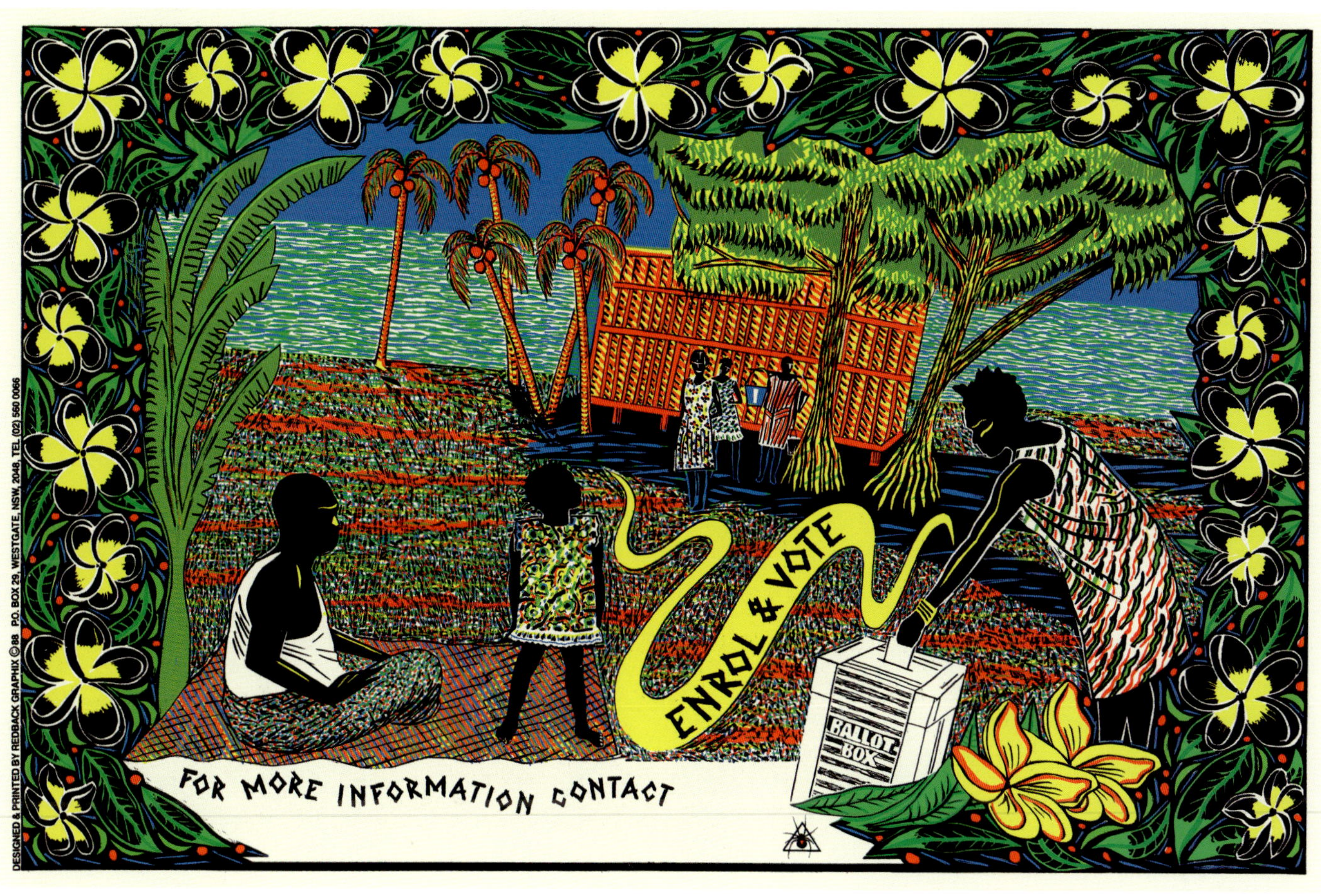


(opposite)
**Marie McMahon** (designer)
**Peter Curtis** (printer)
*Vote* 1987

(above)
**Marie McMahon** (designer)
**Peter Curtis** (printer)
*Enrol and vote – Torres Strait Islands* 1987

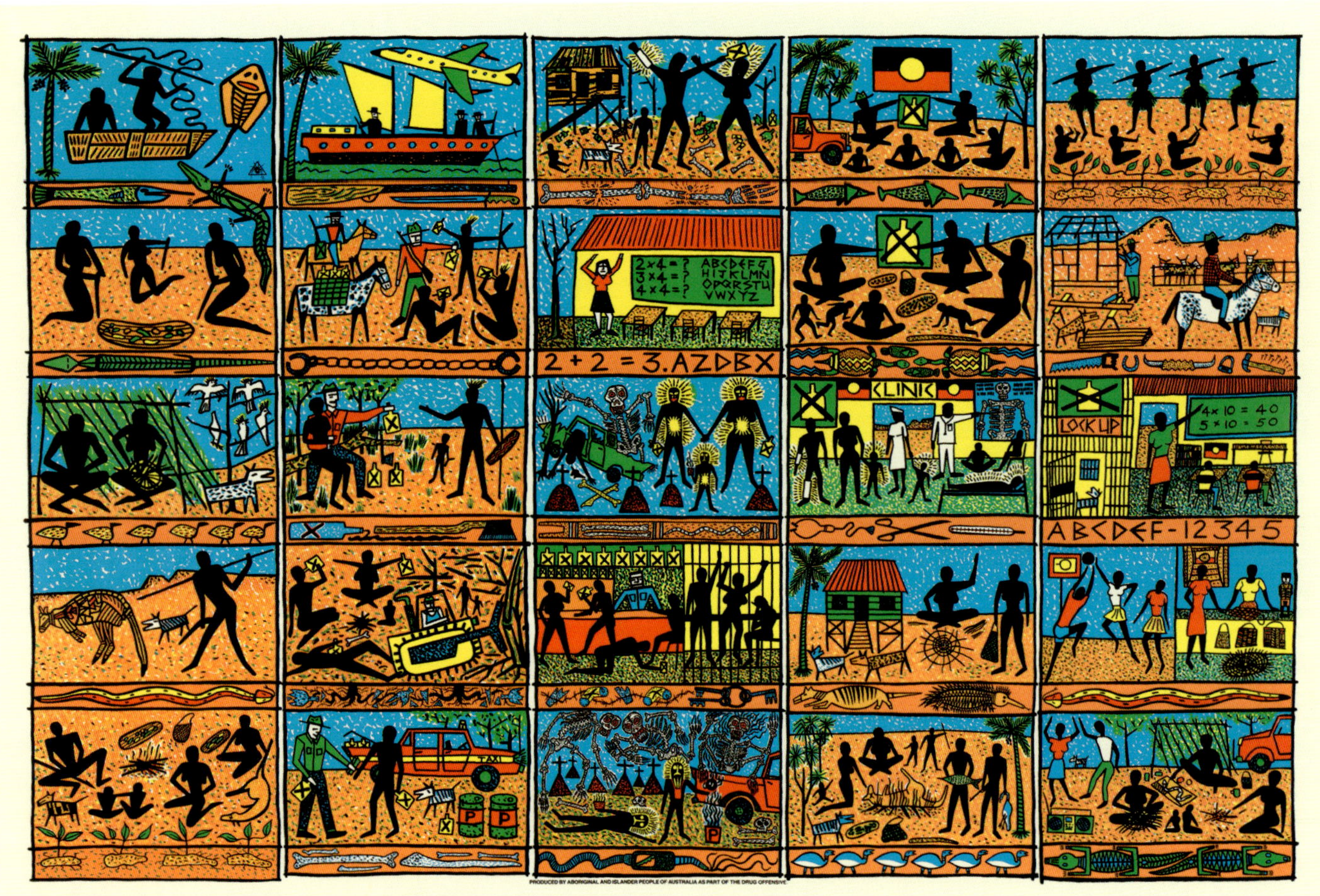
2×4=?
3×4=?
4×4=?
ABCDEFG
HIJKLMN
OPQRSTU
VWXYZ
2+2 = 3.AZDBX
CLINIC
LOCK UP
4×10 = 40
5×10 = 50
ABCDEF-12345
TAXI
P
P
P
PRODUCED BY ABORIGINAL AND ISLANDER PEOPLE OF AUSTRALIA AS PART OF THE DRUG OFFENSIVE

It is as though the intersection of these two symbolic systems, Indigenous and non-Indigenous, over-animates the surface. A similar exuberance is apparent in *Enrol and vote*. McMahon frames a central illustration of a girl casting a vote against a backdrop of a remote island setting, with an intricate border of plants and frangipani flowers, in the style of fabrics from the Torres Strait Islands. The patterned border, however, refuses to be contained and the fecund foliage verges on occupying the composition and marginalising the 'scene' proper.

Commissions for posters aimed at the Aboriginal community changed Redback's approach to composition. Since the posters were targeted at non-English speaking communities, their message needed to be conveyed primarily through images. Whereas the majority of the Wollongong posters flanked a central image with bands of text, many of the posters produced in Sydney display a greater integration of pictorial and textual elements. Others, such as *Big grog story* 1988, *Pregnancy* 1988, and *Beat the grog* 1986 used no text at all. *Beat the grog*, a poster designed by Callaghan and printed with Alder in 1986, tackles the issue of alcohol abuse through the form of a storyboard. Divided into four sections, the composition shows a schematic, chronological account of the introduction of alcohol into Aboriginal communities by the Europeans, disintegration of traditional practices and, in the last frame, its restoration as a result of abstinence. Callaghan's concept for the poster emerged from a truly mind-bending conflation of influences – the expressionless faces found in Aboriginal paintings and Governor Arthur's pictograph poster advocating equal justice for blacks and whites pasted up in 1828.[36] Two years later, Callaghan's follow-up poster on the same subject, *Big grog story*, elaborates on the earlier poster's formal strategies. Divided into twenty-five sections, the poster narrates the devastation wrought by European contact through pictograms and illustrations – snakes, roots, bones, petrol pumps, birds, tools, broken bottles, swords, guns, dolphins and turtles. It is easy to criticise the baldness of these posters, to describe them as simplistic, even patronising, but as posters addressing non-English-speaking Aboriginal communities, they conveyed their message with unambiguous clarity.

(opposite)
**Michael Callaghan** (designer)
**Peter Curtis** (printer)
*Big grog story* 1988

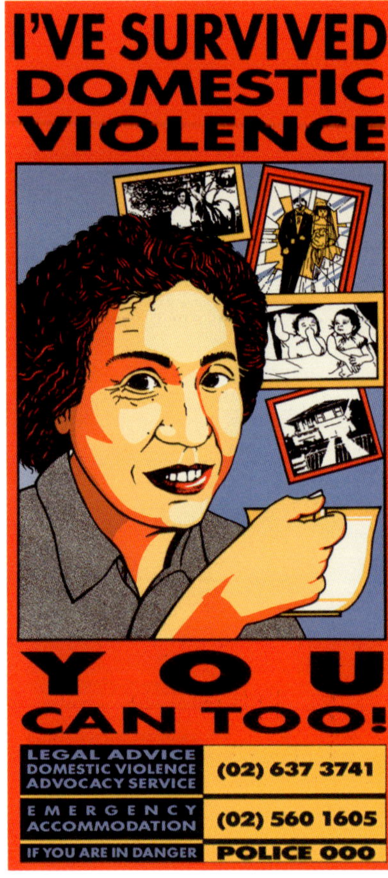


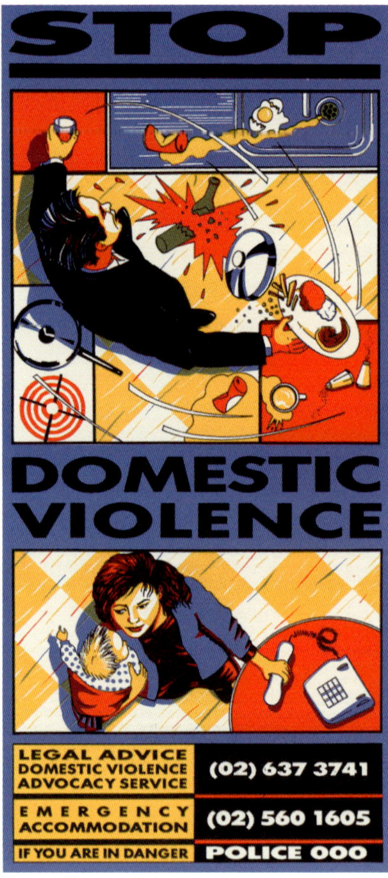


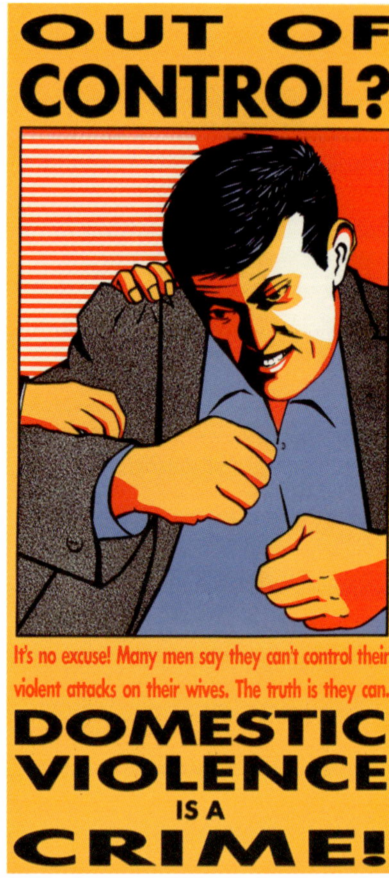


(above left)
**Leonie Lane** (designer)
*I've survived domestic violence* 1988

(above middle)
**Leonie Lane** (designer)
*Stop domestic violence* 1988

(above right)
**Leonie Lane** (designer)
*Out of control? Domestic violence is a crime* 1988

## Diversification

By the late 1980s the number of commissions for screenprinted posters had dropped. Callaghan claimed that people didn't 'read' them any more. In fact, the communication industries – design, advertising and marketing – were undergoing significant changes. Along with the popularisation of personal computers and desktop publishing, advertising and communication models were being challenged by savvy and cynical consumers desensitised to traditional marketing strategies. In the early 1990s, this fragmentation would be countered by 'niche' marketing with advertisers exploiting new technologies to target consumer groups. The escalating cost of materials and the enormous wages bill for each poster was making it difficult for screenprinted posters to compete with offset printing. They were seen as a luxurious rather than cost-effective option for clients. Burdened by mortgage repayments, Alder and Callaghan sold the screenprinting side of the business in 1990. Increasingly Redback diversified to concentrate on corporate identity, T-shirts and wrapping paper.

Computers, initially introduced to assist with typesetting, enabled the studio to venture into publication design. Of the transition Alder remarked, 'I just didn't feel as though I could relate to that medium very easily.'[37] Callaghan, Lane and Cockram, on the other hand, embraced computers. They investigated the creative and technical capabilities of the early computer graphic applications, experimenting with the limits of layout and typography. Callaghan and Cockram's brochure for CAAMA richly integrates illustrative, photographic and typographic elements to create a densely textured pictorial space. And while the number of types used by Redback always remained relatively small, the explosion of bitmap fonts did reach the studio by way of influences. Graphic designer Neville Brody, art director of seminal English style bible, *The Face*, brought a punk sensibility to his manipulation of early modern typography. Copies of the magazine were often lying around the studio. Redback's redesign of stationery for the Department of Arts, Sport Environment and the Territories bears the hallmarks of Brody's playful typographic gymnastics.

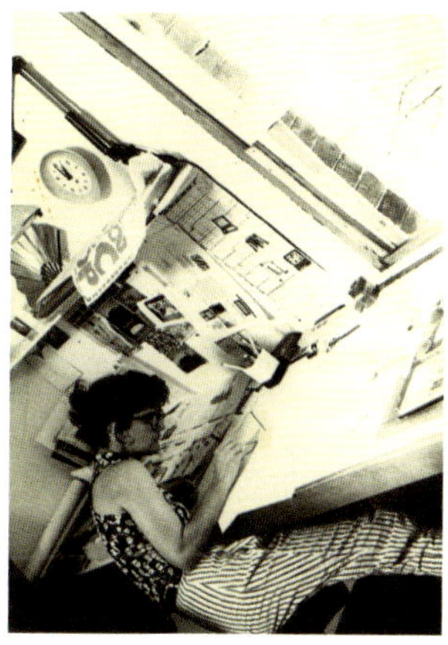

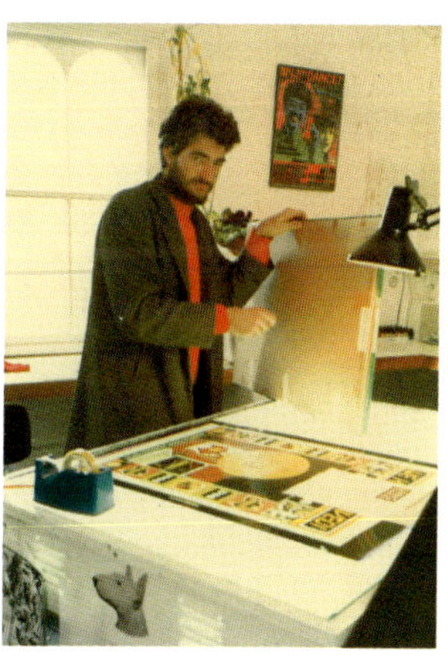

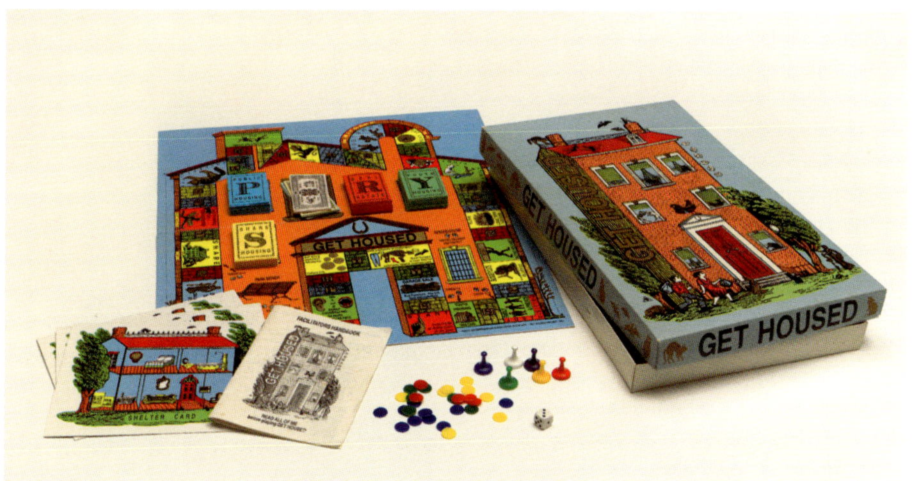


(left)
**Leonie Lane** (designer)
**Paul Cockram** (film planner)
**Stephen Lees** (printer)
Board game: *Get housed* 1989

(above top)
Leonie Lane, 1987
Photograph courtesy of Peter Curtis

Paul Cockram, 1986
Photograph courtesy of Leonie Lane

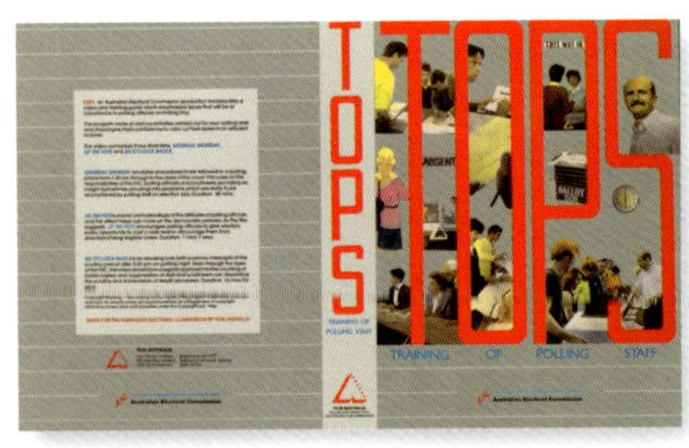


1

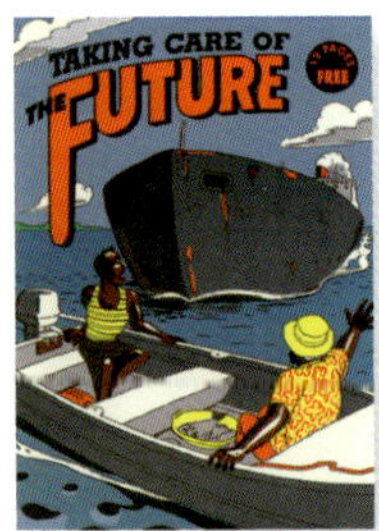


2

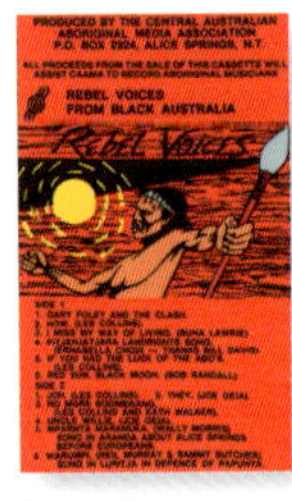


3

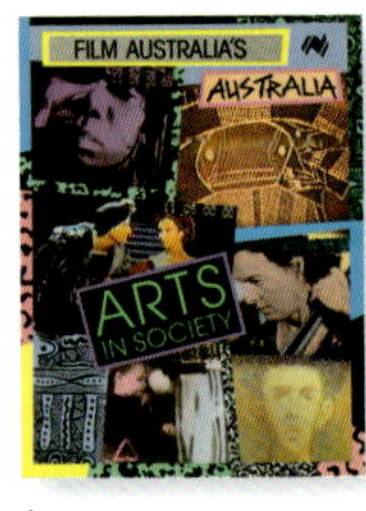


4

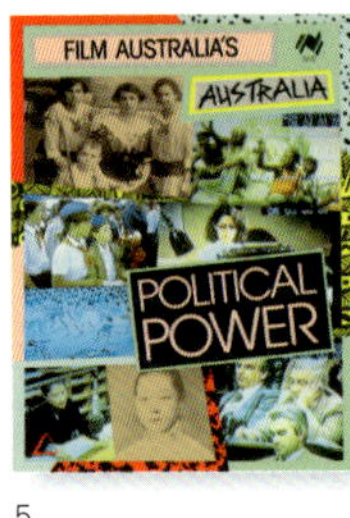


5

1 **Leonie Lane** (designer) Folder: *TOPS (Training of polling staff)* 1986

2 **Tony Thorne** (designer), **Alistair Legge** (author), **Paul Cockram** (film planner) Booklet: *Taking care of the future* 1990

3 **Ray Young** (designer and printer) Cassette cover: *Rebel Voices from Black Australia* 1984–85

4 **Michael Callaghan**, **Jan Mackay** and **Leonie Lane** (designers), **Paul Cockram** (film planner) Video cover: *Film Australia's Australia – Arts in society* 1986

5 **Michael Callaghan** and **Leonie Lane** (designers), **Paul Cockram** (film planner) Video cover: *Film Australia's Australia – Political power* 1986

6 **Michael Callaghan** (designer) and **Alison Alder** (printer) Wrapping paper: *Imparja* 1986

7 **Osmond Kantilla** (designer and printer's assistant), **Ray Young** (printer) Wrapping paper: *Pumpuni* 1986

8 **Neville Namarnyil**k (designer and printer's assistant), **Ray Young** (printer) Wrapping paper: *Oenpelli* 1986

9 **Leonie Lane** (designer) Leaflet: *Overseas Study Awards for Aboriginal people* 1987

10 **Alison Alder** (designer and printer) Card: *Seasonal greetings* c. 1985

11 **Michael Callaghan** (designer) Sticker: *The drug offensive* 1986

12 **Leonie Lane** (designer) Letterhead: *Hibiscus Films Ltd* 1986

13 **Michael Callaghan** and **Leonie Lane** (designers) **Paul Cockram** (film planner) Publication: *Australia Council 1988–89 Annual Report* c. 1990

14 **Leonie Lane** (designer) Tea towel: *Change – not charity* 1993

15 **Michael Callaghan** (designer and printer) **Gregor Cullen** (designer and printer) *AVS Calendar 1982 Oct – Dec* 1981

16 **Stephen Lees** (illustrator) **Leonie Lane** (designer) Leaflet: *Wharfies – a history of the Waterside Workers' Federation of Australia* c. 1985

17 **Marie McMahon** and **Michael Callaghan** (designers) Sticker: *Beat the grog* (blue) 1986

18 **Marie McMahon** and **Michael Callaghan** (designers) Sticker: *Beat the grog* (yellow) 1986

19 **Michael Callaghan** (designer) **Paul Cockram** (film planner) Brochure: *Karnta* 1995

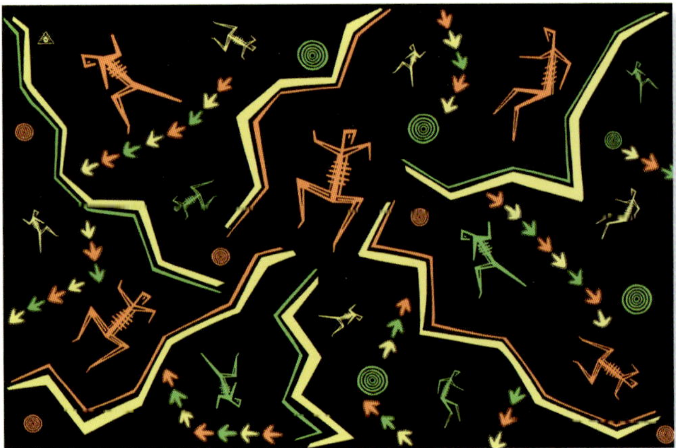

6

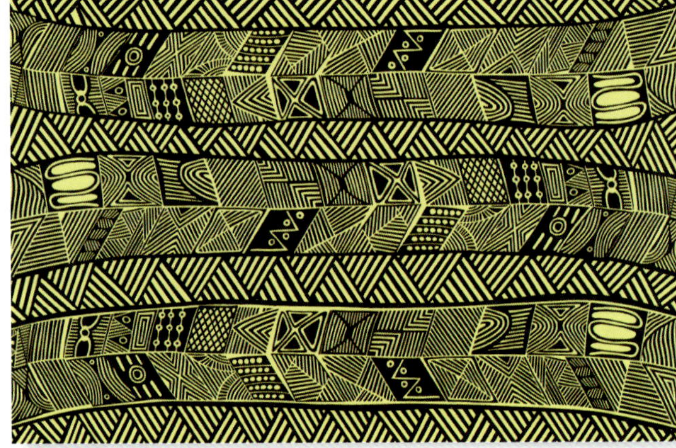

7

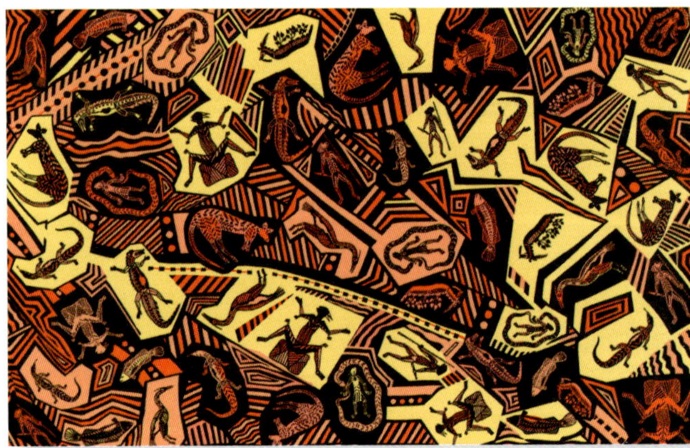

8

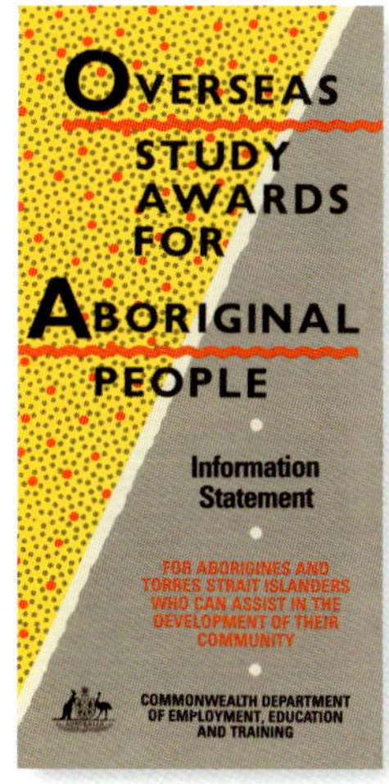


9

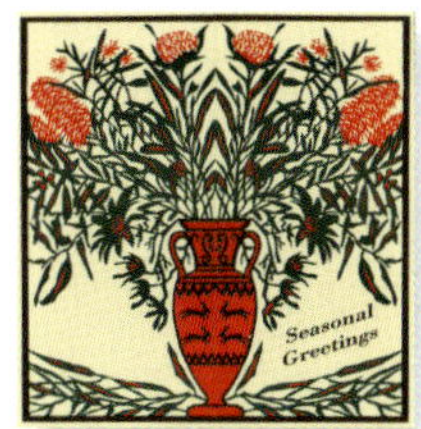


10

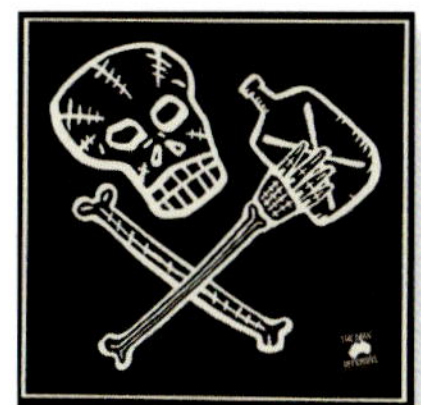

11

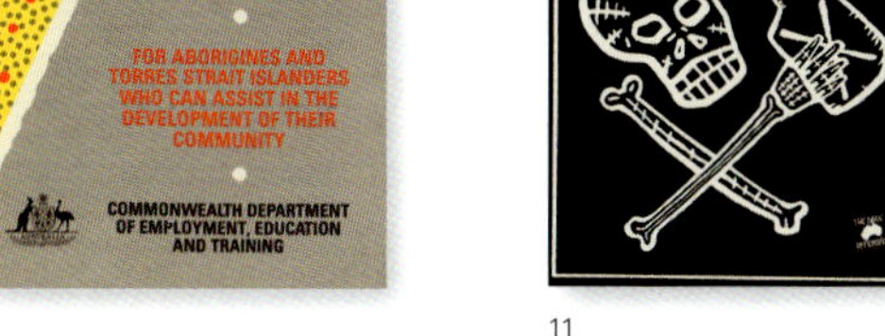


12

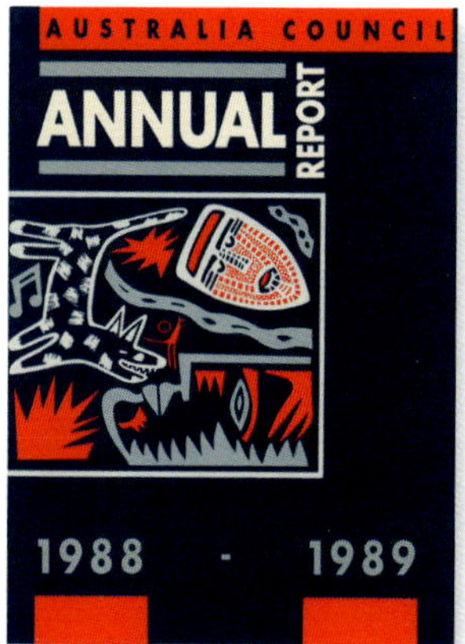


13

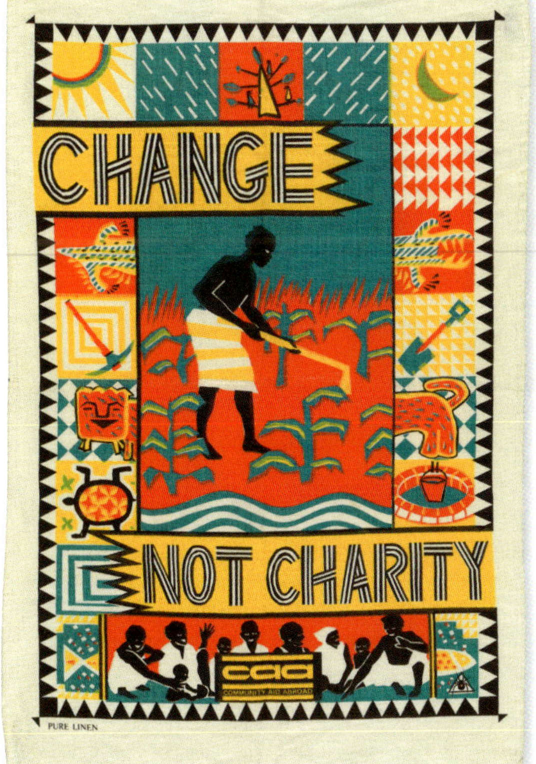


14

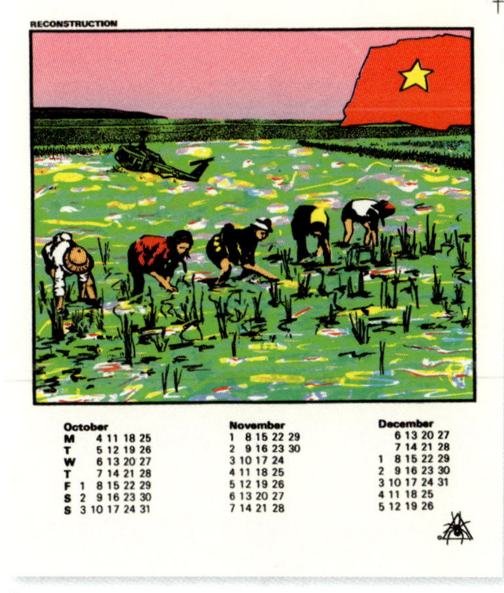


15

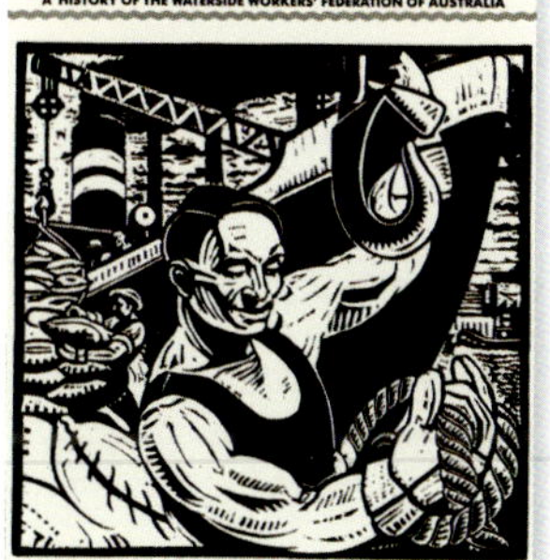


16

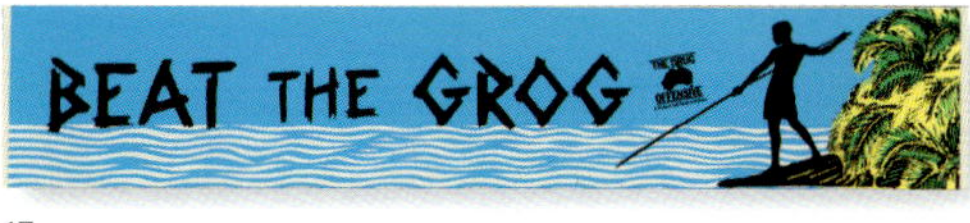


17



18

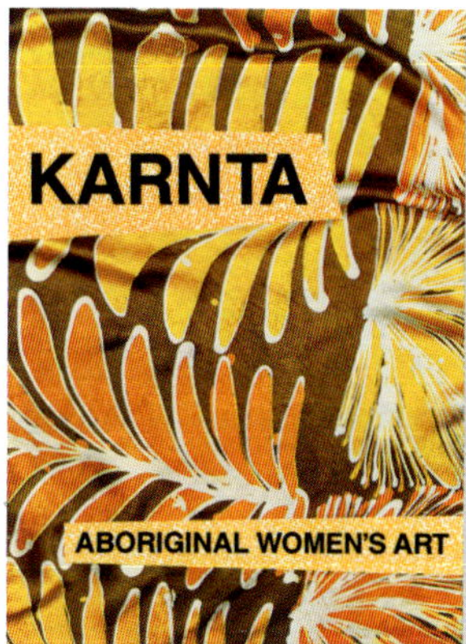


19

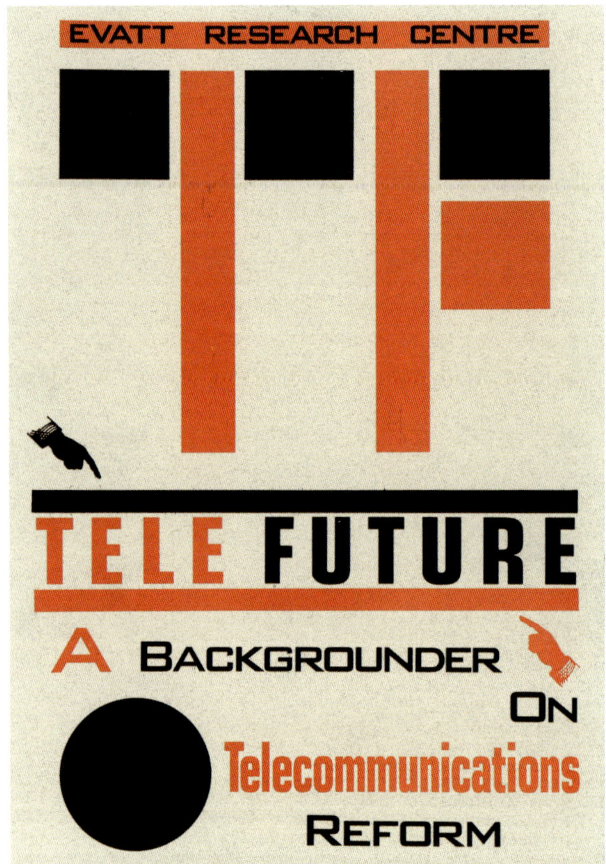


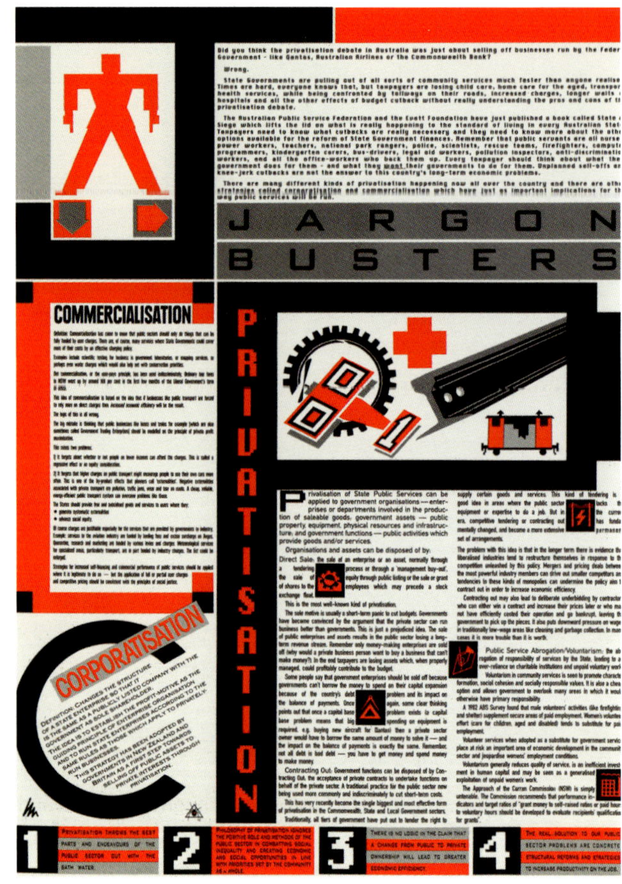


Charles Merewether described Redback's status as a state-supported professional business, as belonging in a 'half-way house'.[38] The problems associated with generating income and still representing the underdog were shared by other screenprinting workshops around Australia in the 1980s. For many years the federal government not only provided grants for individual projects and wages, but frequently commissioned work too. With a downturn in the economy in the early 1990s, many of the programs aimed at addressing social issues were scrapped. The jobs dried up. Alder and Callaghan moved next door to a smaller studio, no longer able to afford the Annandale premises and they parted company soon after. Alder commented, 'It was time to move on.'[39] Callaghan reflected, '[It's] like the Peter Pan story – all the other kids go home, you can't just keep making posters!.'[40] Alder, who had been visiting the Northern Territory to work with Aboriginal communities during the dry season, moved to Tennant Creek. After a serious illness, Callaghan returned to design and continues to operate Redback Graphix as a design studio, focusing on mainly web-based projects.

## After Redback

Art and politics, how do you bring them together? That's the question that Redback posed. Actually add to that *and get paid*. This is the problem that the studio unwaveringly pursued for fifteen-odd years. It relied on rat cunning, a nose for sniffing out opportunities and sheer resourcefulness. Redback occupied many spheres – both the art world and communication industries, the public and private sectors – tapping into diverse networks in order to keep working. There are few instances when these worlds intersected. That is why it is easy to overlook Redback's many successes: you need to cast a wide net to take in their sizeable achievements.

Redback sought to engage with the world through its posters, and its artists were prepared to travel to do so. Unsurprisingly, the world responded in kind and was fascinated. Redback's involvement in international poster exhibitions in England, Japan and France offer proof of this. Its inclusion in numerous national and state gallery collections, in Australia as well as abroad, is further testament to its good reputation. The advertising industry, both in Australia and overseas, also recognised Redback's work. Redback posters won national awards in categories such as Community Service Campaign and were selected twice as finalists in the London International Advertising Awards.

Other outfits may have capitalised on the mood of the 1980s with more success (Mambo comes to mind – the two had plenty in common, an irreverent sense of humour and a background in fine art, although crucially Mambo's passion was for propagating a laidback lifestyle and not political engagement), but if one examines Redback's immense output, something becomes clear. There was always a sense of a bigger project directing the studio, a commitment to addressing issues faced by the disenfranchised and those on the margins. That 'community' originated in the cities of Wollongong and Sydney, but reached as far north as the Torres Strait Islands and across the Pacific to Los Angeles.

(opposite left)
**Michael Callaghan** (designer)
*Telefuture* c. 1989

(opposite right)
**Michael Callaghan** (designer)
*Jargon busters* 1989

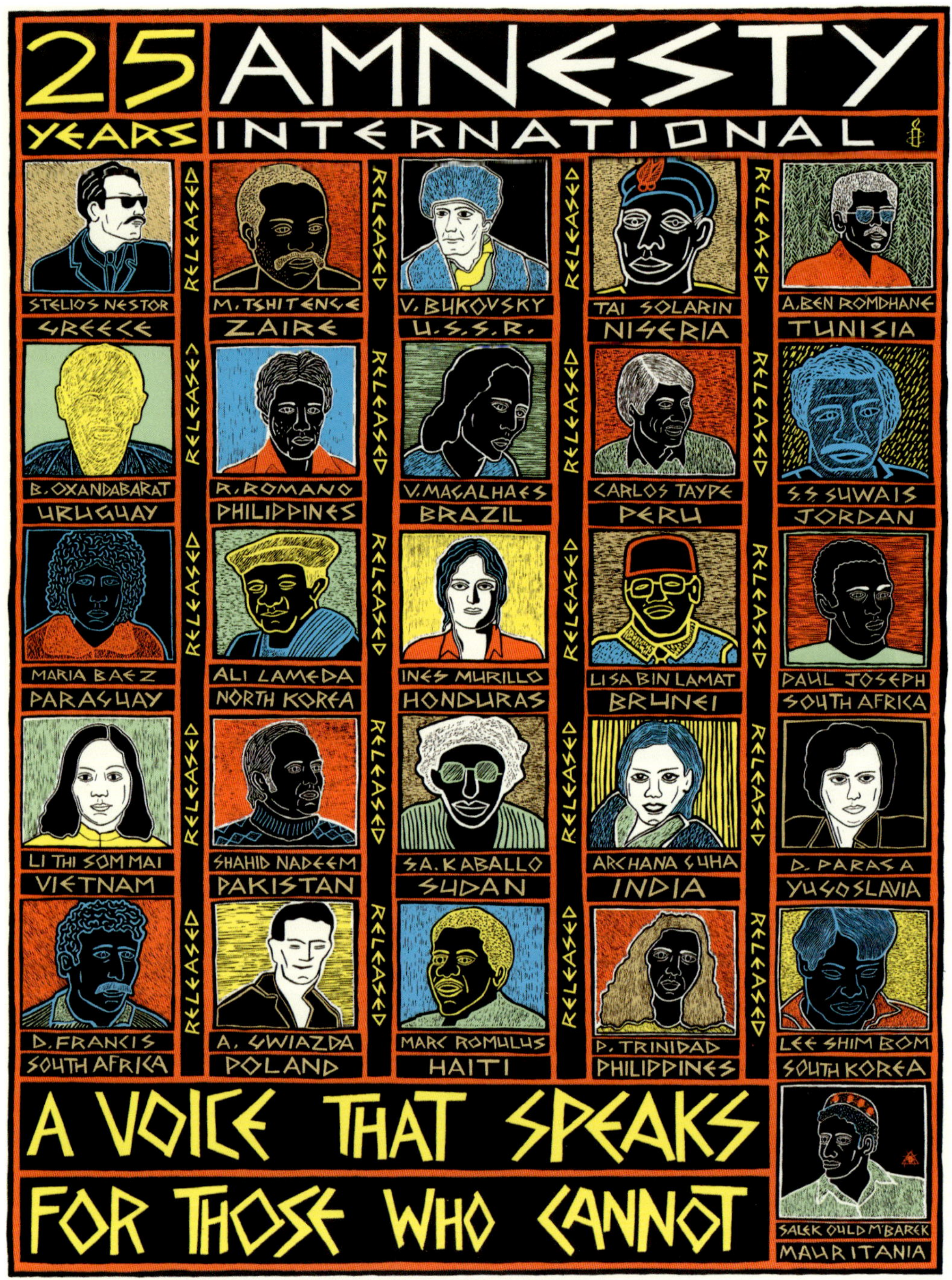

25 YEARS
AMNESTY INTERNATIONAL
STELIOS NESTOR
GREECE
RELEASED
M. TSHITENGE
ZAIRE
RELEASED
V. BUKOVSKY
U.S.S.R.
RELEASED
TAI SOLARIN
NIGERIA
RELEASED
A. BEN ROMDHANE
TUNISIA
B. OXANDABARAT
URUGUAY
RELEASED
R. ROMANO
PHILIPPINES
RELEASED
V. MAGALHAES
BRAZIL
RELEASED
CARLOS TAYPE
PERU
RELEASED
S.S. SUWAIS
JORDAN
MARIA BAEZ
PARAGUAY
RELEASED
ALI LAMEDA
NORTH KOREA
RELEASED
INES MURILLO
HONDURAS
RELEASED
LISA BIN LAMAT
BRUNEI
RELEASED
PAUL JOSEPH
SOUTH AFRICA
LI THI SOM MAI
VIETNAM
RELEASED
SHAHID NADEEM
PAKISTAN
RELEASED
S.A. KABALLO
SUDAN
RELEASED
ARCHANA GUHA
INDIA
RELEASED
D. PARAGA
YUGOSLAVIA
D. FRANCIS
SOUTH AFRICA
RELEASED
A. GWIAZDA
POLAND
RELEASED
MARC ROMULUS
HAITI
RELEASED
D. TRINIDAD
PHILIPPINES
RELEASED
LEE SHIM BOM
SOUTH KOREA
A VOICE THAT SPEAKS
FOR THOSE WHO CANNOT
SALEK OULD M'BAREK
MAURITANIA
AN INTERNATIONAL YEAR OF PEACE PROJECT PRODUCED IN ASSOCIATION WITH AMNESTY INTERNATIONAL AUSTRALIA WITH ASSISTANCE FROM THE AUSTRALIA COUNCIL AND THE DEPARTMENT OF FOREIGN AFFAIRS

Redback's posters, with their emphatic slogans, arresting images and vivid colours, confront the viewer with a terrible urgency. They say to us: life matters, action counts. Not in any sloppy way either but in lush, perfectly registered, five colour screenprints. It is fitting then, that while Redback emerged from the ashes of an exhausted Earthworks to establish something new, decades later, sassy screenprints should surface again.

In Melbourne and to a lesser extent in other Australian state capitals, stencil art has erupted again, covering the sparse surfaces of city walls and footpaths. Generally small in scale and executed in one colour, these 'images of dissent' combine the aesthetics of left-wing propaganda with B-grade movies. Unlike the posters of Earthworks or Redback, the graphic symbols and illustrations of stencil art rarely possess a direct political message. But stencil art's personal, idiosyncratic visual language resonates. In the current economic and political context of global terror, these spray-painted pictograms of revolution and resistance, daytime TV and comic books, reflect the mixed-up times we live in. This new form of printmaking is reclaiming the streets. Life matters, action counts.

(opposite)
**Michael Callaghan** (designer)
**Alison Alder** (printer)
*25 years Amnesty International* 1987

# Endnotes

1 Roger Butler, 'Colin Little: poster maker', in *Colin Little retrospective*, exhibition catalogue, Canberra: Bitumen River Gallery, 1983, p. 1.

2 Ellen Lupton, *Design writing, research: writing on graphic design*, London: Phaidon Press, 1996, p. 198.

3 David Crowley, 'Protest and propaganda', in Margaret Timmers (ed). *The power of the poster*, London: V&A Publications, 1998, p. 130.

4 Charles Merewether, 'The art of serious dancing' in *Redback Graphix Posters 1979–1985*, exhibition catalogue, Wollongong: Wollongong City Gallery, 1987, p. 1.

5 Therese Kenyon, *Under a hot tin roof: art, passion and politics at the Tin Sheds Art Workshop*, Sydney: State Library of New South Wales Press, 1995, p. 48.

6 Ellen Lupton, 'Design and production in the mechanical age', in Maud Lavin (ed.), *Graphic design in the mechanical age: selections from the Merrill C. Berman Collection*, London: Yale University Press, 1998, p. 60.

7 Lupton, 1998, p. 14.

8 Lupton, 1998, p. 19.

9 Kenyon, p. 48.

10 Rick Poyner (ed), *Design without boundaries: visual communication in transition*, London: Booth-Clibborn Editions, 1988, p. 270.

11 Julie Ewington, 'Political postering', in Paul Taylor (ed). *Anything goes: art in Australia 1970–1980*, Melbourne: Art & Text, 1984, p. 97.

12 Kenyon, p. 51.

13 Julia Church, *Pressing issues: contemporary posters from local co-operative presses*, exhibition catalogue, Melbourne: State Library of Victoria, 1990, p. 2.

14 Church, p. 2.

15 Ewington, p. 97.

16 Roger Butler, *The streets as art galleries – walls sometimes speak: poster art in Australia*, Canberra: National Gallery of Australia, 1993, p. 55.

17 Clare Williamson, *Signs of the times: political posters in Queensland 1907–1990*, exhibition catalogue, Brisbane: Queensland Art Gallery, 1991, p. 4.

18 Williamson, p. 4.

19 Michael Callaghan, interview by Anna Zagala at Elizabeth Bay, 24 August 2001.

20 Lee-Anne Hall, 'Who is Bill Posters? An examination of six Australian socially concerned alternative print media organisations', *Caper 27*, 1988, p. 4.

21 Hall, p. 4.

22 Butler, 1993, p. 5.

23 Michael Callaghan was *Greetings'* producer for the first two years of the project's life. Once the film went into production he relinquished the role in order to concentrate on his role as art director.

24 Merewether, p. 1.

25 Gregor Cullen, interview with Anna Zagala at the University of Wollongong, 7 August 2001.

26 Michael Callaghan, interview with Anna Zagala at Elizabeth Bay, 24 August 2001.

27 Michael Callaghan, interview with Anna Zagala at Elizabeth Bay, 24 August 2001.

28 Callaghan, Cullen and Lane visited Japan in 1982; Callaghan and Cullen travelled to Los Angeles in 1984.

29 Among the artists included in *Australia: nine contemporary artists* were Mike Parr, Lyndal Jones, John Davis, Stelarc and John Nixon.

30 Ewington, *Right here right now: Australia 1988*, Adelaide: Adelaide Festival of Arts, 1988.

31 Gregor Cullen, interview with Anna Zagala, at the University of Wollongong, 7 August 2001.

32 Alison Alder, interview by telephone with Anna Zagala, at Acton, Canberra, 26 September 2001.

33 Marie McMahon, interview with Anna Zagala, at Coogee, Sydney, 25 July 2003.

34 Marie McMahon, interview with Anna Zagala, at Coogee, Sydney, 25 July 2003.

35 McQuisten defines visual and graphic language as 'a combination of elements, style, symbolism, typography, atmosphere or tone, historical and artistic references and so forth – which communicates a message in a particular way'. Liz McQuisten, *Graphic agitation*, London: Phaidon Press, 1993, p. 8.

36 Ann Stephen, 'Now we are 10: Let's read Redback' in *Redback Graphix: now we are 10*, exhibition catalogue, Sydney: Redback Graphix, 1987, p. 10.

37 Alison Alder, interview by telephone with Anna Zagala, at Acton, Canberra, 26 September 2001.

38 Merewether, p. 2.

39 Alison Alder, interview by telephone with Anna Zagala, at Acton, Canberra, 26 September 2001.

40 Michael Callaghan, interview with Anna Zagala, at Elizabeth Bay, Sydney, 24 August 2001.

REDBACK POSTERS 1979–94

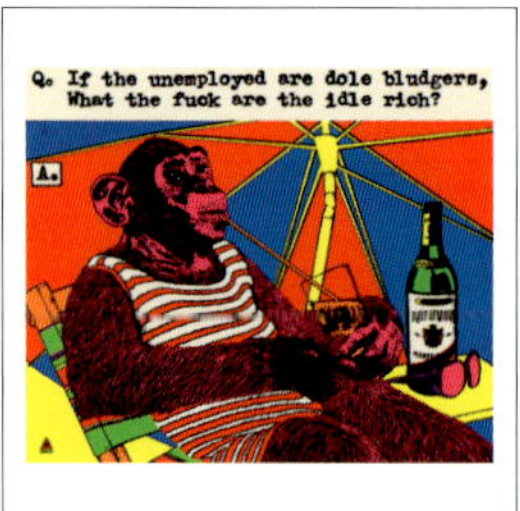

1

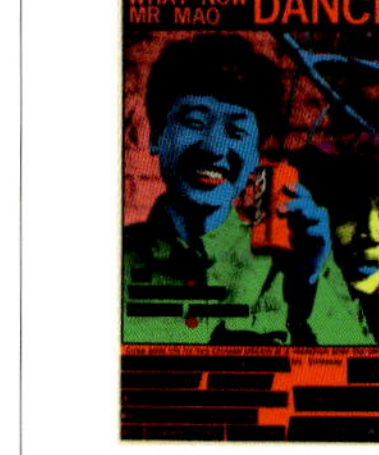

2

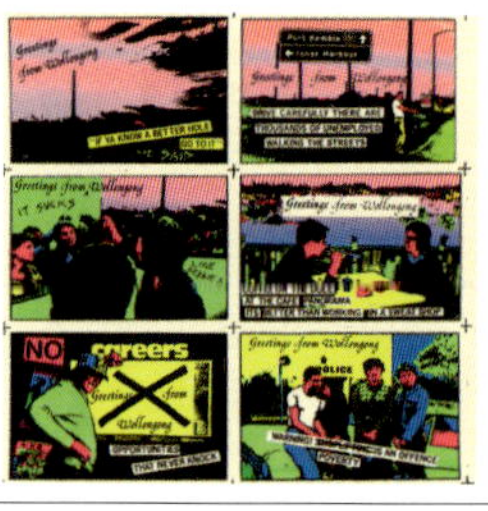
3

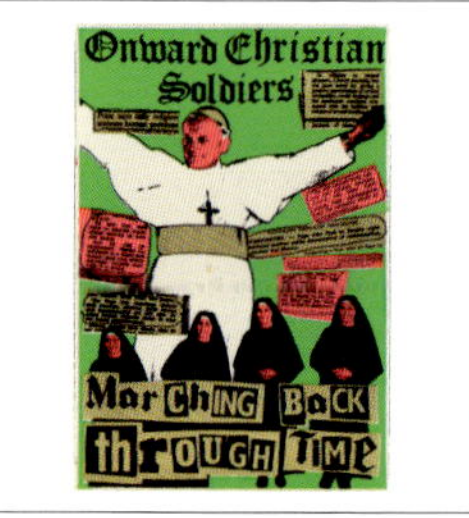

4

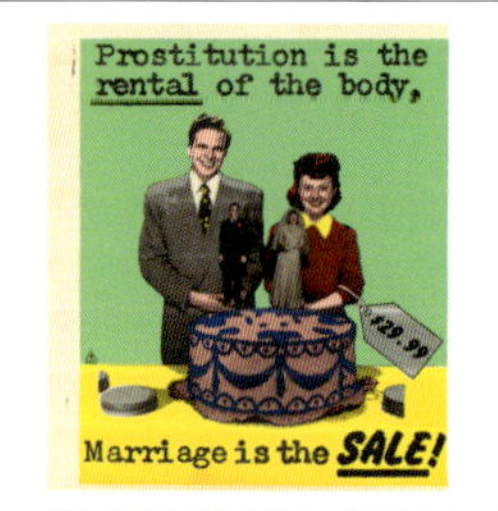

5

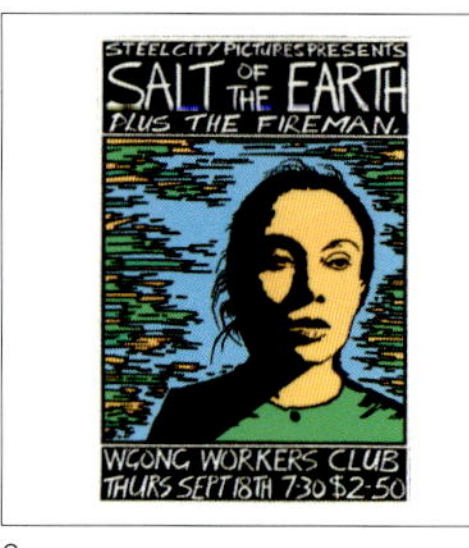

6

7

8

**Principal partners**

Michael Callaghan—born Australia 1952
Gregor Cullen—born Australia 1954
Leonie Lane—born Australia 1955
Alison Alder—born Australia 1958

**List of works**

This list of posters produced by Redback Graphix 1979–1994 was compiled by Roger Butler, Jaklyn Babington and Sarina Noordhuis-Fairfax with the generous and enthusiastic assistance of the artists and printers who have been involved with Redback Graphix over the years.

Measurements are in centimetres, height preceding width.

All works are in the collection of the National Gallery of Australia unless otherwise credited.

1 **Michael CALLAGHAN** (designer and printer)
**Steel City Pictures** (client)
*If the unemployed are dole bludgers, what the fuck are the idle rich?* 1979 Griffith University, Brisbane
screenprint, printed in colour, from five stencils on thin white wove paper
printed image 70.4 x 82.6 cm sheet 71.8 x 84.2 cm
1987.1398

2 **Michael CALLAGHAN** (designer and printer)
**Griffith University Students Union** (client)
*What now Mr Mao, dance?* 1979 Griffith University, Brisbane
screenprint, printed in colour, from five stencils on thin white wove paper
printed image 74.4 x 49.8 cm sheet 76.0 x 51.0 cm
1987.1393

3 **Michael CALLAGHAN** (designer and printer)
**Steel City Pictures** (client)
*Greetings from Wollongong postcards—version 1 (single sheet)* 1979 Griffith University, Brisbane
screenprint, printed in colour, from five stencils on thin white wove paper
sheet 63.0 x 97.0 cm
Gift of Andrew Speirs 1984
1984.395.AB

4 **Michael CALLAGHAN & others** (designers and printers)
**Queensland Film and Drama Centre** (client)
*Onward Christian soldiers* 1979 Griffith University, Brisbane
screenprint, printed in colour, from four stencils on thin white wove paper
printed image 74.4 x 49.4 cm
sheet 76.0 x 50.8 cm
1987.1394

5 **Michael CALLAGHAN** (designer and printer)
**Cherie BRADSHAW** (designer)
Australia 1960–1994
**Lynette FINCH** (printer)
born Australia 1959
*Prostitution is the rental of the body, marriage is the sale!* c. 1979 Griffith University, Brisbane
screenprint, printed in colour, from five stencils on thin white wove paper
printed image 83.2 x 68.4 cm
sheet 88.0 x 76.0 cm
2007.1396

6 **Michael CALLAGHAN** (designer and printer)
**Steel City Pictures** (client)
*Salt of the earth* 1980 Tin Sheds, Sydney
screenprint, printed in colour, from four stencils on thin white wove paper
printed image 74.4 x 49.6 cm
sheet 76.0 x 51.0 cm
Gift of the Philip Morris Arts Grant 1982
1983.1963

7 **Michael CALLAGHAN** (designer and printer)
**Mary CALLAGHAN** (designer)
born Australia 1955
**Steel City Pictures** (client)
*Nice poster* 1980 Tin Sheds, Sydney
screenprint, printed in colour, from five stencils on thin white wove paper
printed image 87.4 x 65.6 cm
sheet 88.2 x 66.6 cm
Gift of the Philip Morris Arts Grant 1982
1983.1979

8 **Michael CALLAGHAN** (designer and printer)
**Steel City Pictures** (client)
*With babes + banners* 1980 Tin Sheds, Sydney
screenprint, printed in colour, from five stencils on thin white wove paper
printed image 88.4 x 66.0 cm
sheet 90.0 x 68.0 cm
1982.934

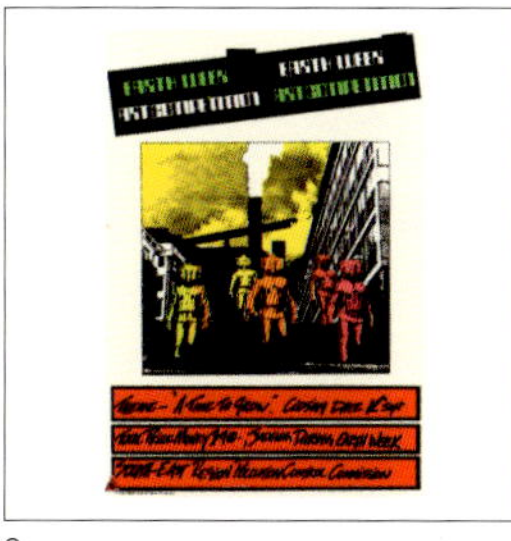

9

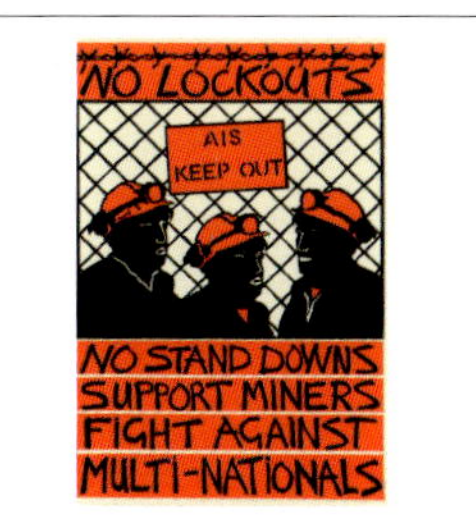


10

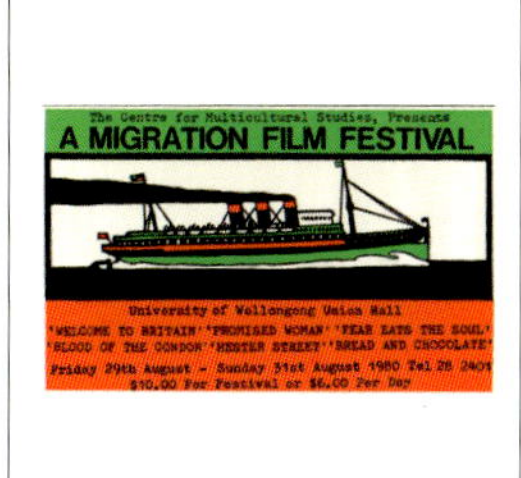


11

IMAGE UNAVAILABLE

12

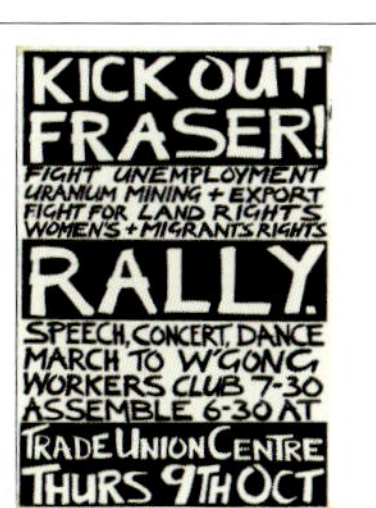


13

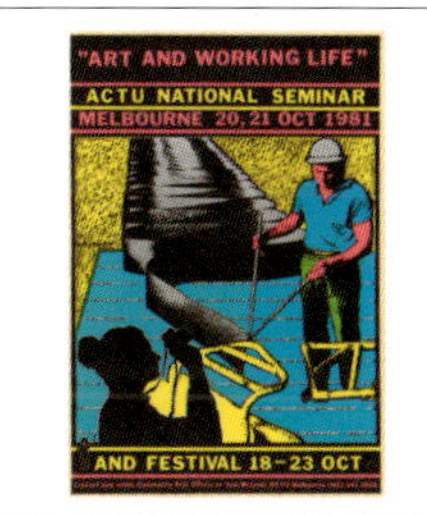


14

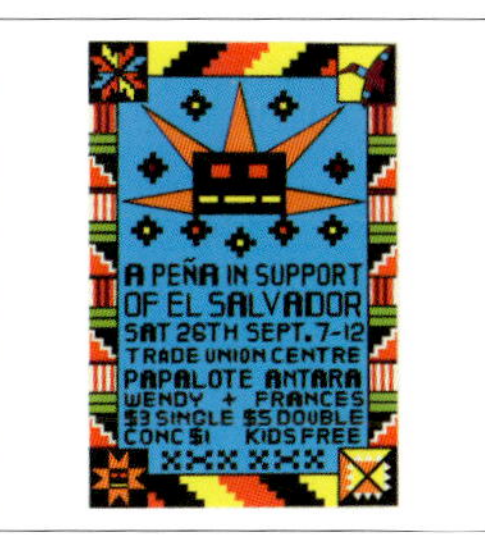


15

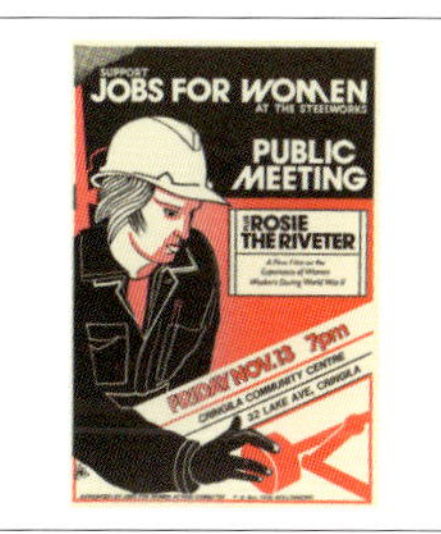


16

9 **Gregor CULLEN** (designer and printer)
**South-East Region Pollution Control Commission** (client)
*Earth week: art competition* 1980 Tin Sheds, Sydney
screenprint, printed in colour, from five stencils on thin white wove paper
printed image 72.0 x 48.2 cm
sheet 75.2 x 50.4 cm
Gift of the Philip Morris Arts Grant 1982
1983.1973

10 **Gregor CULLEN** (designer and printer)
**Miners' Federation** (client)
*No lockouts* 1980 Tin Sheds, Sydney
screenprint, printed in red and black ink, from two stencils on thin white wove paper
printed image 74.7 x 49.8 cm
sheet 76.0 x 51.0 cm
Private collection

11 **Michael CALLAGHAN** (designer and printer)
**Centre for Multicultural Studies, University of Wollongong** (client)
A *migration film festival* 1980 Tin Sheds, Sydney
screenprint, printed in colour, from three stencils on thin white wove paper
printed image 56.4 x 89.6 cm
sheet 58.0 x 91.0 cm
Gift of the Philip Morris Arts Grant 1982
1983.1823

12 **Michael CALLAGHAN** (designer)
**Gregor CULLEN** (designer and printer)
**Australian Council of Trade Unions (ACTU)** (client)
*Art and working life conference* c. 1980 Tin Sheds, Sydney
screenprint, printed in black ink, from one stencil on thin white wove paper
sheet 51.0 x 76.0 cm
Private collection

13 **Michael CALLAGHAN** (designer and printer)
**Gregor CULLEN** (designer and printer)
**South Coast Labour Council** (client)
*Kick out Fraser! rally (Trade Union Centre)* 1981 Wollongong
screenprint, printed in black ink, from one stencil on thin white wove paper
printed image 73.8 x 49.2 cm
sheet 76.0 x 50.8 cm
Gift of the Philip Morris Arts Grant 1982
1983.1864

14 **Michael CALLAGHAN** (designer)
**Gregor CULLEN** (designer and printer)
**Australia Council** and **Australian Council of Trade Unions (ACTU)** (clients)
*Art and working life conference* 1981 Wollongong
screenprint, printed in colour, from four stencils on thin white wove paper
printed image 74.8 x 49.4 cm
sheet 75.8 x 50.8 cm
Private collection

15 **Michael CALLAGHAN** (designer and printer)
**Marie McMAHON** (designer)
born Australia 1953
**El Salvador Support Group** (client)
*A Peña in support of El Salvador* 1981 Wollongong
screenprint, printed in colour, from four stencils on thin white wove paper
printed image 74.6 x 49.4 cm
sheet 76.0 x 51.0 cm
1987.1321

16 **Gregor CULLEN** (designer and printer)
**Jobs for Women Action Committee** (client)
*Rosie the riveter* 1981 Wollongong
screenprint, printed in colour, from two stencils on thin white wove paper
printed image 73.6 x 48.8 cm
sheet 76.0 x 50.8 cm
Gift of Gregor Cullen 2008
2008.252

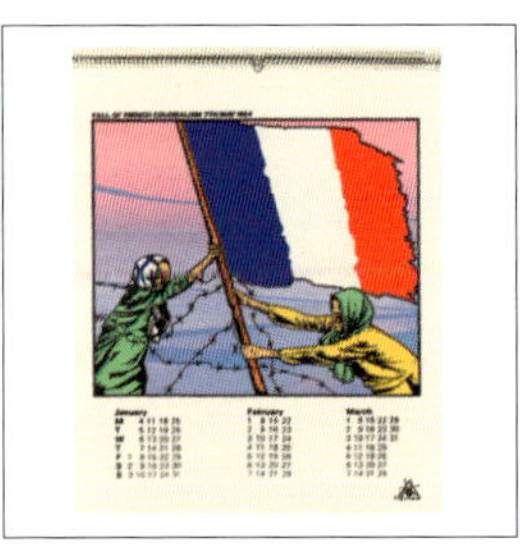

17

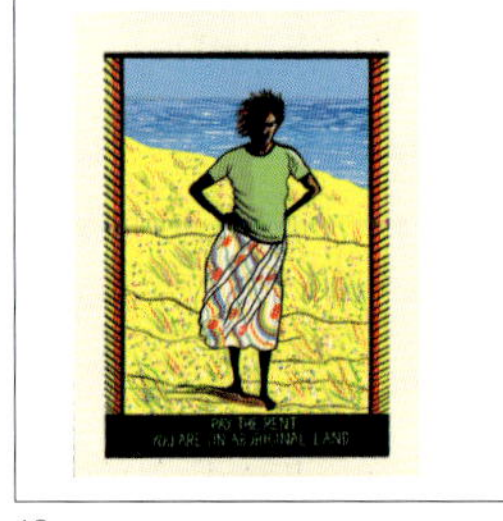

18

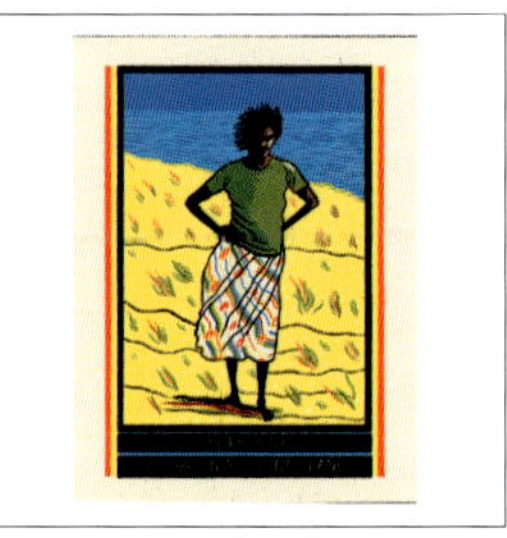

19

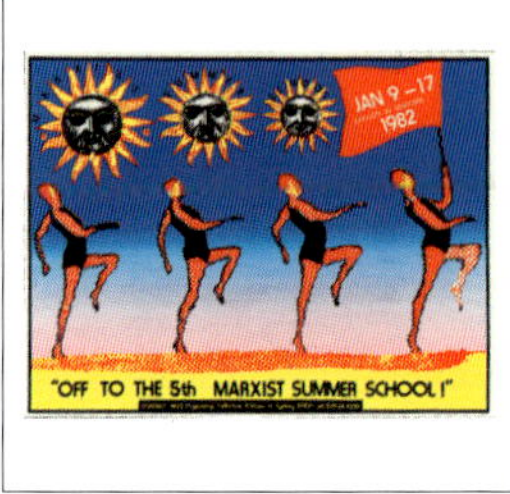


20

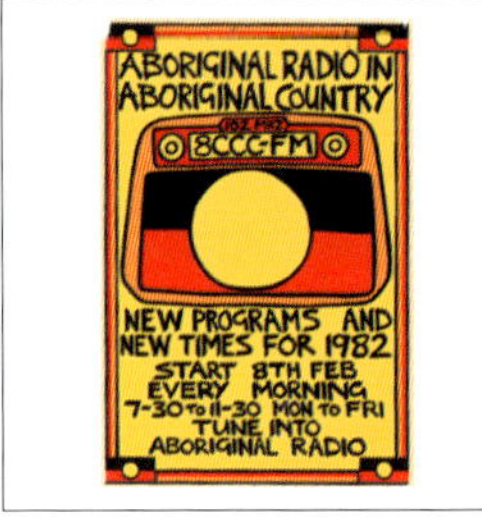


21

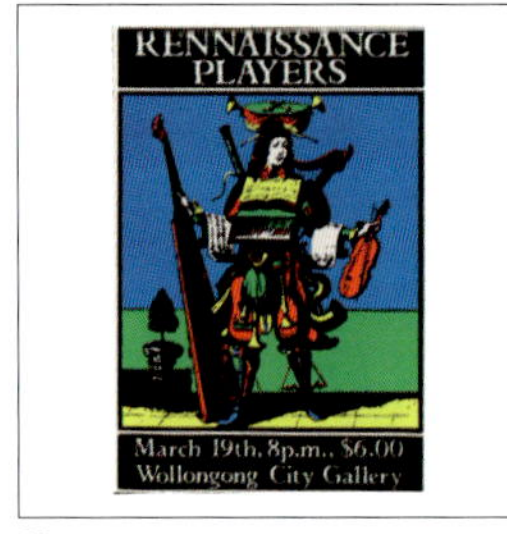


22

23

24

17 **Michael CALLAGHAN** (designer and printer)
**Gregor CULLEN** (designer and printer)
**Australia–Vietnam Society (AVS)** (client)
*AVS calendar* 1982 Wollongong, 1981
screenprint, printed in colour, each from multiple stencils on thin white wove paper
sheet 49.4 x 40.0 cm
Gordon Darling Australia Pacific Print Fund 2008
2008.277.1-4

18 **Marie McMAHON** (designer and printer)
*Pay the rent: you are on Aboriginal land* [*1*] 1981
screenprint, printed in colour, from multiple stencils
printed image 65.3 x 45.8 cm
sheet 76.0 x 56.0 cm
93.30

19 **Marie McMAHON** (designer and printer)
*Pay the rent: you are on Aboriginal land* [*2*] 1982
screenprint, printed in colour, from multiple stencils
printed image 67.2 x 45.0 cm
sheet 76.0 x 56.0 cm
93.31

20 **Ann STEPHEN** (designer and printer)
born Australia 1951
**Gregor CULLEN** (designer and printer)
**Marxist Summer School Organising Committee** (client)
*Marxist summer school* 1982 Wollongong
screenprint, printed in colour, from four stencils on thin white wove paper
printed image 49.4 x 63.8 cm
sheet 51.2 x 76.0 cm
1987.1348

21 **Michael CALLAGHAN** (designer and printer)
**Central Australian Aboriginal Media Association (CAAMA)** (client)
*Aboriginal radio in Aboriginal country* 1982 Wollongong
screenprint, printed in colour, from multiple stencils on thin white wove paper
printed image 74.4 x 48.8 cm
sheet 75.8 x 50.5 cm
Private collection

22 **Michael CALLAGHAN** (designer and printer)
**Gregor CULLEN** (designer and printer)
**Wollongong City Gallery** (client)
*Renaissance players* 1982 Wollongong
screenprint, printed in colour, from four stencils on thin white wove paper
printed image 74.8 x 49.4 cm
sheet 76.0 x 51.0 cm
1987.1338

23 **Michael CALLAGHAN** (designer and printer)
**Gregor CULLEN** (designer and printer)
**Theatre South** (client)
*Vocations* 1982 Wollongong
screenprint, printed in colour, from four stencils on thin white wove paper
printed image 49.6 x 74.4 cm
sheet 51.2 x 76.0 cm
1987.1330

24 **Michael CALLAGHAN** (designer and printer)
**Nick SOUTHALL** (printer's assistant)
born Australia 1962
**El Salvador Support Committee** (client)
*The daily oppression* 1982 Wollongong
screenprint, printed in colour, from five stencils on thin white wove paper
printed image 97.4 x 60.8 cm
sheet 102.0 x 64.4 cm
1987.1359

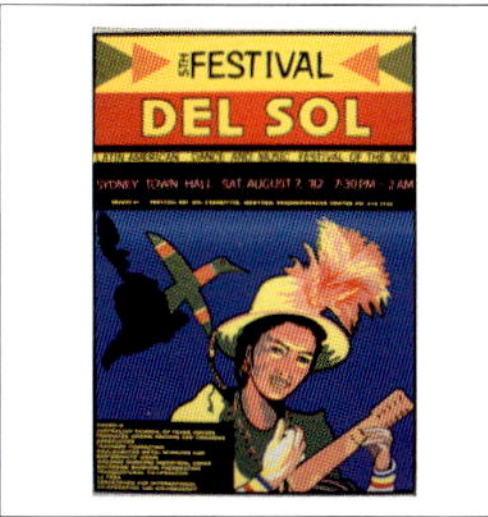

25

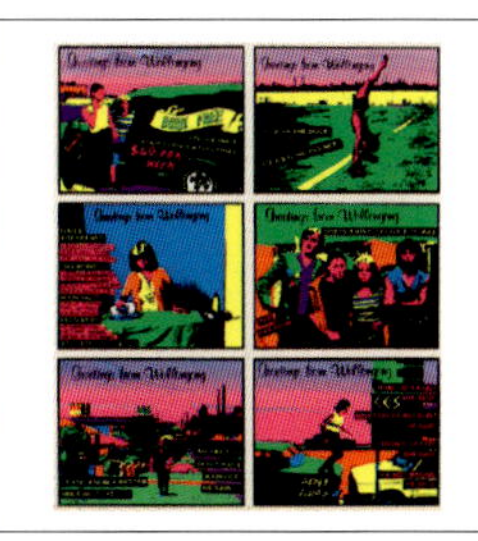
26

27

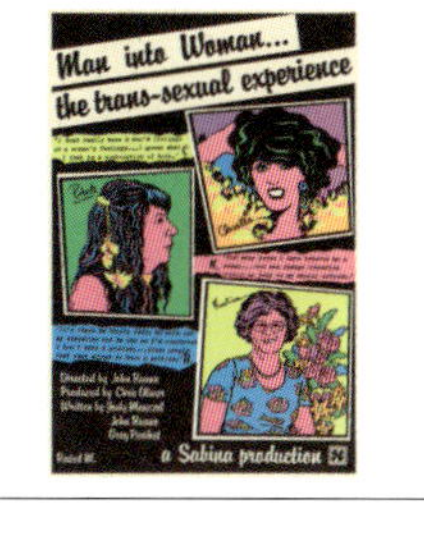

28

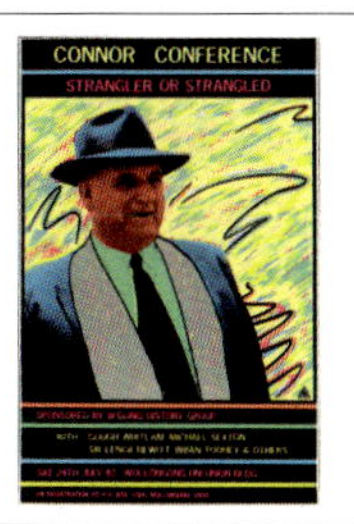

29

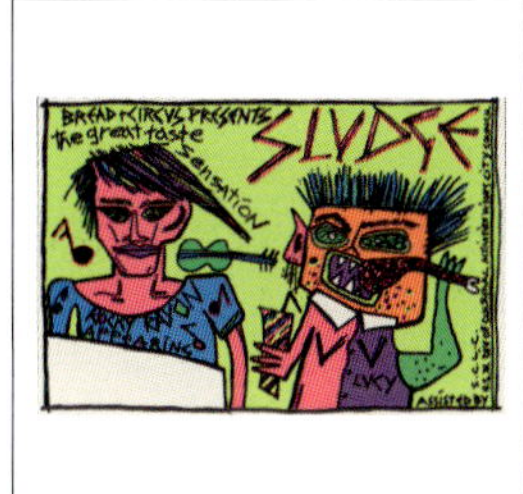
30

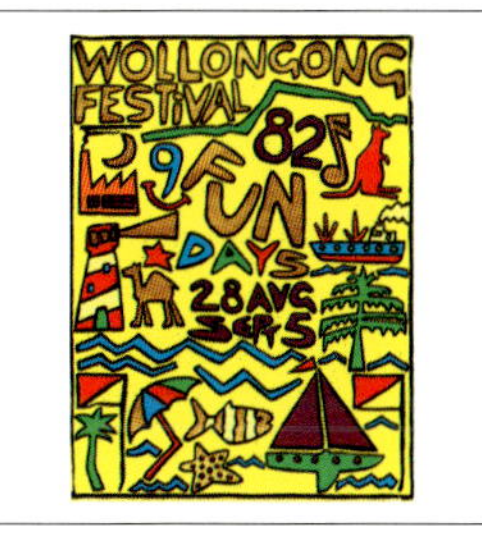

31

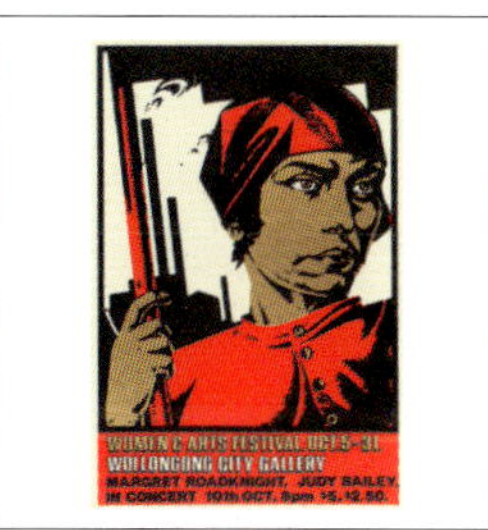
32

25 **Marie McMAHON** (designer and printer)
**Festival del Sol Committee** (client)
*Festival del sol* 1982 Wollongong
screenprint, printed in colour, from multiple stencils on thin white wove paper
sheet 76.0 x 51.0 cm
Private collection

26 **Michael CALLAGHAN** (designer and printer)
**Steel City Pictures** (client)
*Greetings from Wollongong postcards—version 2 (single sheet)* 1982 Wollongong
screenprint, printed in colour, from five stencils on thin white wove paper
printed image 40.4 x 38.9 cm
sheet 62.8 x 45.8 cm
Gordon Darling Australia Pacific Print Fund, 2008
2008.310

27 **Michael CALLAGHAN** (designer and printer)
**Nick SOUTHALL** (printer's assistant)
born Australlia 1962
**Steel City Pictures** (client)
*Greetings from Wollongong* 1982 Wollongong
screenprint, printed in colour, from five stencils on thin white wove paper
printed image 59.4 x 87.4 cm
sheet 61.0 x 89.0 cm
1987.1363

28 **Ruth WALLER** (designer)
born Australia 1955
**Michael CALLAGHAN** (printer)
**Sabina Productions** (client)
*Man into woman* 1982 Wollongong
screenprint, printed in colour, from four stencils on thin off-white paper
printed image 74.5 x 49.2 cm
sheet 76.0 x 50.6 cm
Gordon Darling Australia Pacific Print Fund 2008
2008.294

29 **Michael CALLAGHAN** (designer and printer)
**Gregor CULLEN** (designer and printer)
**Wollongong History Group** (client)
*Connor conference* 1982 Wollongong
screenprint, printed in colour, from seven stencils on thin white wove paper
printed image 91.8x 58.8 cm
sheet 93.0 x 60.0 cm
1987.1366

30 **Michael CALLAGHAN** (designer and printer)
**Bread and Circus Theatre Company** (client)
*Sludge* 1982 Wollongong
screenprint, printed in colour, from four stencils on thin white wove paper
printed image 59.8 x 87.4 cm
sheet 61.0 x 89.0 cm
1987.1358

31 **Michael CALLAGHAN** (designer and printer)
**Wollongong City Festival Committee** (client)
*Wollongong festival* 1982 Wollongong
screenprint, printed in colour, from five stencils on thin white wove paper
sheet 76.0 x 102.0 cm
Private collection

32 **Gregor CULLEN** (designer and printer)
**Wollongong City Gallery** (client)
*Women and arts festival* 1982
screenprint, printed in colour, from three stencils on thin white wove paper
printed image 73.4 x 48.2 cm
sheet 78.6 x 50.8 cm
Gift of Gregor Cullen 2008
2008.268

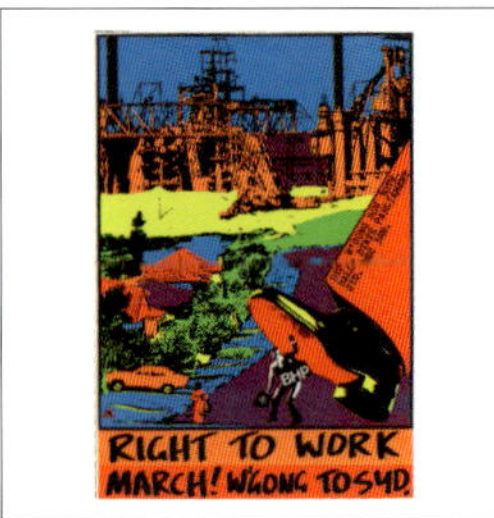


33

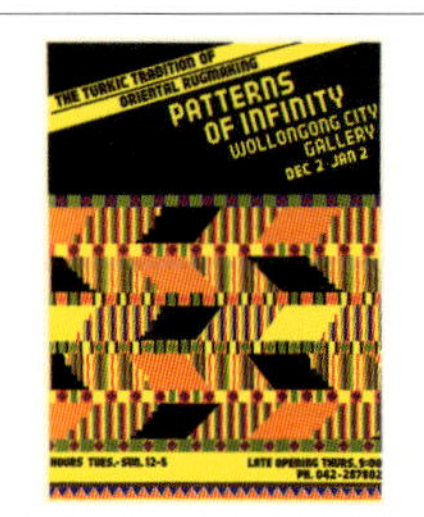


34

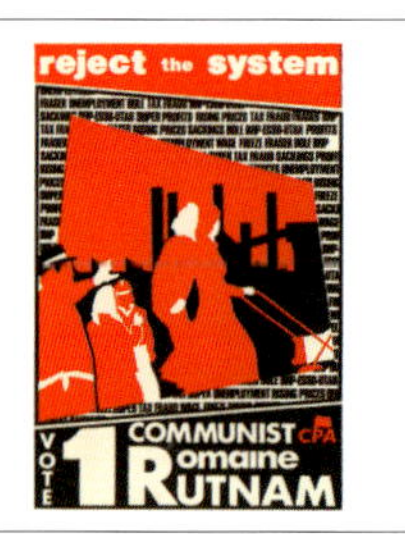


35

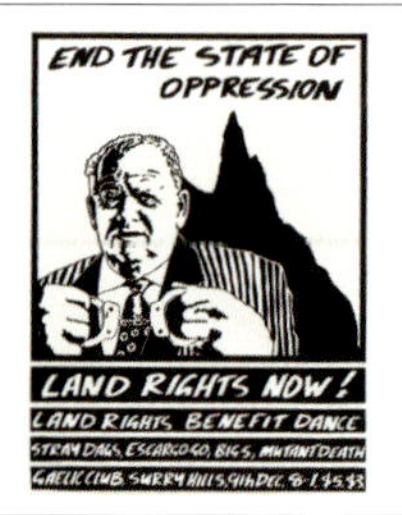


36

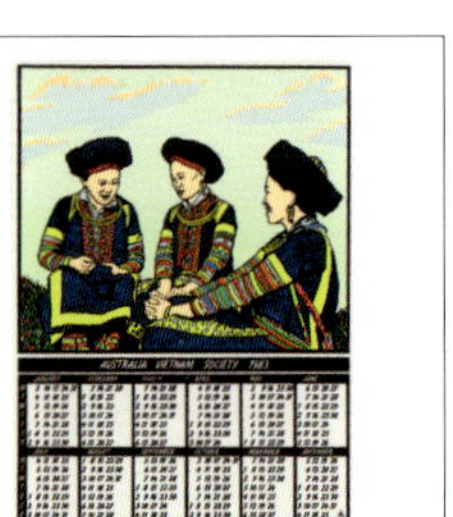

37

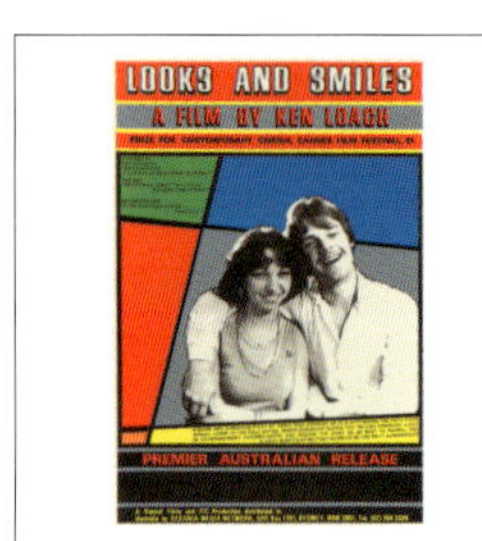


38

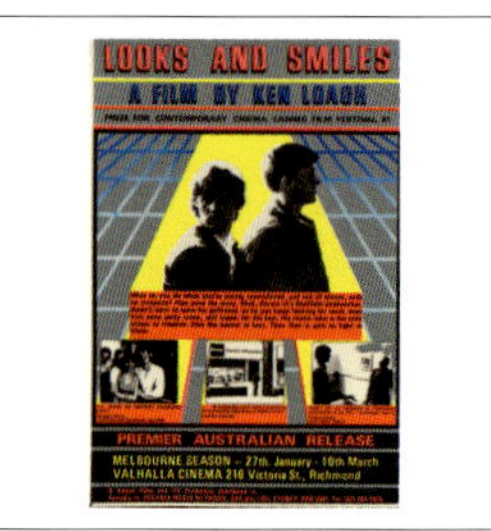


39

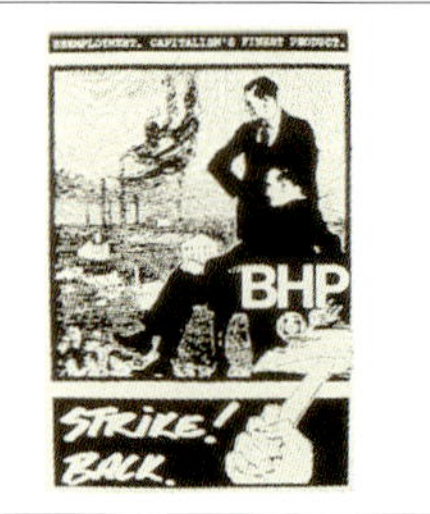


40

33 **Gregor CULLEN** (designer and printer)
**South Coast Labour Council** (client)

*Right to work march!* 1982 Wollongong
screenprint, printed in colour, from four stencils on thin white wove paper
printed image 87.8 x 59.4 cm
sheet 89.0 x 61.0 cm
Gift of Andrew Paterson 1984
1984.362

34 **Marie McMAHON** (designer and printer)
**Wollongong City Gallery** (client)

*Patterns of infinity* 1982 Wollongong
screenprint, printed in colour, from multiple stencils on thin white wove paper
printed image 74.4 x 54.0 cm
sheet 76.0 x 56.0 cm
Private collection

35 **Gregor CULLEN** (designer and printer)
**Nick SOUTHALL** (printer)
**Communist Party of Australia** (client)

*Reject the system* 1982 Wollongong
screenprint, printed in colour, from two stencils on thin white wove paper
printed image 90.0 x 59.6 cm
sheet 91.2 x 61.0 cm
1987.1360

36 **Gregor CULLEN** (designer and printer)
**Deborah NESBITT** (printer)
born Australia 1958
**Land Rights Support Group (Strawberry Hills)** (client)

*End the state of oppression* 1982
screenprint, printed in black ink, from one stencil
printed image 99.5 cm x 73.4 cm
sheet 102.2 x 76.0 cm
Roger Butler Fund 1994
94.307

37 **Michael CALLAGHAN** (designer and printer)
**Australia–Vietnam Society (AVS)** (client)

*AVS calendar 1983* 1982 Wollongong
screenprint, printed in colour, from seven stencils on thin white wove paper
printed image 74.0 x 53.6 cm
sheet 76.2 x 55.8 cm
1987.1335

38 **Gregor CULLEN** (designer and printer)
**Oceania Media Network** (client)

*Looks and smiles* [1] 1983 Wollongong
screenprint, printed in colour, from five stencils on thin white wove paper
printed image 74.6 x 49.8 cm
sheet 76.0 x 51.0 cm
1987.1339

39 **Gregor CULLEN** (designer and printer)
**Oceania Media Network** (client)

*Looks and smiles* [2] 1983 Wollongong
screenprint, printed in colour, from five stencils on thin white wove paper
printed image 74.6 x 49.8 cm
sheet 76.0 x 51.0 cm
Gordon Darling Australia Pacific Print Fund 2008
2008.639

40 **Gregor CULLEN** (designer and printer)
**Percy LEASON** (print after)
**Port Kembla Branch of the Federated Ironworkers Association** (client)

*BHP—strike back!* 1983 Wollongong
screenprint, printed in black ink, from one stencil on thin white wove paper
sheet 76.0 x 56.0 cm
Private Collection

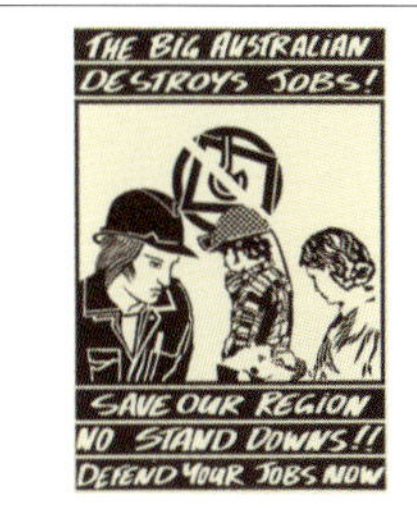


41

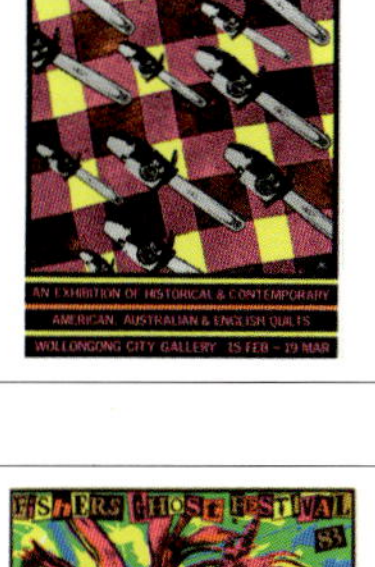


42

43



44



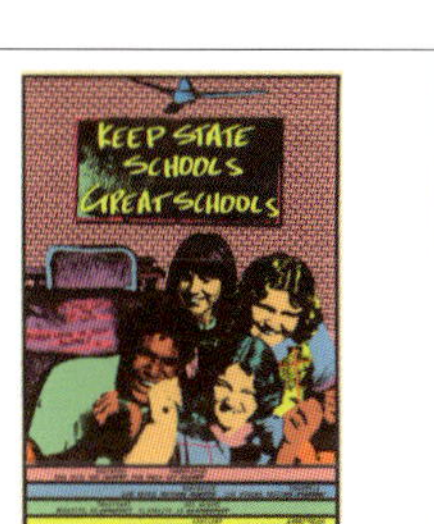


45

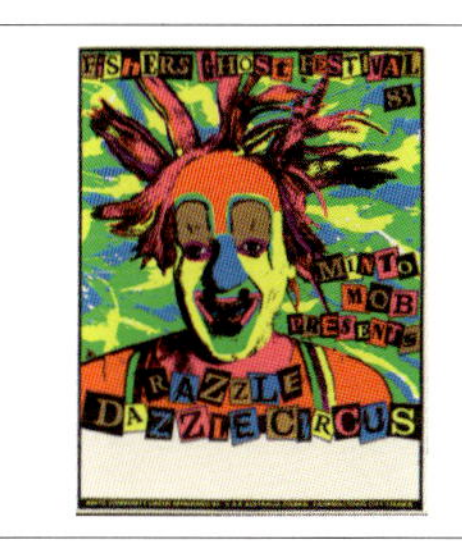


46

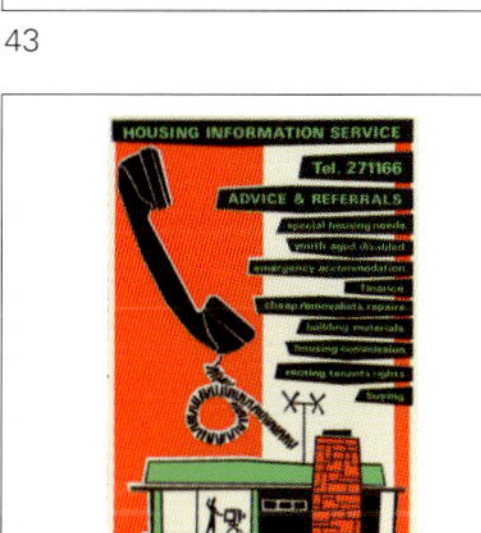


47

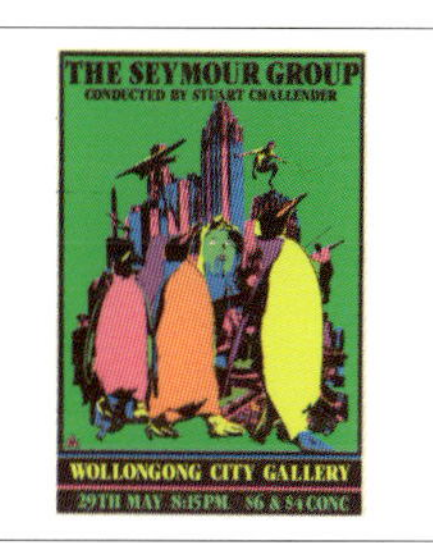


48

41 **Gregor CULLEN** (designer and printer)
**Miners' Federation** (client)

*The big Australian* 1983 Wollongong
screenprint, printed in black ink, from one stencil on thin white wove paper
printed image 74.6 x 49.4 cm
sheet 75.8 x 50.8 cm
Private collection

42 **Gregor CULLEN** (designer and printer)
**Wollongong City Gallery** (client)

*Over the top* 1983 Wollongong
screenprint, printed in colour, from four stencils on thin white wove paper
printed image 74.6 x 49.6 cm
sheet 76.0 x 51.0 cm
1987.1319

43 **Gregor CULLEN** (designer and printer)
**Artspace, Visual Arts Ltd** (client)

*A different perspective* 1983 Wollongong
screenprint, printed in colour, from five stencils on thin white wove paper
printed image 74.8 x 49.8 cm
sheet 76.0 x 51.0 cm
1987.1325

44 **Gregor CULLEN** (designer and printer)
**Wollongong City Gallery** (client)

*Flamenco guitar* 1983 Wollongong
screenprint, printed in colour, from two stencils on thin white wove paper
printed image 74.4 x 49.2 cm
sheet 76.0 x 51.0 cm
1987.1313

45 **Gregor CULLEN** (designer and printer)
**NSW Teachers Federation** (client)

*Keep state schools great schools* 1983 Wollongong
screenprint, printed in colour, from eight stencils on thin white wove paper
sheet 51.0 x 76.0 cm
Gordon Darling Australia Pacific Print Fund 2008
2008.303

46 **Michael CALLAGHAN** (designer and printer)
**Gregor CULLEN** (designer and printer)
**Fishers Ghost Festival Committee** (client)

*Fishers Ghost festival* 1983 Wollongong
screenprint, printed in colour, from five stencils on thin white wove paper
printed image 100.2 x 74.0 cm
sheet 102.2 x 76.0 cm
1987.1381

47 **Michael CALLAGHAN** (designer and printer)
**Gregor CULLEN** (designer and printer)
**Illawarra Community Housing Trust** (client)

*Housing Information Service* 1983 Wollongong
screenprint, printed in colour, from three stencils on thin white wove paper
printed image 74.2 x 49.0 cm
sheet 76.0 x 51.0 cm
1987.1320

48 **Gregor CULLEN** (designer and printer)
**Wollongong City Gallery** (client)

*The Seymour group* 1983 Wollongong
screenprint, printed in colour, from five stencils on off-white paper
printed image 74.8 x 49.6 cm
sheet 75.8 x 51.0 cm
Gordon Darling Australia Pacific Print Fund 2008
2008.301

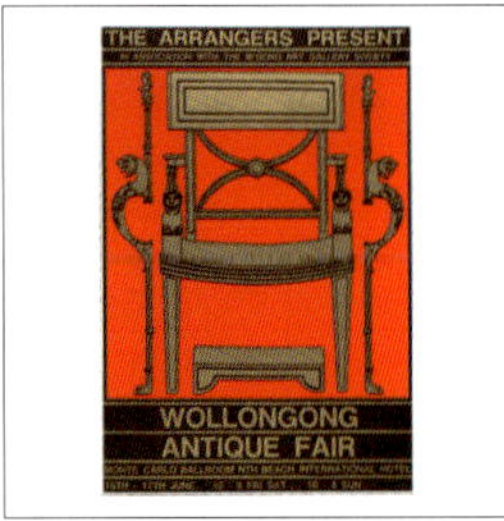


49

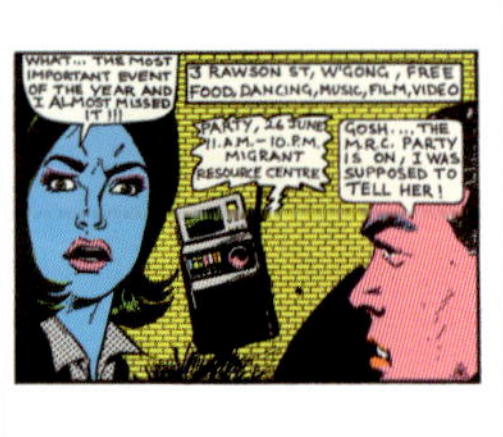


50

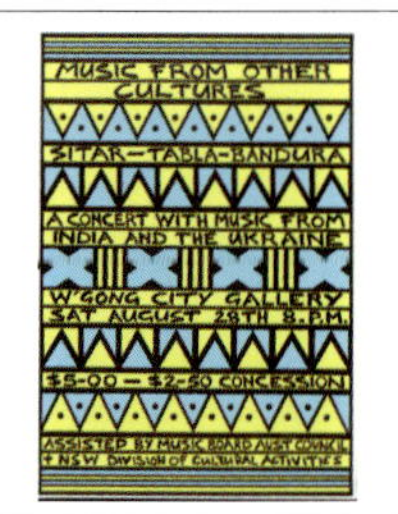


51

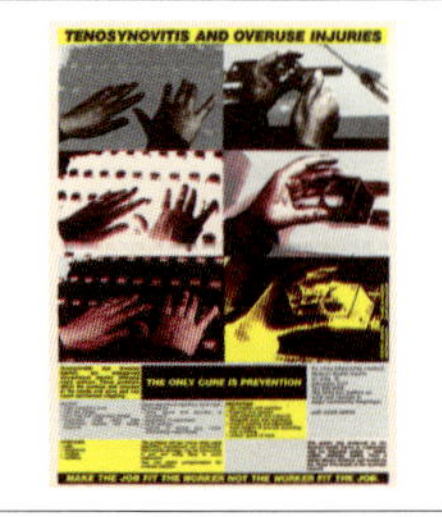


52

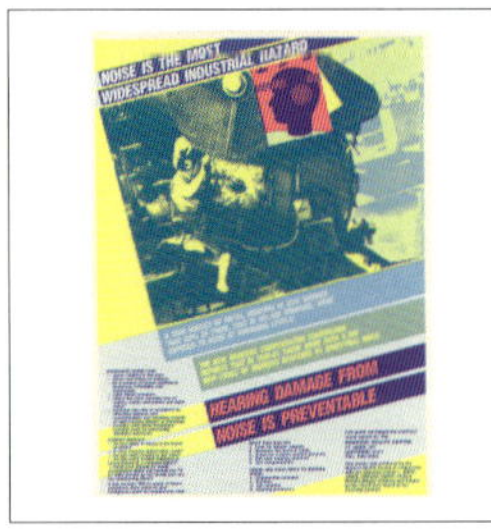


53

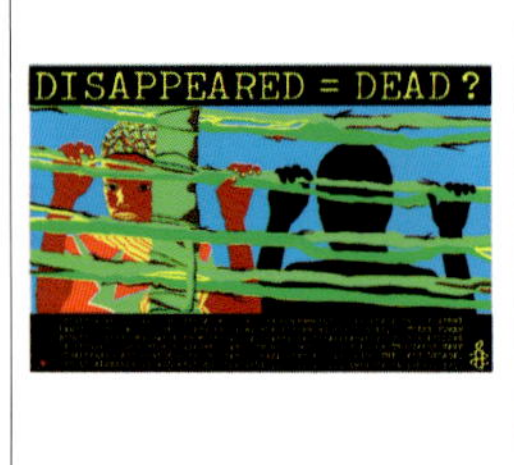


54

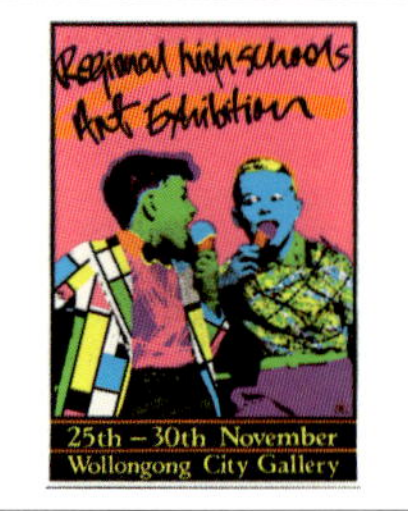


55

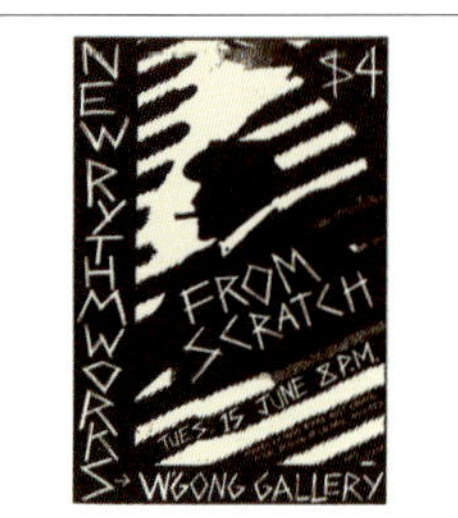


56

49 **Michael CALLAGHAN** (designer and printer)
**Gregor CULLEN** (designer and printer)
**The Arrangers** (client)
*The Arrangers present Wollongong Antique Fair* 1983 Wollongong
screenprint, printed in colour, from three stencils on thin white wove paper
printed image 74.8 x 49.8 cm
sheet 76.0 x 51.0 cm
1987.1311

50 **Michael CALLAGHAN** (designer and printer)
**Gregor CULLEN** (designer and printer)
**Migrant Resource Centre** (client)
*Migrant Resource Centre party* 1983 Wollongong
screenprint, printed in colour, from nine stencils on thin white wove paper
printed image 49.8 x 70.0 cm
sheet 50.8 x 71.4 cm
1987.1352

51 **Michael CALLAGHAN** (designer and printer)
**Gregor CULLEN** (designer and printer)
**Marie McMAHON** (designer)
**Wollongong City Gallery** (client)
*Music from other cultures* 1983 Wollongong
screenprint, printed in colour, from three stencils on thin white wove paper
printed image 74.8 x 49.8 cm
sheet 76.0 x 51.0 cm
1987.1347

52 **Marie McMAHON (**designer and printer)
**Julie DONALDSON** (photographer)
born Australia 1955
**Lidcombe Workers Health Centre** (client)
*Tenosynovitis and overuse injuries* 1983 Wollongong
screenprint, printed in colour, from four stencils on thin white wove paper
printed image 74.2 x 52.8 cm
sheet 76.0 x 56.0 cm
Gordon Darling Australia Pacific Print Fund 2008
2008.645

53 **Marie McMAHON** (designer and printer)
**Julie DONALDSON** (photographer)
**Lidcombe Workers Health Centre** (client)
*Industrial noise* 1983
screenprint, printed in colour, from four stencils on thin white wove paper
printed image 74.0 x 53.4 cm
sheet 76.0 x 55.9 cm
Gordon Darling Australasian Print Fund 2008
2008.302

54 **Michael CALLAGHAN** (designer and printer)
**Gregor CULLEN** (designer and printer)
**Amnesty International Australia (Kiama)** (client)
*Disappeared = Dead* 1983 Wollongong
screenprint, printed in colour, from six stencils on thin white wove paper
printed image 59.2 x 89.8 cm
sheet 60.8 x 91.2 cm
1987.1368

55 **Gregor CULLEN** (designer and printer)
**Wollongong City Gallery** (client)
*Regional High Schools art exhibition* 1983 Wollongong
screenprint, printed in colour, from four stencils on thin white wove paper
printed image 74.0 x 49.0 cm
sheet 76.0 x 50.8 cm
1987.1316

56 **Michael CALLAGHAN** (designer and printer)
**Wollongong City Gallery** (client)
*From scratch* 1983 Wollongong
screenprint, printed in black ink, from one stencil on thin white wove paper
printed image 59.8 x 87.4 cm
sheet 61.0 x 89.0 cm
1987.1342

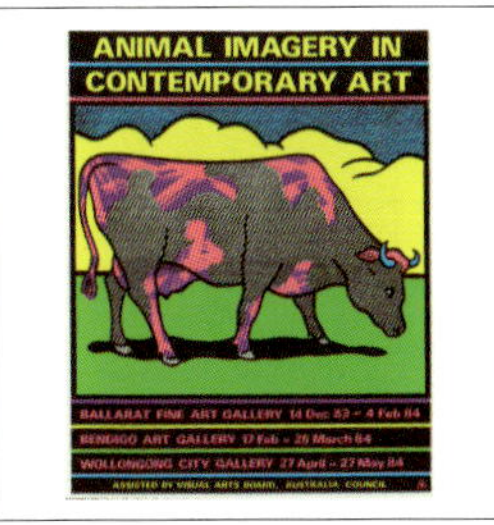

57

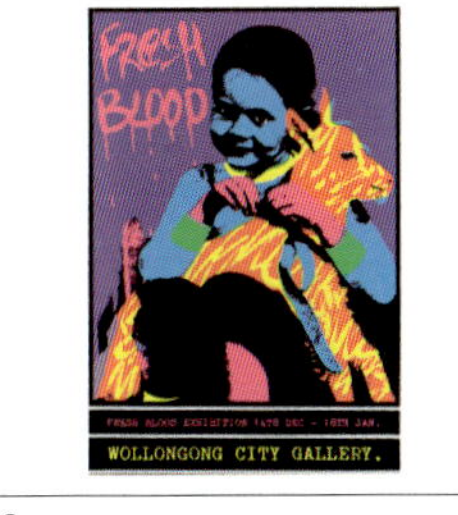

58

59

60

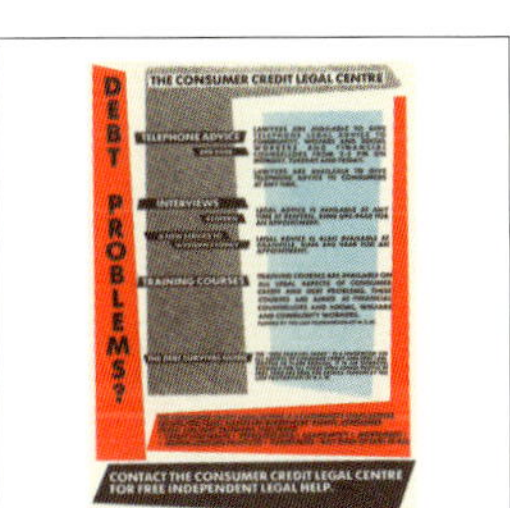

61

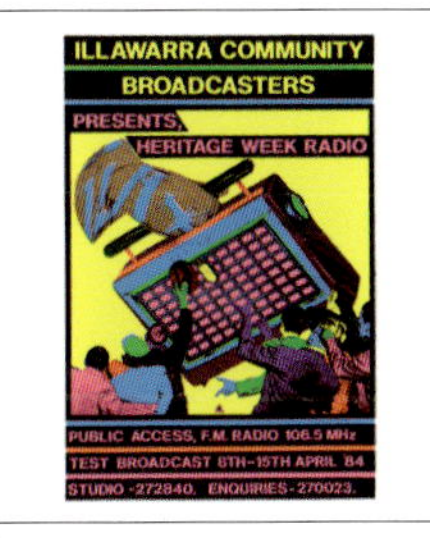

62

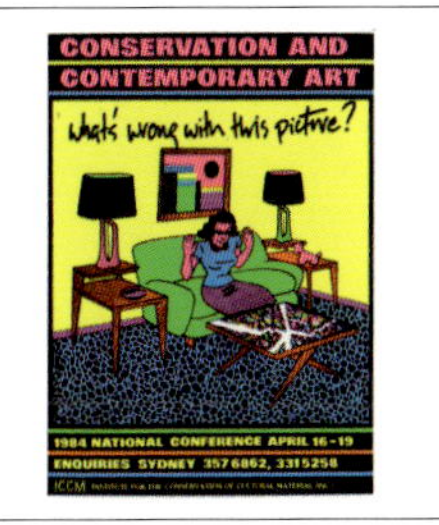

63

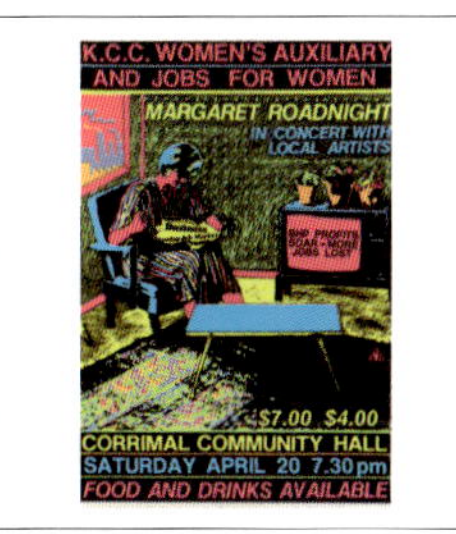

64

57 **Michael CALLAGHAN** (designer and printer)
**Gregor CULLEN** (designer and printer)
**Wollongong City Gallery** (client)
*Animal imagery in contemporary art* 1983 Wollongong
screenprint, printed in colour, from five stencils
on thin white wove paper
printed image 75.8 x 58.8 cm
sheet 77.6 x 60.8 cm
1987.1332

58 **Gregor CULLEN** (designer and printer)
**Wollongong City Gallery** (client)
*Fresh blood* 1983 Wollongong
screenprint, printed in colour, from seven stencils
on thin white wove paper
printed image 74.6 x 50.0 cm
sheet 76.0 x 51.0 cm
Gift of Roger Butler 1985
1985.547

59 **Marie McMAHON** (designer and printer)
**Australia–Vietnam Society (AVS)** (client)
*AVS calendar 1984* Wollongong, 1983
screenprint, printed in colour, from five stencils
on thin white wove paper
printed image 55.4 x 49.0 cm
sheet 59.6 x 52.8 cm
87.1343

60 **Gregor CULLEN** (designer and printer)
**Small Change** (client)
*Small change* 1983
screenprint, printed in colour, from four stencils
printed image 73.4 x 99.3 cm
sheet 75.6 x 102.0 cm
Gordon Darling Australia Pacific Print Fund 2008
2008.630

61 **Alison ALDER** (designer and printer)
**Consumer Credit Legal Centre** (client)
*Debt problems?* 1984
screenprint, printed in colour, from three stencils
printed image 41.0 x 28.7 cm
sheet 42.2 x 29.6 cm
Gordon Darling Australia Pacific Print Fund 2008
2008.653

62 **Michael CALLAGHAN** (designer and printer)
**Gregor CULLEN** (designer and printer)
**Illawarra Community Broadcasters** (client)
*Illawarra Community Broadcasters* 1984 Wollongong
screenprint, printed in colour, from five stencils
on thin white wove paper
printed image 74.2 x 49.2 cm
sheet 76.0 x 51.0 cm
1987.1312

63 **Michael CALLAGHAN** (designer and printer)
**Gregor CULLEN** (designer and printer)
**Institute for Conservation of Cultural Material** (client)
*Conservation and contemporary art* 1984 Wollongong
screenprint, printed in colour, from four stencils
on thin white wove paper
printed image 89.0 x 63.4 cm
sheet 91.0 x 65.0 cm
Gift of Roger Butler 1985
1985.101

64 **Alison ALDER** (designer and printer)
**KCC Women's Auxiliary** (client)
*Jobs for women* 1984 Wollongong
screenprint, printed in colour, from four stencils
on thin white wove paper
printed image 74.0 x 50.0 cm
sheet 76.0 x 50.8 cm
1987.1350

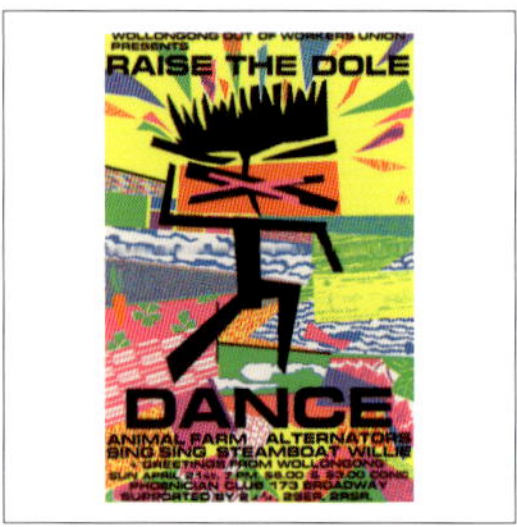


65

66

67

68

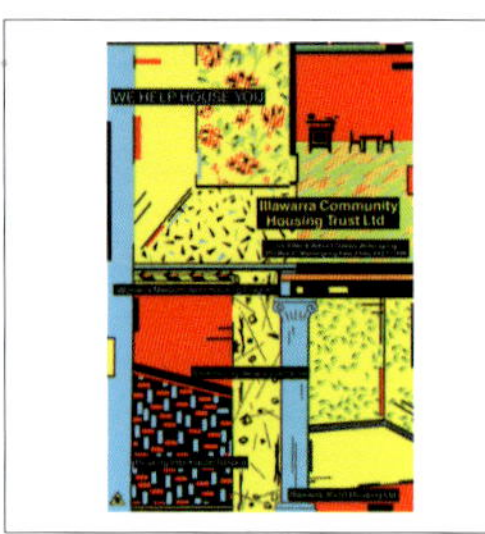


69

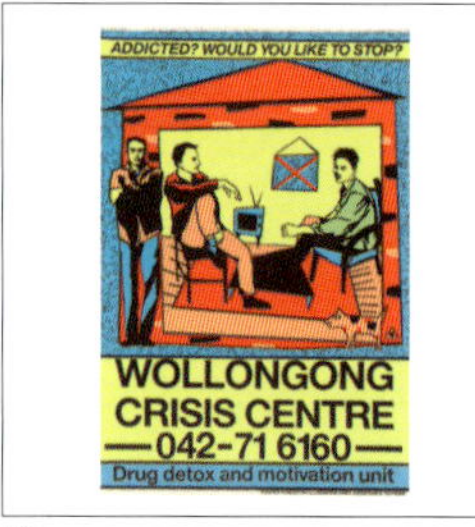


70

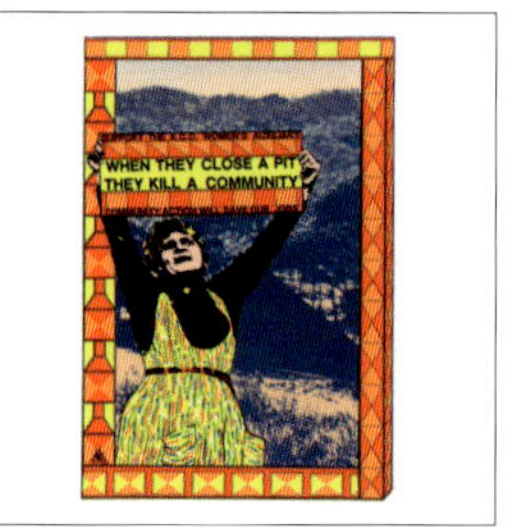


71

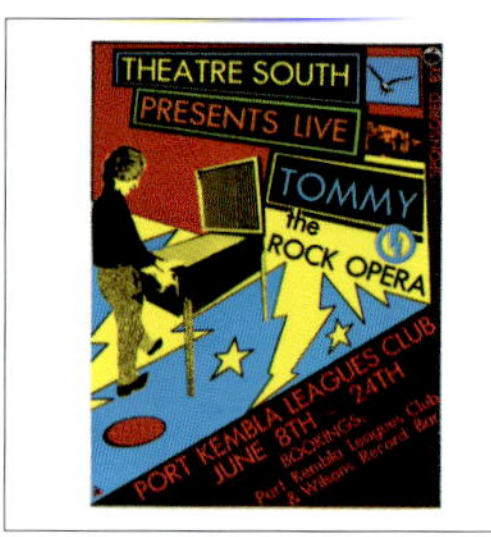


72

65 **Michael CALLAGHAN** (designer and printer)
**Alison ALDER** (printer)
**Sharon PUSELL** (printer's assistant)
born Australia 1963
**Wollongong Out of Workers Union** (client)
*Raise the dole dance* 1984 Wollongong
screenprint, printed in colour, from four stencils
on thin white wove paper
printed image 75.0 x 50.0 cm
sheet 75.0 x 50.0 cm
1987.1329

66 **Alison ALDER** (designer and printer)
**Regional Migrant Health Centre** (client)
*Regional Migrant Health Centre [1 ]* 1984 Wollongong
screenprint, printed in colour, from four stencils
on thin white wove paper
printed image 50.0 x 75.0 cm
sheet 51.0 x 76.0 cm
1987.1318

67 **Alison ALDER** (designer and printer)
**Regional Migrant Health Centre** (client)
*Regional Migrant Health Centre* [2] 1984 Wollongong
screenprint, printed in colour, from four stencils
on thin white wove paper
printed image 74.9 x 49.8 cm
sheet 75.8 x 51.0 cm
Gordon Darling Australia Pacific Print Fund 2008
2008.649

68 **Alison ALDER** (designer and printer)
**Regional Migrant Health Centre** (client)
*Regional Migrant Health Centre* [3] 1984 Wollongong
screenprint, printed in colour, from five stencils
on thin white wove paper
printed image 75.8 x 50.0 cm
sheet 76.2 x 51.0 cm
87.1327

69 **Alison ALDER** (designer and printer)
**Illawarra Community Housing Trust** (client)
*We help house you* 1984 Wollongong
screenprint, printed in colour, from four stencils
on thin white wove paper
printed image 73.8 x 48.4 cm
sheet 73.8 x 48.4 cm
1987.1355

70 **Alison ALDER** (designer and printer)
**Illawarra Area Assistance Scheme** (client)
*Wollongong Crisis Centre* 1984 Wollongong
screenprint, printed in colour, from five stencils
on thin white wove paper
printed image 74.4 x 50.0 cm
sheet 75.0 x 50.0 cm
Gordon Darling Australia Pacific Print Fund 2008
2008.313

71 **Alison ALDER** (designer and printer)
**KCC Women's Auxiliary** (client)
*When they close a pit* 1984 Wollongong
screenprint, printed in colour, from five stencils
on thin white wove paper
printed image 74.4 x 49.4 cm
sheet 76.0 x 51.0 cm
1987.1308

72 **Ray YOUNG** (designer and printer)
born Australia 1951
**Theatre South Wollongong** (client)
*Tommy* 1984 Wollongong
screenprint, printed in colour, from four stencils
on thin white wove paper
printed image 100.2 x 74.4 cm
sheet 102.2 x 76.0 cm
1987.1378

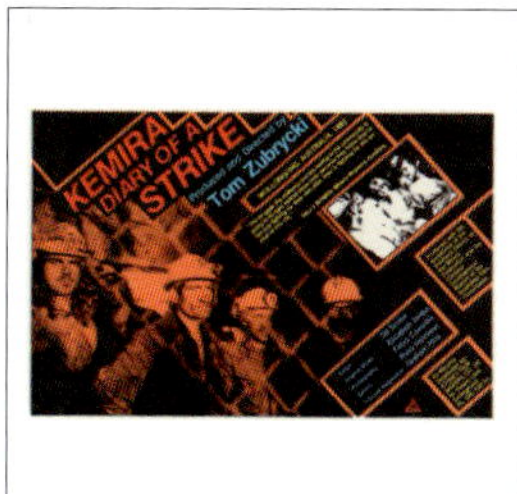

73

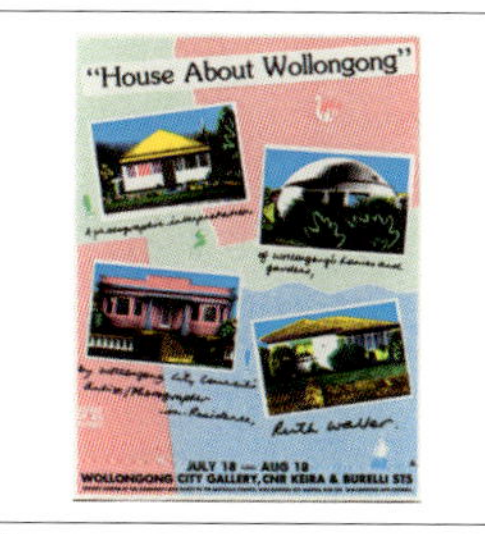

74

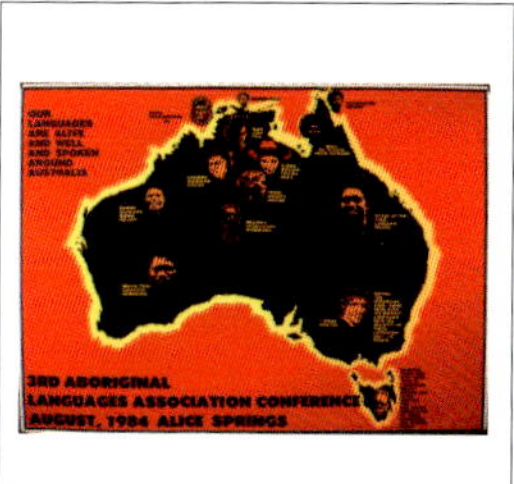

75

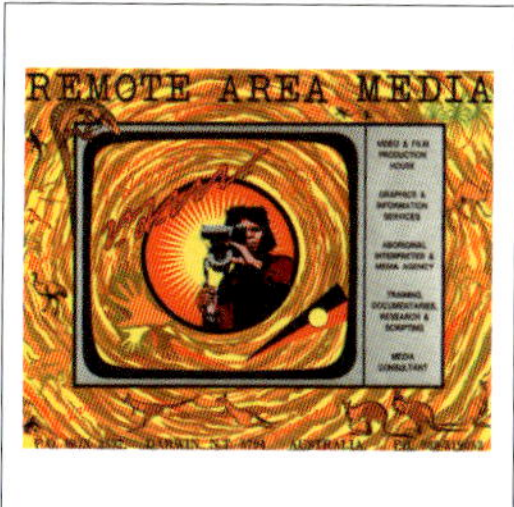

76

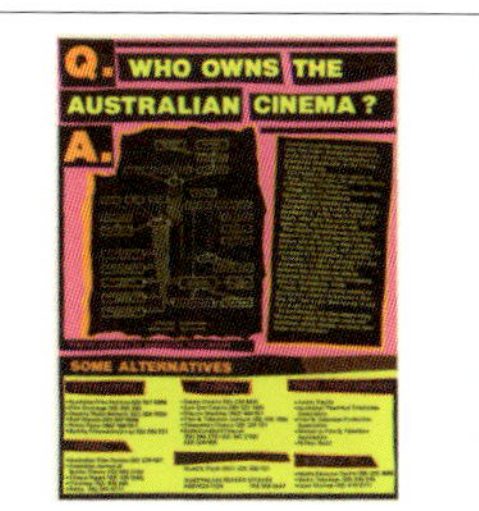

77

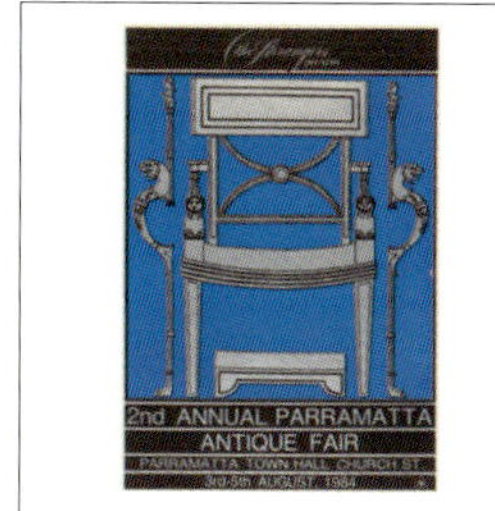

78

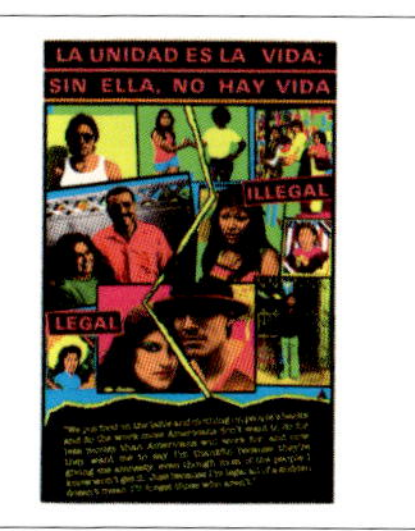

79

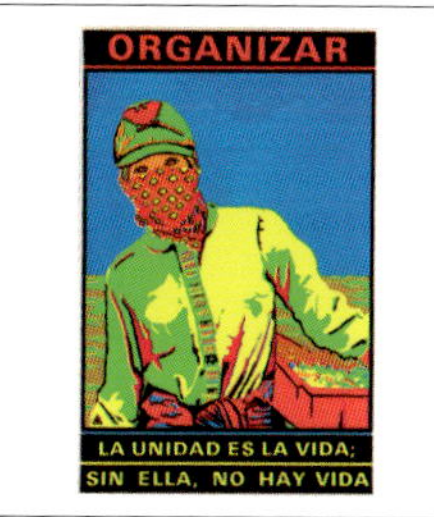

80

73 **Ray YOUNG** (designer and printer)
**Jotz Productions** (client)
*Kemira—diary of a strike* 1984 Wollongong
screenprint, printed in colour, from four stencils on thin white wove paper
printed image 49.2 x 74.2 cm
sheet 51.0 x 76.0 cm
1987.1379

74 **Ruth WALLER** (designer)
**Michael CALLAGHAN** (printer)
**Wollongong City Gallery** (client)
*House about Wollongong* 1984 Wollongong
screenprint, printed in colour, from five stencils on thin white wove paper
printed image 74.4 x 54.4 cm
sheet 76.0 x 56.0 cm
1987.1357

75 **Ray YOUNG** (designer and printer)
**Aboriginal Languages Association** (client)
*3rd Aboriginal Languages Conference* 1984 Wollongong
screenprint, printed in colour, from three stencils on thin white wove paper
sheet 76.0 x 102.0 cm
Private collection

76 **Ray YOUNG** (designer and printer)
**Remote Area Media** (client)
*Remote Area Media* 1984 Wollongong
screenprint, printed in colour, from eight stencils on thin white wove paper
printed image 72.8 x 90.0 cm
sheet 72.8 x 90.0 cm
1987.1376

77 **Michael CALLAGHAN** (designer and printer)
**Gregor CULLEN** (designer and printer)
**Australian Film Commission** (client)
*Who owns Australian cinema?* 1984 Wollongong
screenprint, printed in colour, from three stencils on thin white wove paper
printed image 93.4 x 68.1 cm
sheet 95.1 x 69.6 cm
Gordon Darling Australia Pacific Print Fund 2008
2008.312

78 **Michael CALLAGHAN** (designer and printer)
**Gregor CULLEN** (designer and printer)
**The Arrangers** (client)
*The Arrangers present 2nd annual Parramatta Antique Fair* 1984 Wollongong
screenprint, printed in colour, from three stencils on thin white wove paper
printed image 75.0 x 49.6 cm
sheet 76.0 x 51.0 cm
Gordon Darling Australia Pacific Print Fund 2008
2008.641

79 **Michael CALLAGHAN** (designer and printer)
**Gregor CULLEN** (designer and printer)
**Stephen GRACE** (printer)
**Oscar DUARDO** (printer)
**Richard DUARDO** (facilitator)
**Chicano Cultural Coalition, Los Angeles** (client)
*Illegal/Legal* 1984 Aztlan Multiples, Los Angeles
screenprint, printed in colour, from five stencils on thin white wove paper
printed image 87.4 x 55.2 cm
sheet 89.2 x 57.2 cm
1987.1365

80 **Michael CALLAGHAN** (designer and printer)
**Gregor CULLEN** (designer and printer)
**Oscar DUARDO** (printer)
**Richard DUARDO** (facilitator)
**United Farm Workers Union** (client)
*Organizar* 1984 Aztlan Multiples, Los Angeles
screenprint, printed in colour, from five stencils on thin white wove paper
printed image 87.2 x 55.4 cm
sheet 89.2 x 57.0 cm
1987.1364

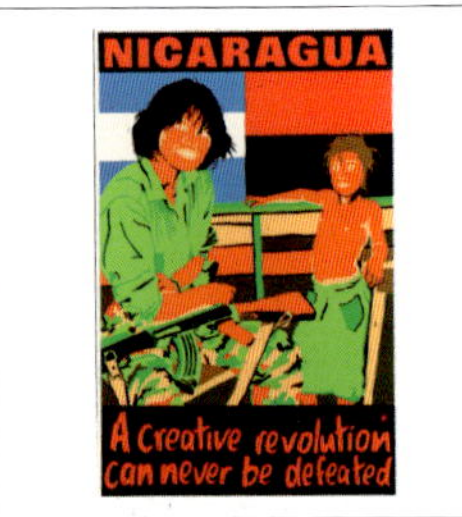

81

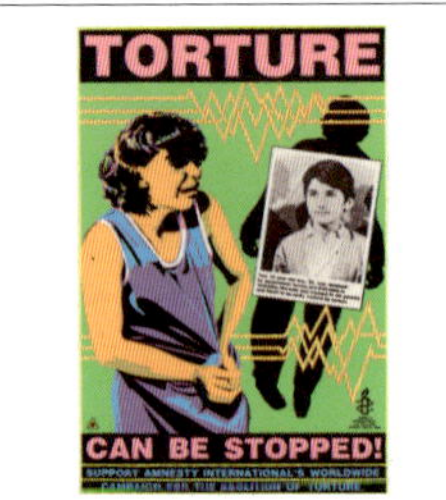

82

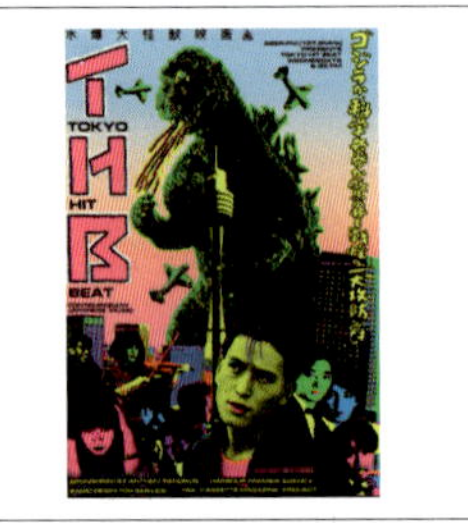

83

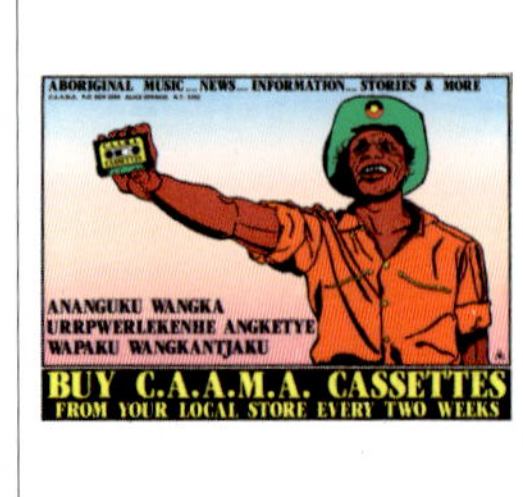

84

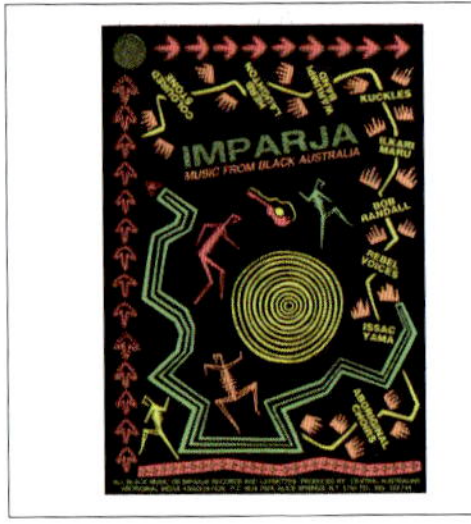

85

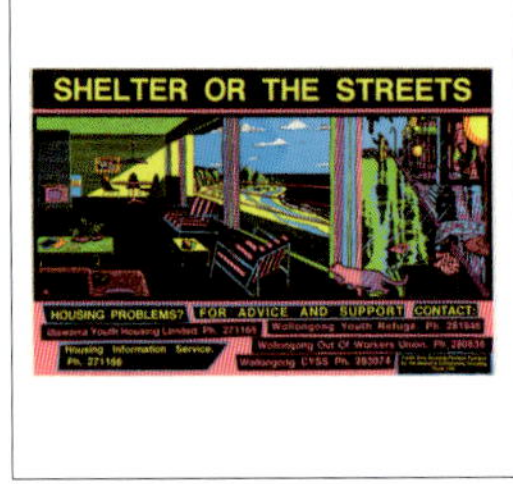

86

87

88

81 **Michael CALLAGHAN** (designer and printer)
**Gregor CULLEN** (designer and printer)
**Committee in Solidarity with Central America and the Caribbean** (client)
*Nicaragua* 1984 Wollongong
screenprint, printed in colour, from six stencils
on thin white wove paper
printed image 74.2 x 49.2 cm
sheet 76.0 x 51.0 cm
1987.1345

82 **Leonie LANE** (designer)
**Ray YOUNG** (printer)
**Amnesty International Australia** (client)
*Torture* 1983 Wollongong
screenprint, printed in colour, from five stencils
on thin white wove paper
printed image 90.6 x 59.4 cm
sheet 91.2 x 61.0 cm
1987.1361

83 **Michael CALLAGHAN** (designer and printer)
**Ray YOUNG** (printer)
**Rick Tanaka** (client)
*Tokyo hit beat* 1984 Wollongong
screenprint, printed in colour, from five stencils
on thin white wove paper
printed image 74.6 x 49.8 cm
sheet 74.6 x 49.8 cm
1987.1328

84 **Michael CALLAGHAN** (designer and printer)
**Jeff STEWART** (illustrator)
born Australia 1950
**Central Australian Aboriginal Media Association (CAAMA)** (client)
*Buy CAAMA cassettes* 1984 Wollongong
screenprint, printed in colour, from six stencils
on thin white wove paper
printed image 74.8 x 100.8 cm
sheet 76.0 x 102.0 cm
Gordon Darling Australasian Print Fund 1984
1984.662

85 **Michael CALLAGHAN** (designer and printer)
**Ray YOUNG** (printer)
**Central Australian Aboriginal Media Association (CAAMA)** (client)
*Imparja music* 1984 Wollongong
screenprint, printed in colour, from five stencils
on thin white wove paper
printed image 74.0 x 49.8 cm
sheet 74.0 x 49.8 cm
1987.1314

86 **Sharon PUSELL** (designer and printer)
**Gregor CULLEN** (printer)
**Illawarra Community Housing Trust** (client)
*Shelter or the streets* 1984 Wollongong
screenprint, printed in colour, from four stencils
on thin white wove paper
printed image 49.8 x 74.8 cm
sheet 51.0 x 76.0 cm
1987.1315

87 **Ray YOUNG** (designer and printer)
**Aboriginal Art Award Committee** (client)
*First National Aboriginal Art Award* 1984 Wollongong
screenprint, printed in colour, from six stencils
on thin white wove paper
printed image 74.6 x 49.8 cm
sheet 76.0 x 51.0 cm
1987.1334

88 **Leonie LANE** (designer and printer)
**Illawarra Housing Trust** (client)
*Steel houses in a steel city* 1984 Wollongong
screenprint, printed in colour, from three stencils
on thin white wove paper
printed image 50.0 x 36.6 cm
sheet 51.0 x 38.0 cm
1987.1322

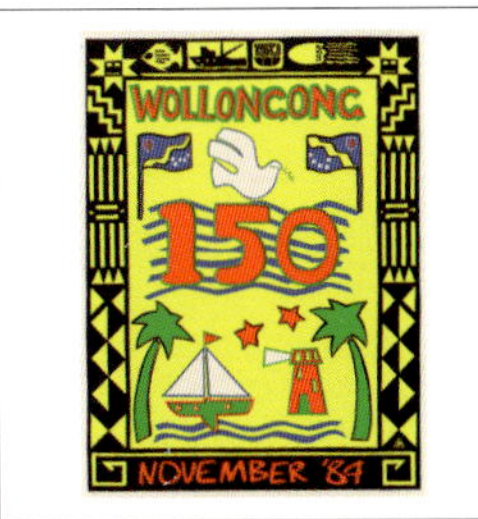


89

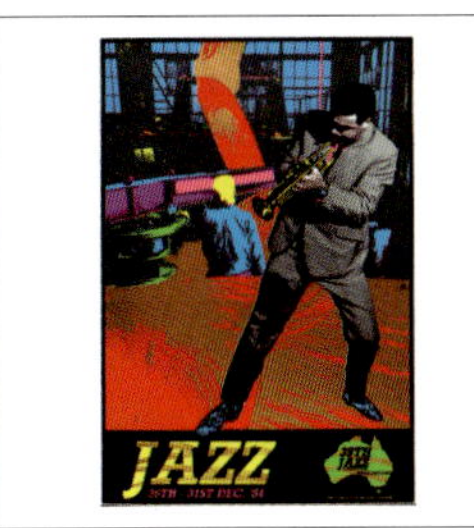


90

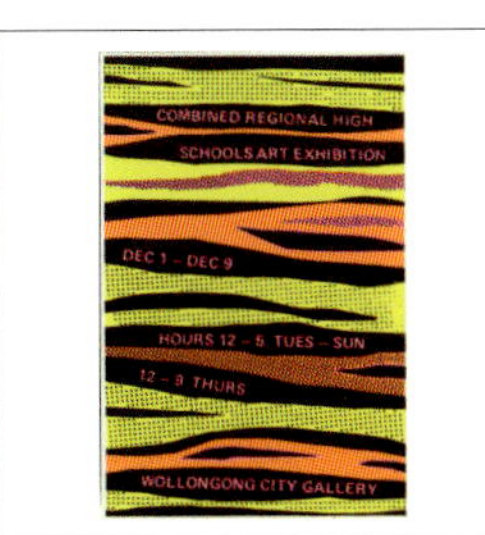


91

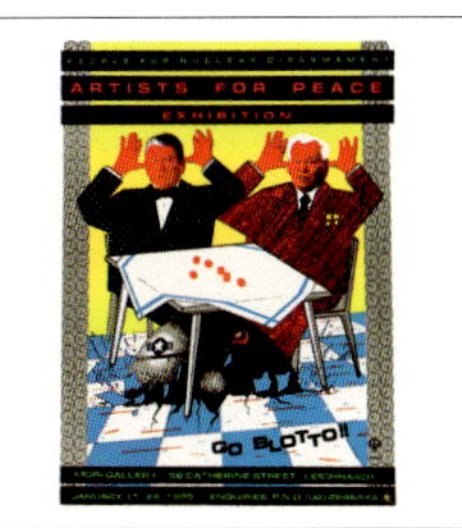


92

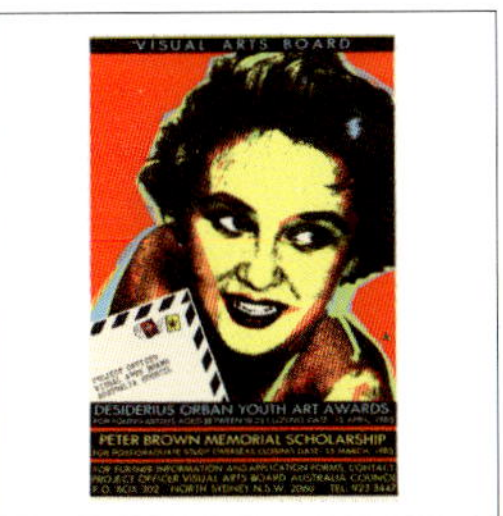


93

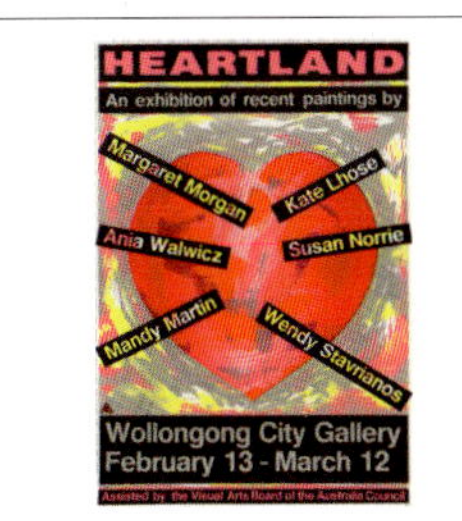


94

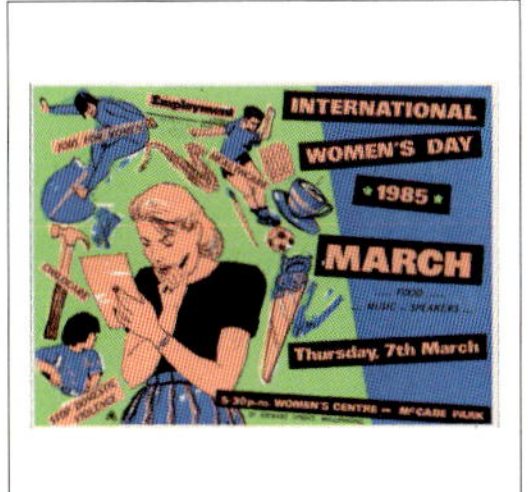


95

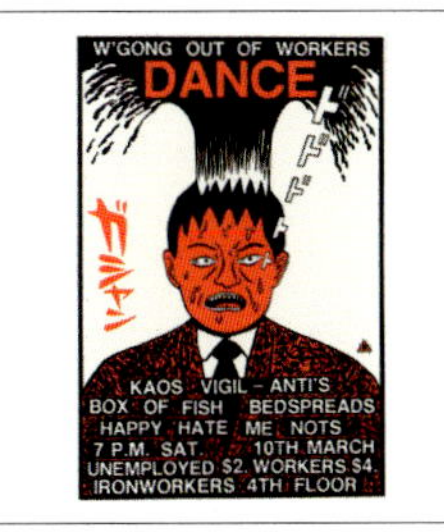


96

89 **Gregor CULLEN** (designer)
**Alison ALDER** (designer and printer)
**Wollongong City Council** (client)
*Wollongong 150th anniversary* 1984 Wollongong
screenprint, printed in colour, from four stencils
on thin white wove paper
printed image 97.6 x 72.0 cm
sheet 102.2 x 76.0 cm
1987.1382

90 **Gregor CULLEN** (designer and printer)
**Kiama Jazz Festival Committee** (client)
*Kiama Jazz Festival* 1984 Wollongong
screenprint, printed in colour, from eight stencils
on thin white wove paper
printed image 75.2 x 50.0 cm
sheet 76.0 x 51.0 cm
1987.1324

91 **Michael CALLAGHAN** (designer)
**Gregor CULLEN** (printer)
**Wollongong City Gallery** (client)
*Combined Regional High Schools Art Exhibition*
1984 Wollongong
screenprint, printed in colour, from three stencils
on thin white wove paper
printed image 61.6 x 40.0 cm
sheet 63.2 x 41.4 cm
1987.1307

92 **Leonie LANE** (designer)
**Ray YOUNG** (printer)
**Artists for Peace and People for Nuclear Disarmament** (clients)
*Go blotto!* 1984 Wollongong
screenprint, printed in colour, from five stencils
on thick white wove paper
printed image 74.0 x 53.2 cm
sheet 76.0 x 55.8 cm
1987.1331

93 **Alison ALDER** (designer and printer)
**Visual Arts and Crafts Board, Australia Council** (client)
*Visual Arts and Crafts Board* 1984 Wollongong
screenprint, printed in colour, from four stencils
on thin white wove paper
printed image 74.0 x 49.4 cm
sheet 76.0 x 51.0 cm
1987.1326

94 **Alison ALDER** (designer and printer)
**Wollongong City Gallery** (client)
*Heartland* 1985 Wollongong
screenprint, printed in colour, from six stencils
on thin white wove paper
printed image 74.2 x 50.8 cm
sheet 76.0 x 51.0 cm
1987.1349

95 **Leonie LANE** (designer and printer)
**Alison ALDER** (printer)
**Wollongong Women's Centre** (client)
*International Women's Day* 1985 Annandale, Sydney
screenprint, printed in colour, from four stencils on thick white wove paper
printed image 37.0 x 49.8 cm
sheet 38.0 x 51.0 cm
1987.1306

96 **Michael CALLAGHAN** (designer and printer)
**Nick SOUTHALL** (printer's assistant)
**Wollongong Out of Workers Union** (client)
*WOW dance* 1985 Wollongong
screenprint, printed in colour, from two stencils
on thin white wove paper
printed image 74.4 x 49.4 cm
sheet 76.0 x 51.0 cm
1987.1310

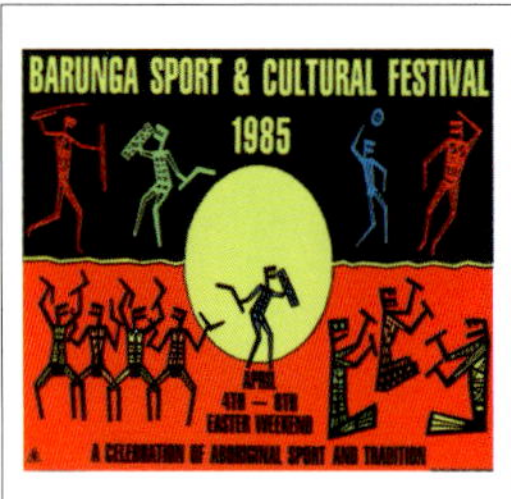

97

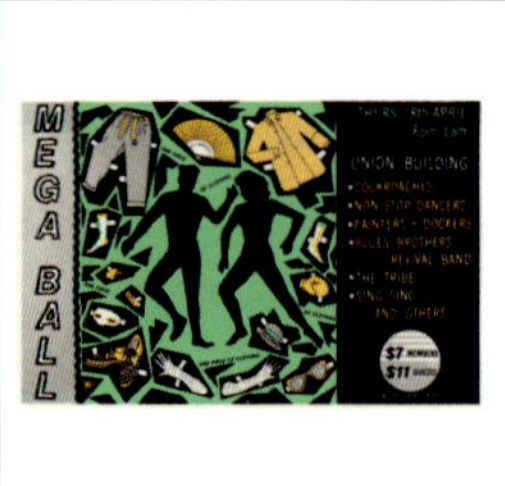

98

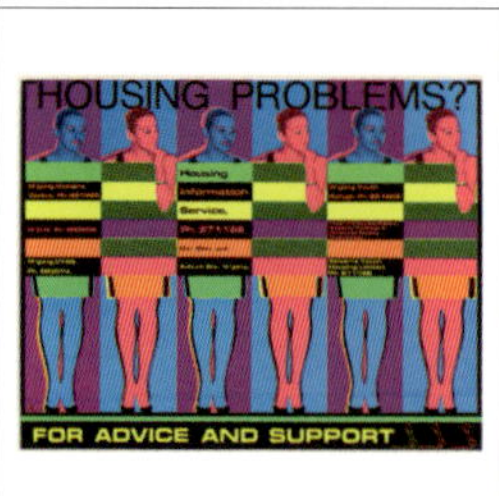

99

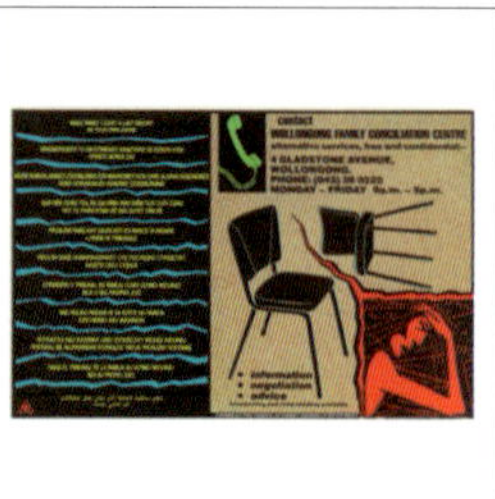
100

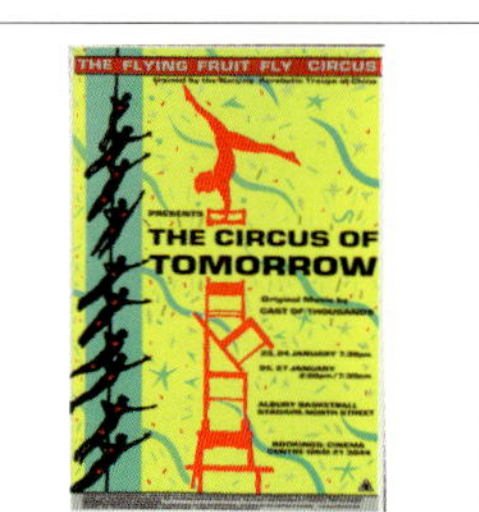

101

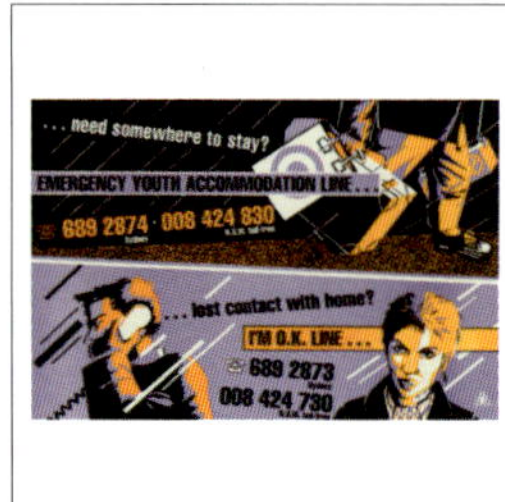

102

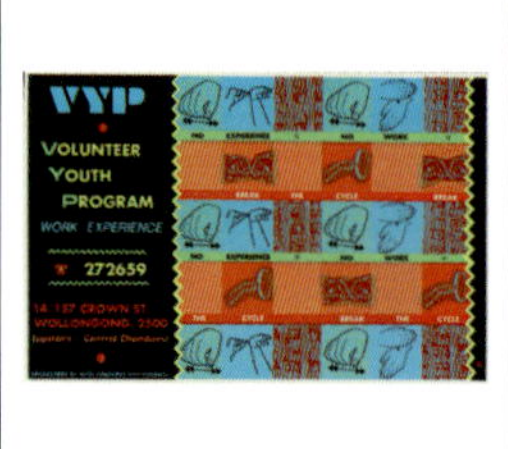

103

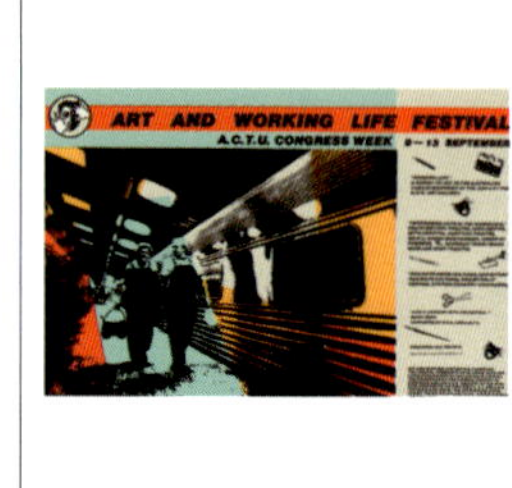

104

97 **Michael CALLAGHAN** (designer and printer)
**Manuel PAMKAL** (original concept)
**Ray YOUNG** (printer)
**Barunga Community Government Council** (client)
*Barunga Festival 1* 1985 Wollongong
screenprint, printed in colour, from four stencils
on thin white wove paper
printed image 49.8 x 74.8 cm
sheet 49.8 x 74.8 cm
1987.1341

98 **Leonie LANE** (designer and printer)
**Wollongong University Student Union** (client)
*Mega ball* 1985
screenprint, printed in colour, from four stencils
on thin white wove paper
printed image 48.8 x 73.6 cm
sheet 50.8 x 75.8 cm
1987.1340

99 **Sharon PUSELL** (designer and printer)
**Illawarra Community Housing Trust** (client)
*Housing problems?* 1985 Wollongong
screenprint, printed in colour, from five stencils
on thin white wove paper
printed image 59.0 x 73.6 cm
sheet 60.8 x 75.0 cm
1987.1369

100 **Ray YOUNG** (designer and printer)
**Federal Attorney General's Department** (client)
*Wollongong Family Conciliation Centre* 1985
Wollongong
screenprint, printed in colour, from four stencils
on thin white wove paper
printed image 50.0 x 75.0 cm
sheet 50.8 x 76.2 cm
Gordon Darling Australia Pacific Print Fund 2008
2008.629

101 **Alison ALDER** (designer and printer)
**Flying Fruit Fly Circus** (client)
*The circus of tomorrow* 1985 Annandale, Sydney
screenprint, printed in colour, from five stencils
on thin white wove paper
printed image 74.4 x 49.8 cm
sheet 76.0 x 51.0 cm
1987.1344

102 **Leonie LANE** (designer and printer)
**THE IMPRESSIONISTS PTY LTD** (printer)
**NSW State Government Youth and Community Services** (client)
*Need somewhere to stay?* 1985 Annandale, Sydney
offset-lithograph, printed in colour, from multiple plates
on white wove paper
printed image 43.0 x 59.4 cm
sheet 43.6 x 59.4 cm
1987.1385

103 **Leonie LANE** (designer and printer)
**Wollongong City Council** (client)
*Volunteer Youth Program* 1985 Wollongong
screenprint, printed in colour, from four stencils
on thin white wove paper
printed image 49.0 x 74.2 cm
sheet 51.0 x 76.0 cm
1987.1351

104 **Alison ALDER** (designer and printer)
**Leonie LANE** (designer and printer)
**Art and Working Life Festival Committee** (client)
*Art and Working Life Festival* Tin Sheds, Sydney 1985
screenprint, printed in colour, from five stencils on thick
thin white wove paper
printed image 49.0 x 73.6 cm
sheet 49.0 x 73.6 cm
1987.1317

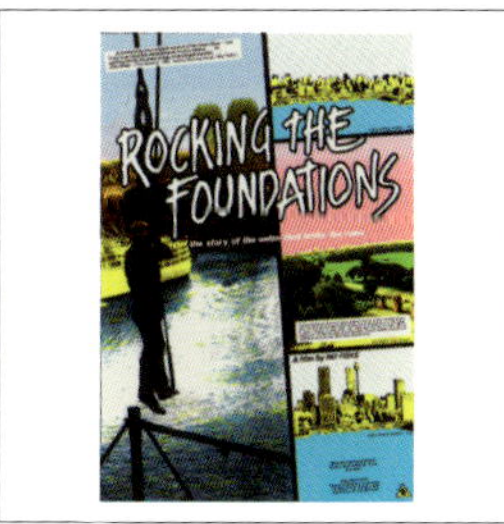

105

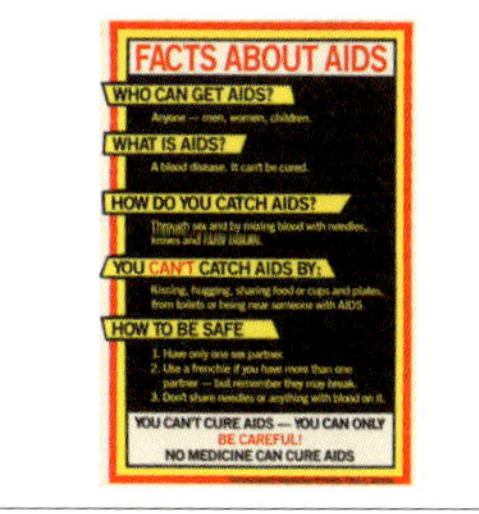

106

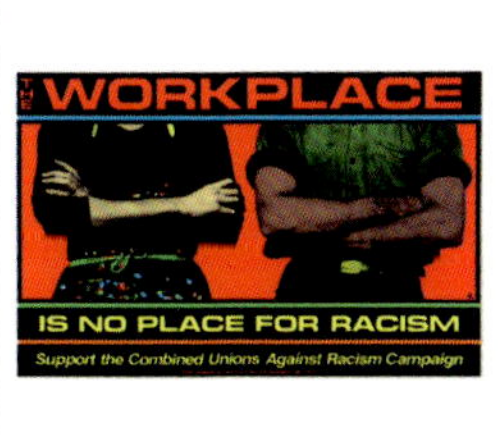

107

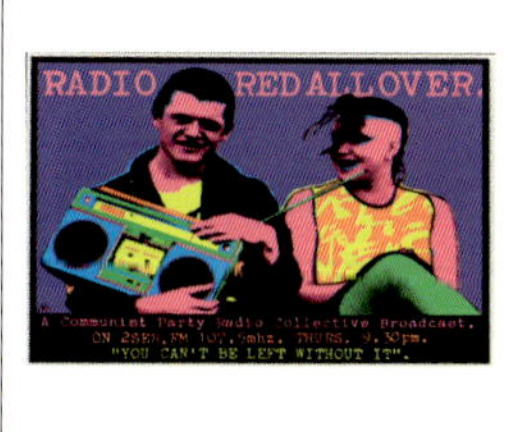

108

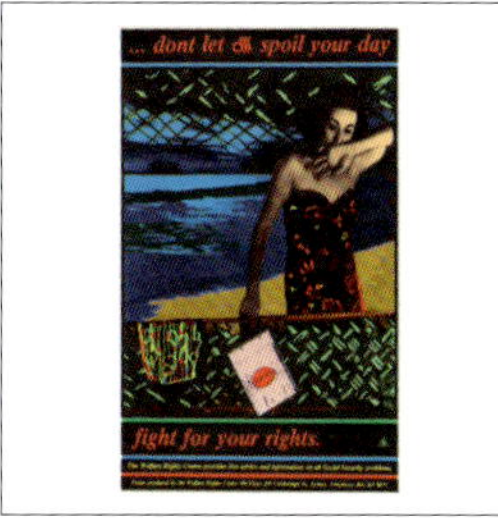

109

110

111

112

105 **LEONIE LANE** (designer)
**Alison ALDER** (printer)
**Sydney Filmmakers Co-operative** (client)
*Rocking the foundations* 1985 Annandale, Sydney
screenprint, printed in colour, from four stencils on thin white wove paper
printed image 73.2 x 48.6 cm
sheet 73.2 x 48.6 cm
1987.1323

106 **Michael CALLAGHAN** (designer and printer)
**Gregor CULLEN** (designer and printer)
**Commonwealth Department of Health** (client)
*Facts about AIDS* 1985 Wollongong
screenprint, printed in colour, from multiple stencils on thin white wove paper
printed image 74.7 x 49.8 cm
sheet 76.3 x 50.8 cm
Private collection

107 **Gregor CULLEN** (designer and printer)
**Combined Unions Against Racism** (client)
*The workplace is no place for racism* 1985 Wollongong
screenprint, printed in colour, from six stencils on thin white wove paper
printed image 54.4 x 74.8 cm
sheet 56.0 x 76.0 cm
1987.1333

108 **Gregor CULLEN** (designer and printer)
**Nick SOUTHALL** (printer's assistant)
**Deborah NESBITT** (printer's assistant)
**Communist Party of Australia** (client)
*Radio red all over* 1985 Wollongong
screenprint, printed in colour, from four stencils on thin white wove paper
printed image 73.8 x 99.6 cm
sheet 76.0 x 102.2 cm
1987.1383

109 **Gregor CULLEN** (designer and printer)
**Welfare Rights Centre** (client)
*Don't let DSS spoil your day* 1985 Annandale, Sydney
screenprint, printed in colour, from six stencils on thin white wove paper
printed image 89.2 x 59.2 cm
sheet 91.0 x 61.0 cm
1987.1367

110 **Michael CALLAGHAN** (designer and printer)
**Ray YOUNG** (printer)
**Central Australian Aboriginal Media Association (CAAMA)** (client)
*Bush radio* 1985 Annandale, Sydney
screenprint, printed in colour, from four stencils on thin white wove paper
printed image 74.2 x 100.0 cm
sheet 74.2 x 100.0 cm
1987.1375

111 **Michael CALLAGHAN** (designer and printer)
**Ray YOUNG** (designer and printer)
**Central Australian Aboriginal Media Association (CAAMA)** (client)
*The 8-KIN network* 1985 Wollongong
screenprint, printed in colour, from six stencils on thin white wove paper
printed image and sheet 102.0 x 152.0 cm
Gift of Alison Alder, 2008
2008.798

112 **Alison ALDER** (designer and printer)
**Broad Left Conference Committee** (client)
*Broad Left Conference* 1986 Annandale, Sydney
screenprint, printed in colour, from four stencils on thin white wove paper
printed image 74.6 x 100.6 cm
sheet 76.0 x 102.0 cm
1987.1380

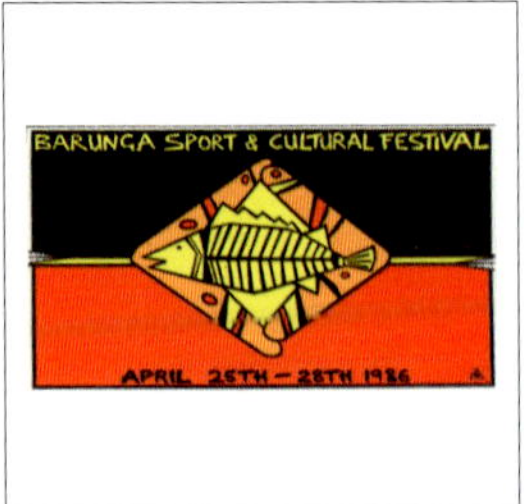


113

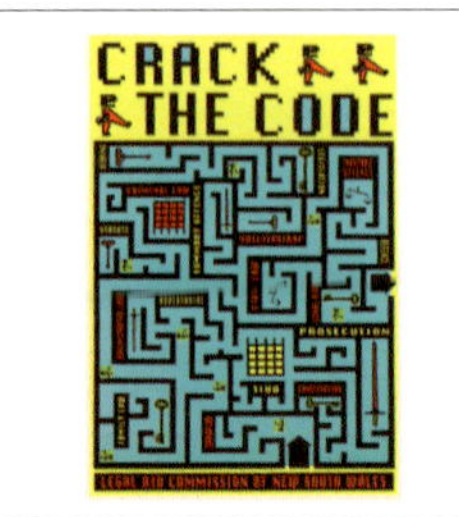


114

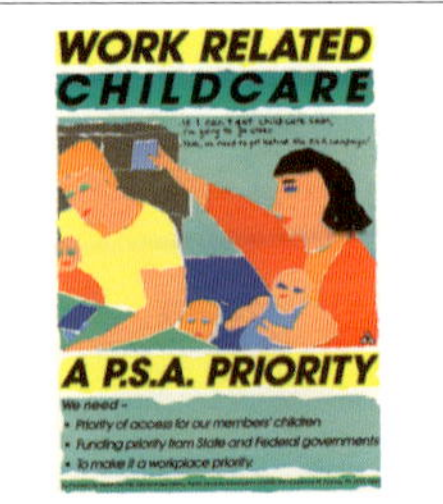


115

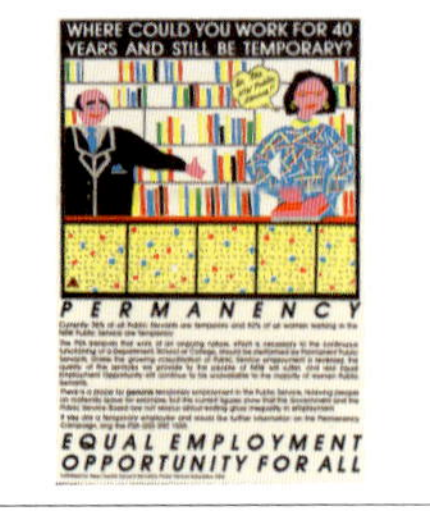


116

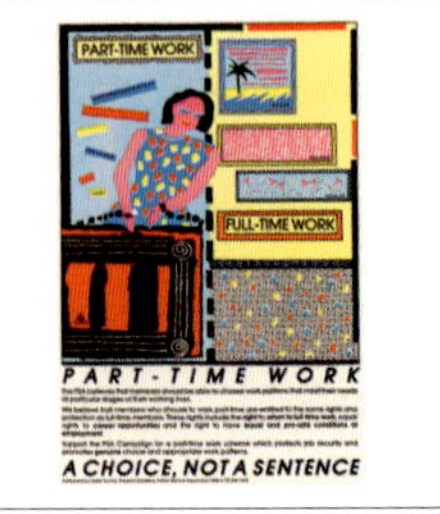


117

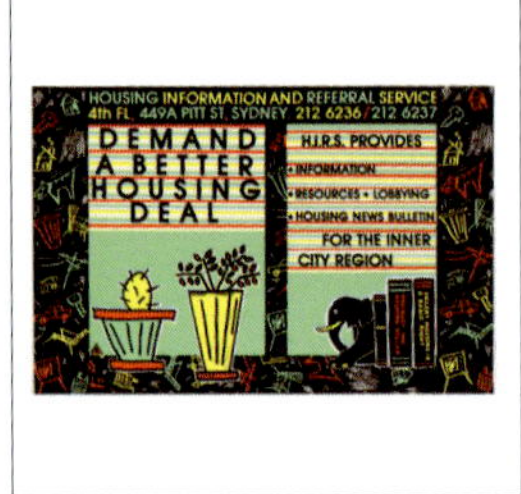


118

119

120

113 **Michael CALLAGHAN** (designer and printer)
**Ray YOUNG** (printer)
**Barunga Community Government Council** (client)
*Barunga Festival 2* 1986 Annandale, Sydney
screenprint, printed in colour, from three stencils on thin white wove paper
printed image 49.4 x 75.6 cm
sheet 50.8 x 76.0 cm
1987.1353

114 **Michael CALLAGHAN** (designer)
**Alison ALDER** (printer)
**Legal Aid Commission** (client)
*Crack the code* 1986 Annandale, Sydney
screenprint, printed in colour, from four stencils on thin white wove paper
printed image 74.0 x 49.6 cm
sheet 76.1 x 50.9 cm
Gordon Darling Australia Pacific Print Fund 2008
2008.642

115 **Alison ALDER** (designer)
**MARTICH-OSTERMAN PRINTING AND PUBLISHING PTY LTD** (printer)
**Public Service Association of NSW** (client)
*Work-related childcare* 1986 Annandale, Sydney
offset-lithograph, printed in colour, on thin white wove paper
printed image 68.2 x 46.8 cm
sheet 69.6 x 47.6 cm
Gordon Darling Australia Pacific Print Fund 2008
2008.650

116 **Alison ALDER** (designer)
**MARTICH-OSTERMAN PRINTING AND PUBLISHING PTY LTD** (printer)
**Public Service Association NSW** (client)
*Permanency* 1986 Annandale, Sydney
offset-lithograph, printed in colour, from multiple plates on thin white wove paper
printed image 73.6 x 47.6 cm
sheet 75.6 x 50.0 cm
1987.1387

117 **Alison ALDER** (designer)
**MARTICH-OSTERMAN PRINTING AND PUBLISHING PTY LTD** (printer)
**Public Service Association NSW** (client)
*Part-time work* 1986 Annandale, Sydney
offset-lithograph, printed in colour, from multiple plates on thin white wove paper
printed image 73.0 x 47.0 cm
sheet 75.0 x 49.2 cm
1987.1386

118 **Alison ALDER** (designer and printer)
**Housing Information and Referral Service** (client)
*Demand a better housing deal* 1986 Annandale, Sydney
screenprint, printed in colour, from four stencils on thin white wove paper
printed image 49.8 x 75.0 cm
sheet 50.8 x 76.2 cm
1987.1392

119 **Ray YOUNG** (designer and printer)
**ROTARY OFFSET PRESS PTY LTD** (printer)
**Mermaid Beach Productions** (client)
*Backlash* 1986 Annandale, Sydney
offset-lithograph, printed in colour, from multiple plates on thin white wove paper
printed image 66.4 x 48.8 cm
sheet 76.0 x 51.0 cm
1987.1391

120 **Leonie LANE** (designer)
**Michael CALLAGHAN** (designer)
**PRINTCRAFT PTY LTD** (printer)
**Australian Film Commission** (client)
*Australian movies well worth watching* 1986 Annandale, Sydney
offset-lithograph, printed in colour, from multiple plates on thin white wove paper
printed image 65.0 x 40.4 cm
sheet 65.0 x 40.4 cm
1987.1389

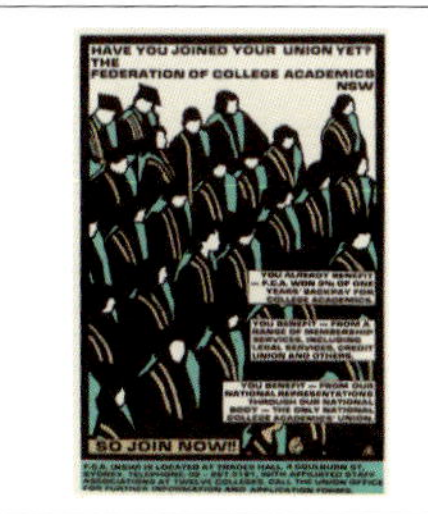

121

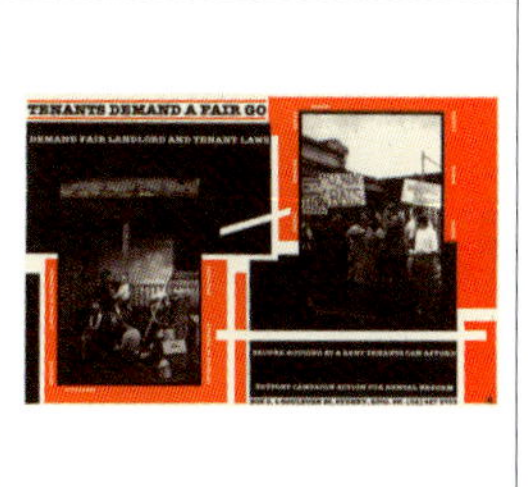


122

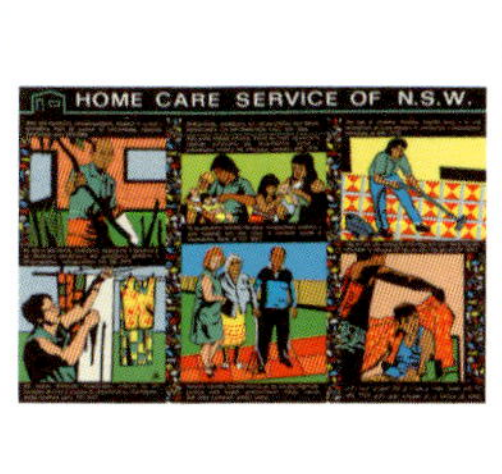


123

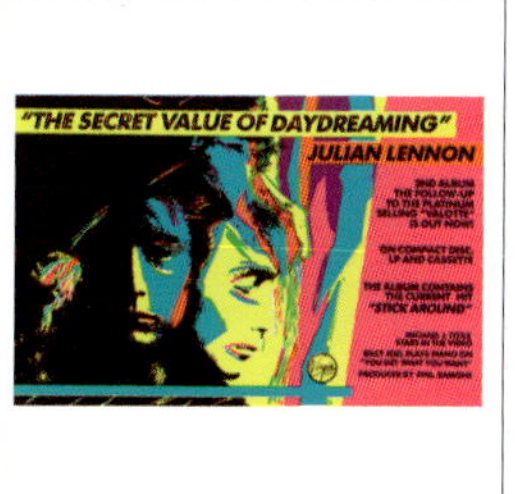


124

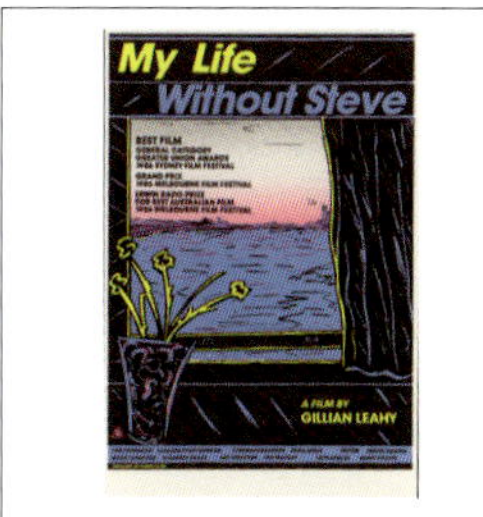


125

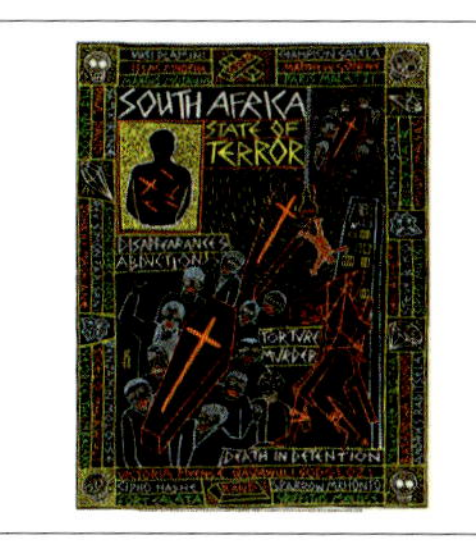


126

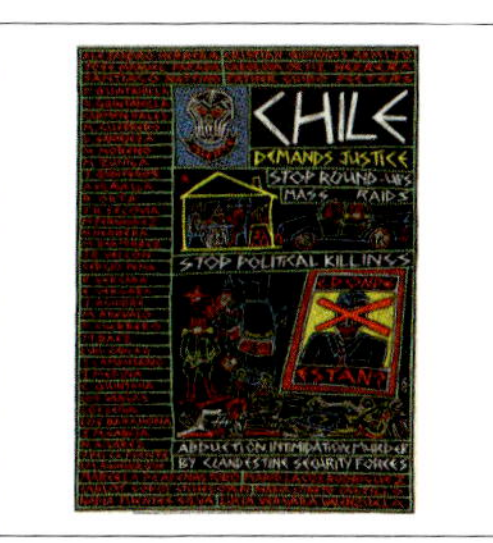


127

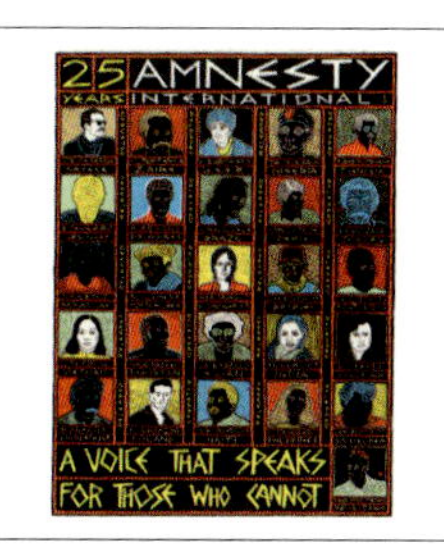


128

121 **Alison ALDER** (designer and printer)
**Federation of College Academics** (client)
*College Academics* 1986 Annandale, Sydney
screenprint, printed in colour, from three stencils on thin white wove paper
printed image 73.6 x 48.0 cm
sheet 76.0 x 50.8 cm
1987.1336

122 **Alison ALDER** (designer and printer)
**Ray YOUNG** (printer)
**Tenants' Union of NSW** and **Shelter NSW** (clients)
*Tenants demand a fair go!* 1986 Annandale, Sydney
screenprint, printed in colour, from two stencils on thin white wove paper
printed image 49.2 x 74.4 cm
sheet 51.0 x 75.6 cm
1987.1354

123 **Alison ALDER** (designer)
**ROTARY OFFSET PRESS** PTY LTD (printer)
**Home Care Service of NSW** (client)
*Home Care Service of NSW* 1986 Annandale, Sydney
offset-lithograph, printed in colour, on thin white wove paper
printed image and sheet 51.6 x 76.2 cm
Gordon Darling Australia Pacific Print Fund 2008
2008.656

124 **Alison ALDER** (designer and printer)
**Virgin Records (Australia)** (client)
*The secret value of daydreaming* 1986 Annandale, Sydney
screenprint, printed in colour, from four stencils
printed image and sheet 59.2 x 89.2 cm
87.1362

125 **Jan MACKAY** (designer)
born Australia 1950
**Alison ALDER** (printer)
**Gillian Leaghy** (client)
*My life without Steve* 1986 Annandale, Sydney
screenprint, printed in colour, from four stencils on thin white wove paper
printed image 70.0 x 48.2 cm
sheet 75.8 x 50.0 cm
1987.1384

126 **Michael CALLAGHAN** (designer)
**Peter CURTIS** (printer)
born Australia 1956
**Amnesty International Australia** (client)
*Amnesty/South Africa* 1986 Annandale, Sydney
screenprint, printed in colour, from four stencils on thin white wove paper
printed image 100.6 x 74.8 cm
sheet 102.2 x 76.1 cm
1987.1400

127 **Michael CALLAGHAN** (designer and printer)
**Alison ALDER** (printer)
**Amnesty International Australia** (client)
*Amnesty/Chile demands justice* 1987 Annandale, Sydney
screenprint, printed in colour, from five stencils on thin white wove paper
printed image 100.0 x 73.9 cm
sheet 102.2 x 76.6 cm
1987.1399

128 **Michael CALLAGHAN** (designer)
**Alison ALDER** (printer)
**Amnesty International Australia** (client)
*25 years Amnesty International* 1987 Annandale, Sydney
screenprint, printed in colour, from six stencils on thin white wove paper
printed image 100.0 x 73.9 cm
sheet 102.2 x 76.6 cm
Gordon Darling Australasian Print Fund 1992
1992.775

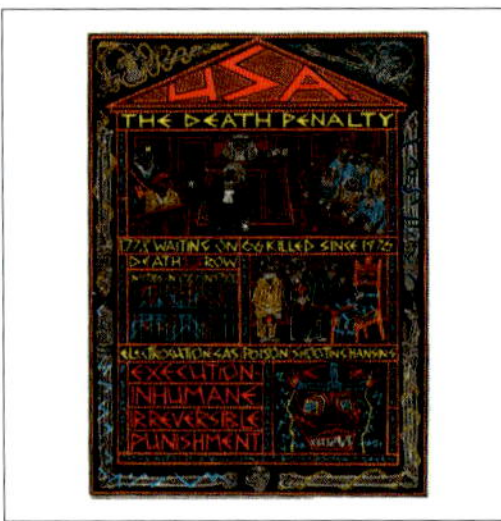

129

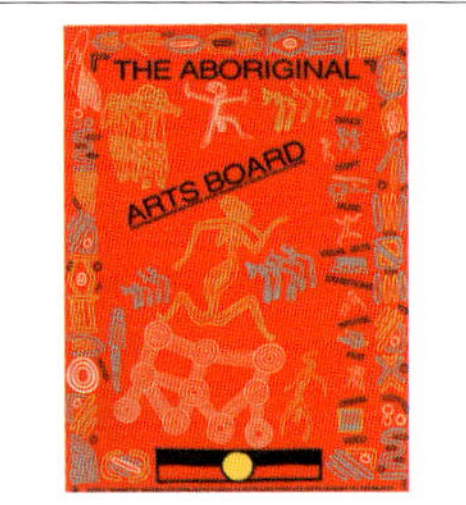

130

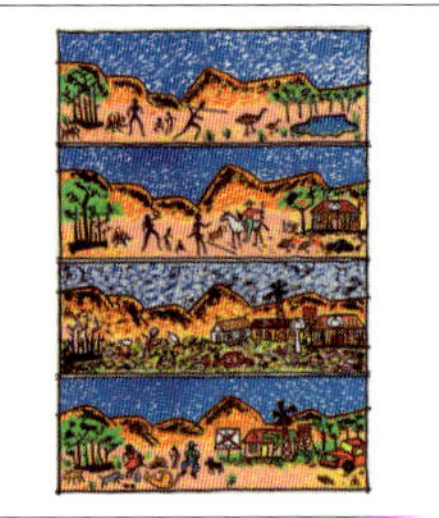
131

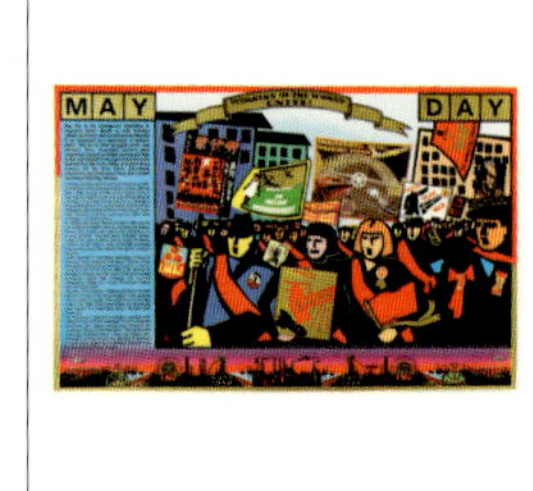

132

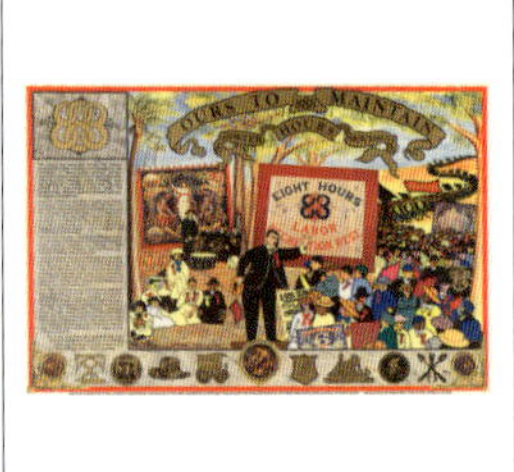
133

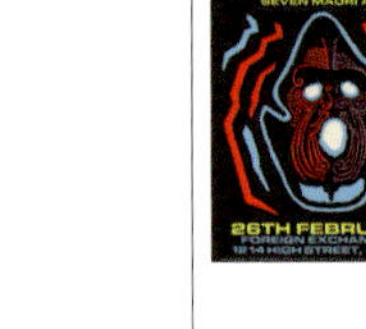

134

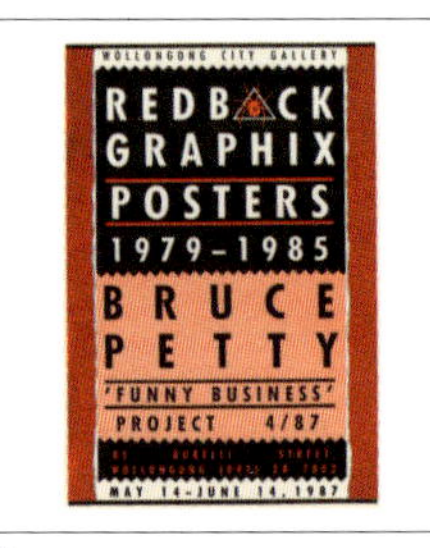

135

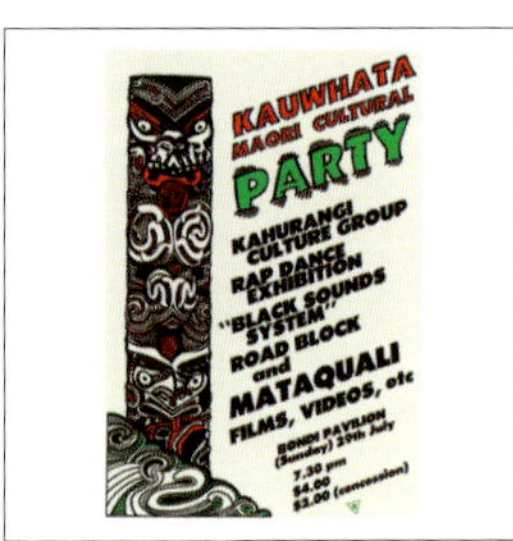

136

129 **Michael CALLAGHAN** (designer)
**Alison ALDER** (printer)
**Amnesty International Australia** (client)
*Amnesty/USA—The death penalty* 1988 Annandale, Sydney
screenprint, printed in colour, from five stencils on thin white wove paper
printed image 100.0 x 73.9 cm sheet 102.2 x 76.6 cm
Gordon Darling Australasian Print Fund 1992
1992.776

130 **Michael CALLAGHAN** (designer)
**Ray YOUNG** (designer and printer)
**Osmond KANTILLA** (designer and printer)
born Australia 1966
**Neville NAMARNYILK** (designer and printer)
born Australia 1966
**Aboriginal Arts Board** (client)
*The Aboriginal Arts Board* 1986
screenprint, printed in colour, from four stencils
printed image and sheet 100.3 x 74.2 cm
Gordon Darling Australia Pacific Print Fund 2008
2008.643

131 **Michael CALLAGHAN** (designer and printer)
**Alison ALDER** (printer)
**Central Australian Aboriginal Media Association (CAAMA)** (client)
*Beat the grog [1]* 1986 Annandale, Sydney
screenprint, printed in colour, from six stencils on thin white wove paper
printed image 90.0 x 60.6 cm sheet 91.8 x 61.4 cm
Gift of Nat Williams 1986
1986.2355

132 **Marie McMAHON** (designer)
**Michael CALLAGHAN** (designer)
**PAUL COCKRAM** (film planner)
born Australia 1951
**Ann STEPHEN** (research)
**Peter CURTIS** (printer)
**Ray YOUNG** (printer)
**Australian Council of Trade Unions (ACTU)** (client)
*May Day* 1986 Annandale, Sydney
screenprint, printed in colour, from five stencils on thin white wove paper
printed image 99.0 x 149.0 cm sheet 100.8 x 151.2 cm
Gordon Darling Fund 1989
1989.634

133 **Marie McMAHON** (designer)
**Michael CALLAGHAN** (designer)
**PAUL COCKRAM** (film planner)
**Ann STEPHEN** (research)
**SNAP ADS PTY LTD** (printer)
**Australian Council of Trade Unions (ACTU)** (client)
*Eight Hour Day* 1987 Annandale, Sydney
screenprint, printed in colour, from five stencils
printed image 108.0 x 158.0 cm sheet 110.0 x 160.0 cm
Gordon Darling Fund 1989
1989.633

134 **Ray YOUNG** (designer and printer)
**Aboriginal Arts Board of the Australia Council** (client)
*Te Ao Marama* 1987 Annandale, Sydney
screenprint, printed in colour, from multiple stencils on thin white wove paper
printed image and sheet 49.2 x 74.2 cm
Gordon Darling Australia Pacific Print Fund 2008
2008.631

135 **Leonie LANE** (designer)
**Alison ALDER** (printer)
**Wollongong City Gallery** (client)
*Redback Graphix Exhibition 1* 1987 Annandale, Sydney
screenprint, printed in red and black ink, from two stencils on thin white wove paper
printed image 74.8 x 49.2 cm sheet 75.8 x 51.0 cm
Gordon Darling Australia Pacific Print Fund 2008
2008.638

136 **Ray YOUNG** (designer and printer)
**Kauwhata–Maori Cultural Party** (client)
*Kauwhata–Maori Cultural Party* 1987 Annandale, Sydney
screenprint, printed in colour, from three stencils on thin white wove paper
printed image 74.0 x 49.0 cm sheet 76.0 x 51.0 cm
1987.1309

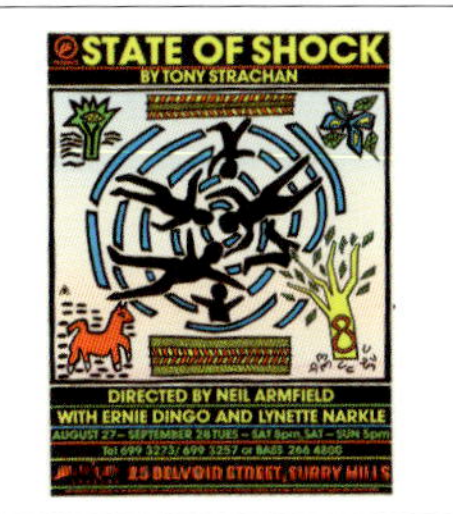


137

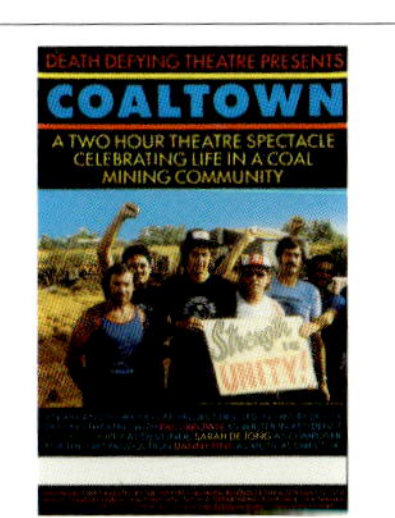


138

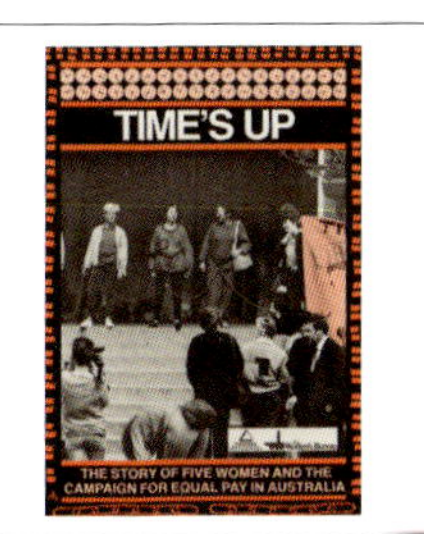


139

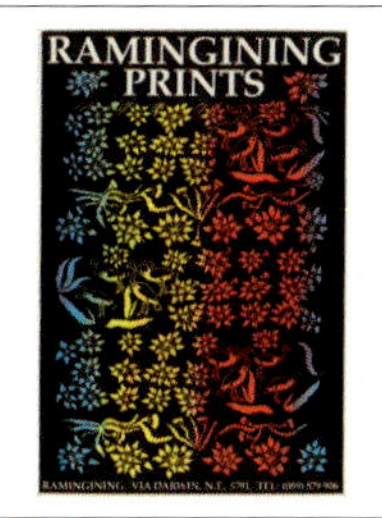


140

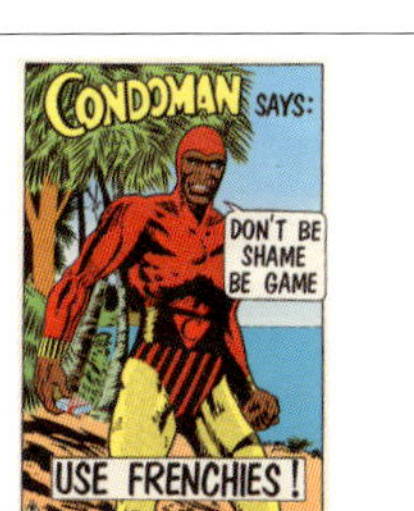


141

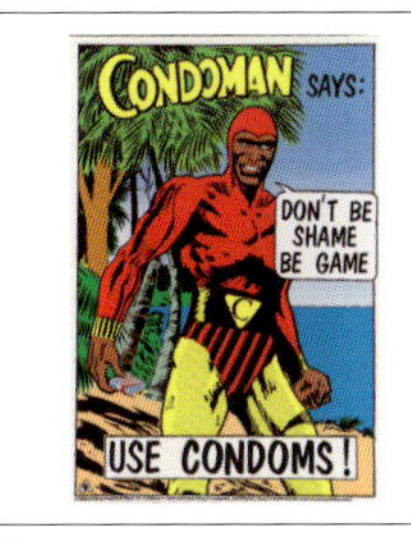


142

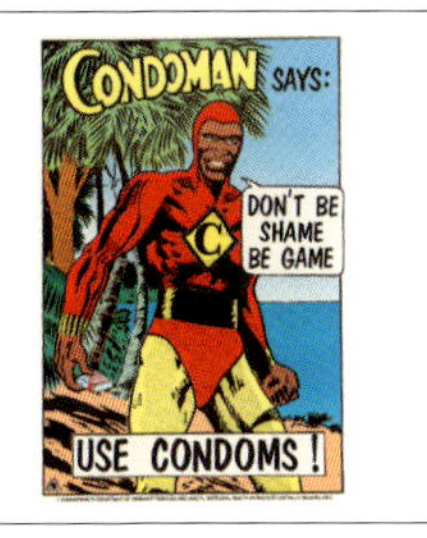


143

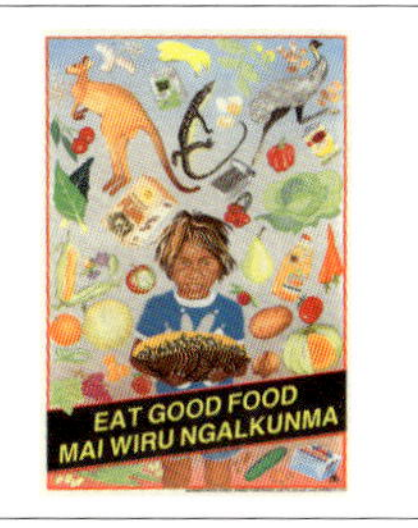


144

137 **Michael CALLAGHAN** (designer)
**Alison ALDER** (printer)
**Belvoir Street Theatre** (client)
*State of shock* 1987 Annandale, Sydney
screenprint, printed in colour, from five stencils on thin white wove paper
printed image and sheet 76.0 x 102.0 cm
1987.1402

138 **Alison ALDER** (designer and printer)
**Death Defying Theatre** (client)
*Coaltown* 1987 Annandale, Sydney
screenprint, printed in colour, from four stencils on thin white wove paper
printed image 74.0 x 49.0 cm sheet 74.0 x 49.0 cm
Gordon Darling Fund 1989
1989.614

139 **Alison ALDER** (designer)
**ROTARY OFFSET PRESS** (printer)
**Film Australia** (client)
*Time's up* 1987 Annandale, Sydney
offset-lithograph, printed in colour
printed image and sheet 64.0 x 43.4 cm
87.1388

140 **JOHNNY BULUNBULUN** (designer)
born Australia 1946
**Michael CALLAGHAN** (designer and printer)
**Ray YOUNG** (designer and printer)
**Ramingining Arts and Craft** (client)
*Ramingining prints* 1987 Annandale, Sydney
screenprint, printed in colour, from four stencils on thin white wove paper
printed image 74.2 x 49.1 cm sheet 75.8 x 50.8 cm
1994.59

141 **Michael CALLAGHAN** (designer)
**Marie McMAHON** (illustrator)
**Paul COCKRAM** (film planner)
**Peter CURTIS** (printer)
**National Campaign Against AIDS (NACAIDS)** (client)
*Condoman says: use frenchies!* [1st version] 1987 Annandale, Sydney
screenprint, printed in colour, from four stencils on thin white wove paper
printed image 74.2 x 49.0 cm sheet 76.2 x 51.0 cm
Gordon Darling Australia Pacific Print Fund 2008
2008.636

142 **Michael CALLAGHAN** (designer)
**Marie McMAHON** (illustrator)
**Paul COCKRAM** (film planner)
**Peter CURTIS** (printer)
**National Campaign Against AIDS (NACAIDS)** (client)
*Condoman says: use condoms!* [2nd version] 1987 Annandale, Sydney
screenprint, printed in colour, from four stencils on thin white wove paper
sheet 76.0 x 50.8 cm
89.628

143 **Michael CALLAGHAN** (designer)
**Marie McMAHON** (illustrator)
**Paul COCKRAM** (film planner)
**SNAP ADS PTY LTD** (printer)
**National Campaign Against AIDS (NACAIDS)** (client)
*Condoman says: use condoms!* [3rd version] 1988 Annandale, Sydney
screenprint, printed in colour, from four stencils on thick white wove paper
printed image 74.2 x 49.0 cm sheet 76.2 x 51.0 cm
Gordon Darling Fund 1989
00.295

144 **Leonie LANE** (designer and printer)
**Peter CURTIS** (printer)
**Nganampa Health Council** (client)
*Eat good food* 1987 Annandale, Sydney
screenprint, printed in colour, from four stencils on thin white wove paper
printed image 89.0 x 59.1 cm sheet 92.0 x 61.5 cm
Gordon Darling Fund 1989
1989.617

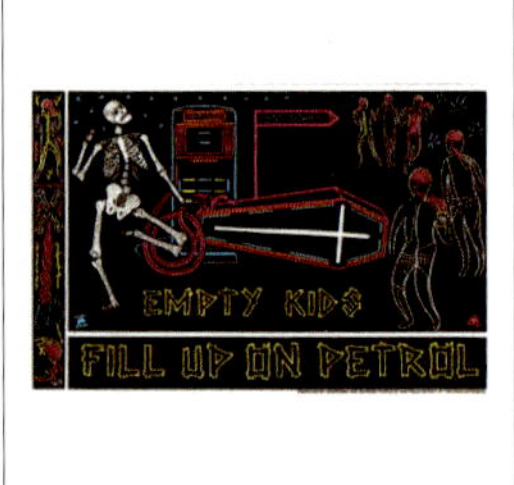

145

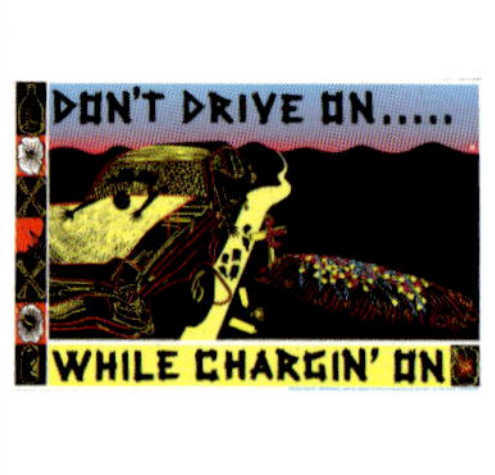


146

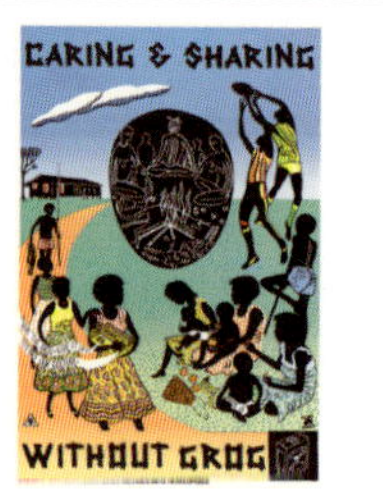


147

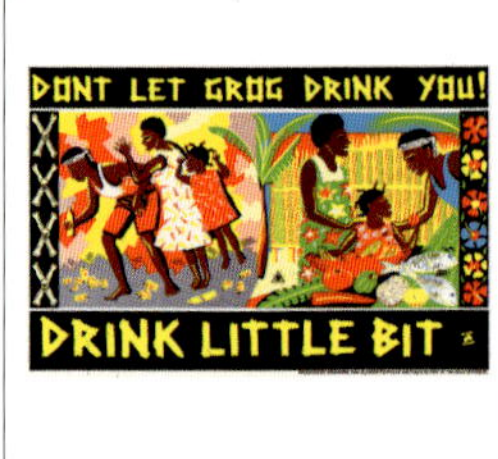


148

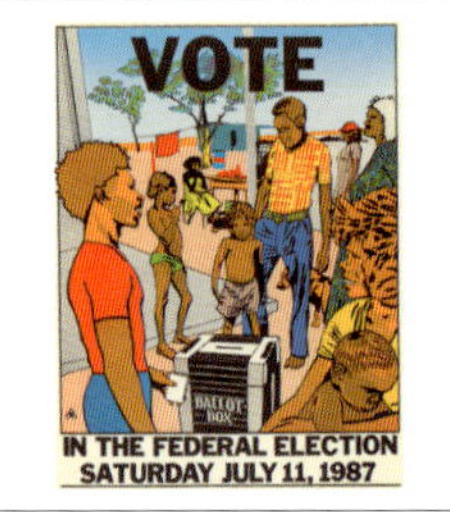


149

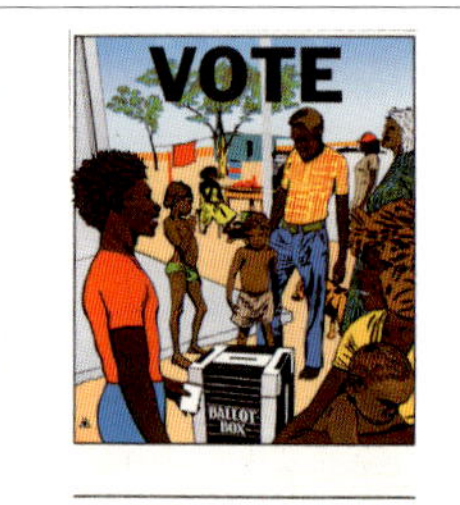


150

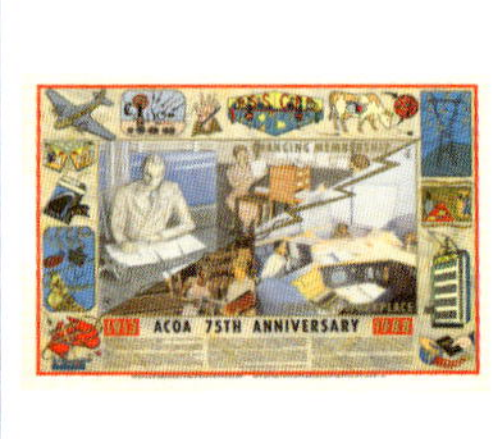


151

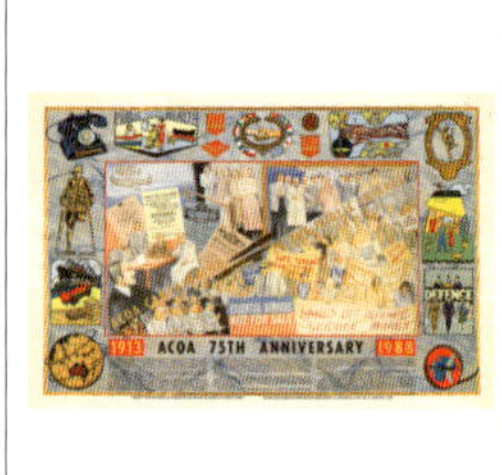


152

145 **Marie McMAHON** (designer)
**Peter CURTIS** (printer)
**National Campaign Against Drug Abuse (NCADA)** (client)
*Empty kids* 1987 Annandale, Sydney
screenprint, printed in colour, from four stencils on thick white wove paper
printed image 49.0 x 73.8 cm sheet 51.0 x 76.0 cm
Gordon Darling Fund 1989
1989.625

146 **Marie McMAHON** (designer)
**Peter CURTIS** (printer)
**National Campaign Against Drug Abuse (NCADA)** (client)
*Don't drive on* 1987 Annandale, Sydney
screenprint, printed in colour, from four stencils on thin white wove paper
printed image 49.4 x 75.0 cm sheet 50.6 x 76.0 cm
Gordon Darling Fund 1989
1989.623

147 **Marie McMAHON** (designer)
**Peter CURTIS** (printer)
**National Campaign Against Drug Abuse (NCADA)** (client)
*Caring and sharing without grog* 1987 Annandale, Sydney
screenprint, printed in colour, from four stencils on thin white wove paper
printed image 73.8 x 48.2 cm sheet 76.0 x 50.8 cm
Gordon Darling Fund 1989
1989.622

148 **Marie McMAHON** (designer)
**Peter CURTIS** (printer)
**National Campaign Against Drug Abuse (NCADA)** (client)
*Drink little bit* 1987 Annandale, Sydney
screenprint, printed in colour, from four stencils on thick white wove paper
printed image 49.2 x 74.0 cm sheet 51.0 x 76.2 cm
Gordon Darling Fund 1989
1989.619

149 **Marie McMAHON** (designer)
**Peter CURTIS** (printer)
**Aboriginal and Torres Strait Islander Education & Information Service (ATSIEIS)** and **Australian Electoral Commission (AEC)** (clients)
*Vote in the federal election July 11* 1987 Annandale, Sydney
screenprint, printed in colour, from four stencils on thin white wove paper
printed image 100.0 x 74.0 cm sheet 102.0 x 76.0 cm
Gordon Darling Australia Pacific Print Fund 2008
2008.644

150 **Marie McMAHON** (designer)
**Peter CURTIS** (printer)
**Australian Electoral Commission (AEC)** (client)
*Vote* 1987 Annandale, Sydney
screenprint, printed in colour, from four stencils on thin white wove paper
printed image 88.6 x 74.2 cm sheet 102.3 x 76.3 cm
Gordon Darling Fund 1989
1989.620

151 **Michael CALLAGHAN** (designer)
**Marie McMAHON** (designer)
**Vickie LEE** (designer)
born Australia 1961
**Paul COCKRAM** (film planner)
**SNAP ADS PTY LTD** (printer)
**Administrative and Clerical Officers Association (ACOA)** (client)
*ACOA 75th anniversary—changing membership, changing workplace* 1988 Annandale, Sydney
screenprint, printed in colour, from five stencils on thin white wove paper
printed image 99.0 x 150.0 cm sheet 109.4 x 160.0 cm
Gordon Darling Australasian Print Fund 1993
1993.1954

152 **Michael CALLAGHAN** (designer)
**Marie McMAHON** (designer)
**Vickie LEE** (designer)
**Paul COCKRAM** (film planner)
**SNAP ADS PTY LTD** (printer)
**Administrative and Clerical Officers Association** (client)
*ACOA 75th anniversary—campaigning in the public interest* 1988 Annandale, Sydney
screenprint, printed in colour, from multiple stencils on thin white wove paper
printed image 99.0 x 150.0 cm sheet 109.4 x 160.0 cm
Gordon Darling Australasian Print Fund 1993
1993.1955

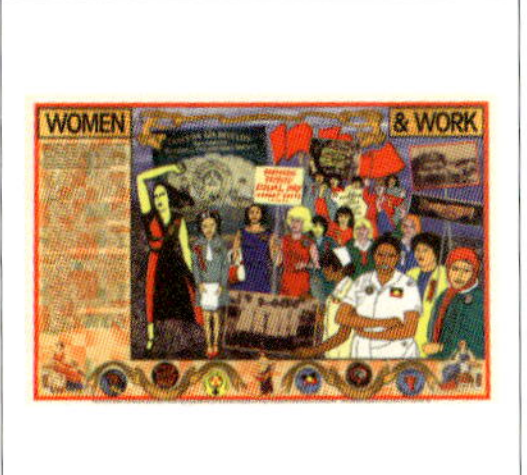


153

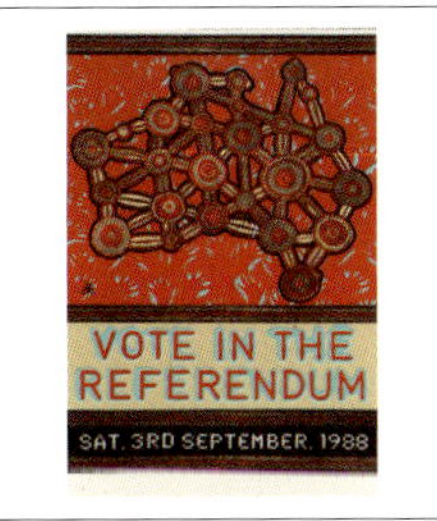


154

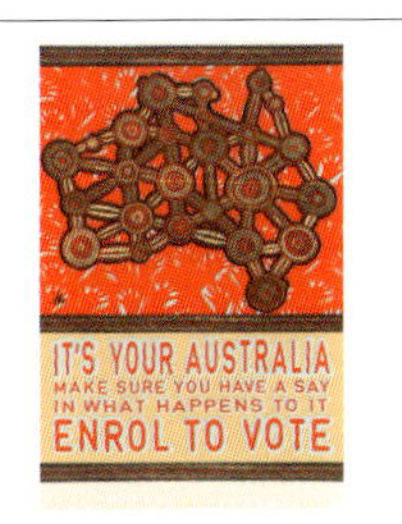


155

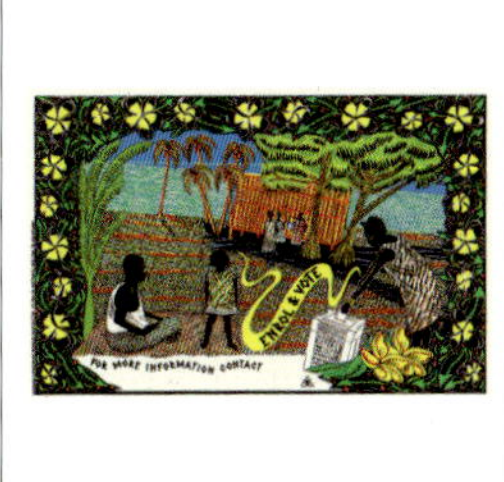

156

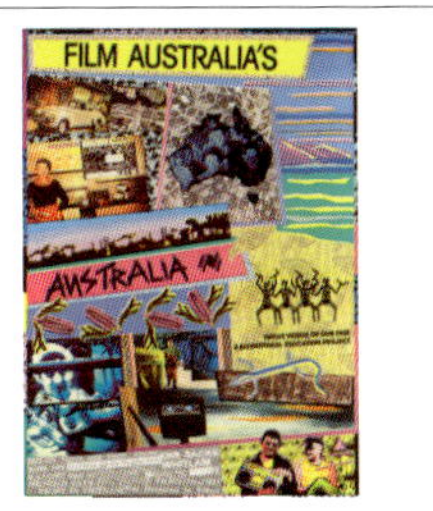

157

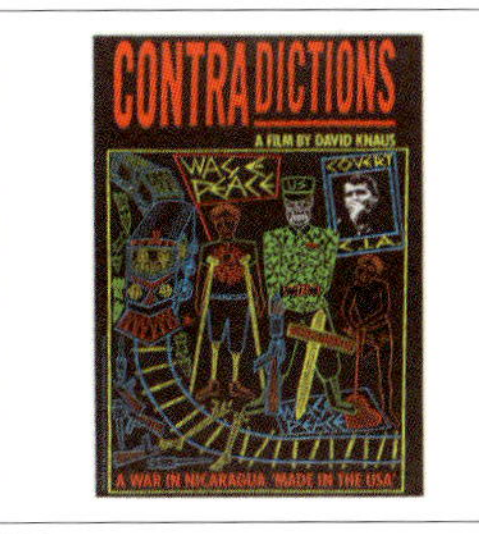


158

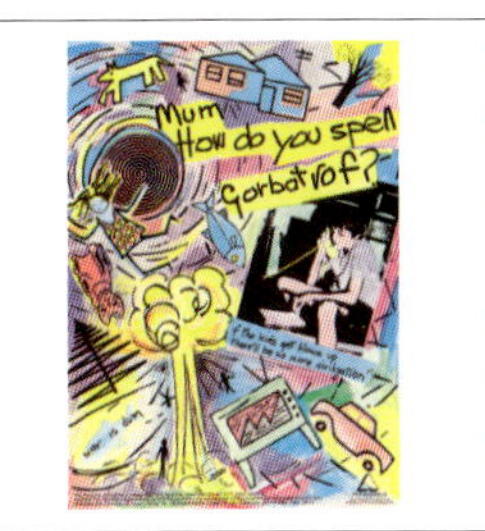


159

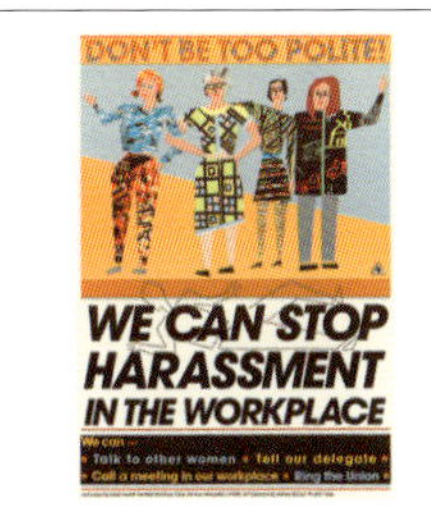


160

153 **Marie McMAHON** (designer)
**Michael CALLAGHAN** (designer)
**Paul COCKRAM (**film planner)
**Ann STEPHEN** (research)
**SNAP ADS PTY LTD** (printer)
**Australian Council of Trade Unions (ACTU)** (client)
*Women and work* 1988 Annandale, Sydney
screenprint, printed in colour, from five stencils
on thin white wove paper
printed image 99.0 x 149.8 cm sheet 104.8 x 155.4 cm
Gordon Darling Australasian Print Fund 1993
1993.1952

154 **Stephen LEES** (designer and printer)
born Australia 1954
**Aboriginal and Torres Strait Islander Education & Information Service (ATSIEIS)** and **Australian Electoral Commission (AEC)** (clients)
*Vote in the Referendum* 1988
screenprint, printed in colour, from four stencils
on thin white wove paper
printed image 70.6 x 49.8 cm sheet 76.0 x 49.8 cm
Gordon Darling Fund 1989
1989.632

155 **Stephen LEES** (designer and printer)
**Aboriginal and Torres Strait Islander Education & Information Service (ATSIEIS)** and **Australian Electoral Commission (AEC)** (clients)
*Enrol to vote* [*hands*] 1988
screenprint, printed in colour, from five stencils
on thin white wove paper
printed image 70.4 x 49.2 cm sheet 76.2 x 49.2 cm
Gordon Darling Australia Pacific Print Fund 2008
2008.314

156 **Marie McMAHON** (designer)
**Peter CURTIS** (printer)
**Australian Electoral Commission (AEC)** (client)
*Enrol and vote—Torres Strait Islands* 1988 Annandale, Sydney
screenprint, printed in colour, from five stencils
on thin white wove paper
printed image 48.0 x 73.4 cm sheet 51.0 x 76.2 cm
Gordon Darling Fund 1989
1989.626

157 **Michael CALLAGHAN** (designer)
**Jan MACKAY** (designer)
**PRINTCRAFT PTY LTD** (printer)
**Film Australia** (client)
*Film Australia's Australia* 1988 Annandale, Sydney
offset-lithograph, printed in colour, on smooth white paper
printed image and sheet 89.2 x 63.0 cm
87.1401

158 **Michael CALLAGHAN** (designer)
**Alison ALDER** (printer)
**David Knause** and **FILM AUSTRALIA** (clients)
*Contradictions* 1988 Annandale, Sydney
screenprint, printed in colour, from six stencils
on thin white wove paper
printed image 100.2 x 70.0 cm sheet 101.8 x 72.0 cm
Gordon Darling Australia Pacific Print Fund 2008
2008.635

159 **Jan MACKAY** (designer)
**PRINTCRAFT PTY LTD** (printer)
**Film Australia** (client)
*How do you spell Gorbatrof?* 1988 Annandale, Sydney
offset-lithograph, printed in colour, on thin white wove paper
printed image 68.2 x 48.2 cm sheet 68.2 x 48.2 cm
1987.1390

160 **Alison ALDER (**designer)
**ROTARY OFFSET PRESS** PTY LTD (printer)
**Public Service Association of NSW** (client)
*Don't be too polite* 1988 Annandale, Sydney
offset-lithograph, printed in colour, on thin white wove paper
printed image 67.2 x 45.6 cm sheet 69.0 x 47.4 cm
Gordon Darling Australia Pacific Print Fund 2008
2008.318

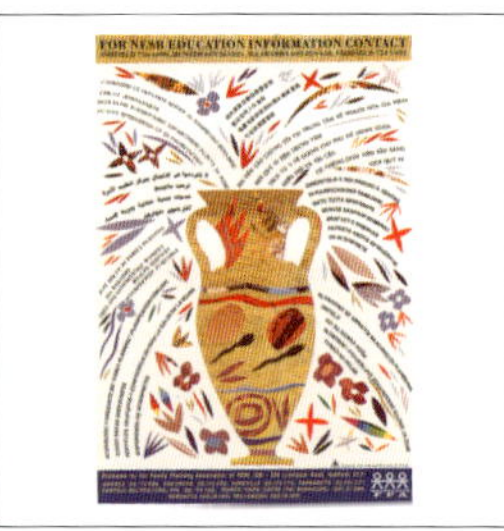

161

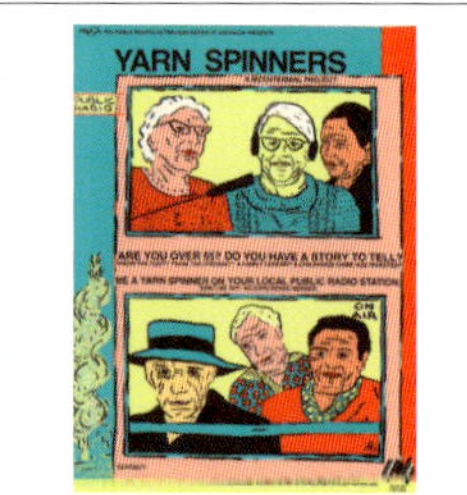


162

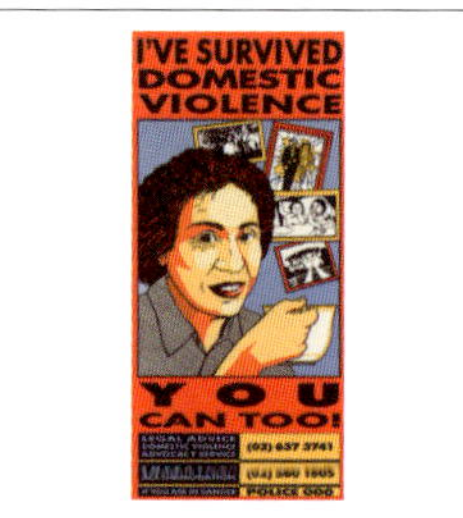


163

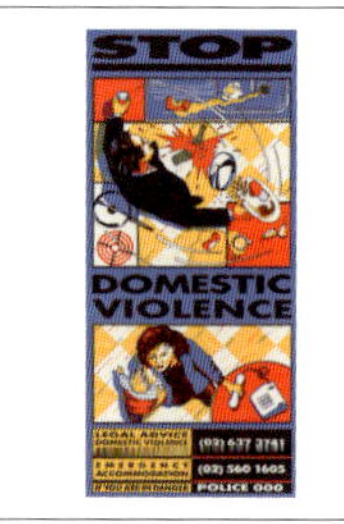


164

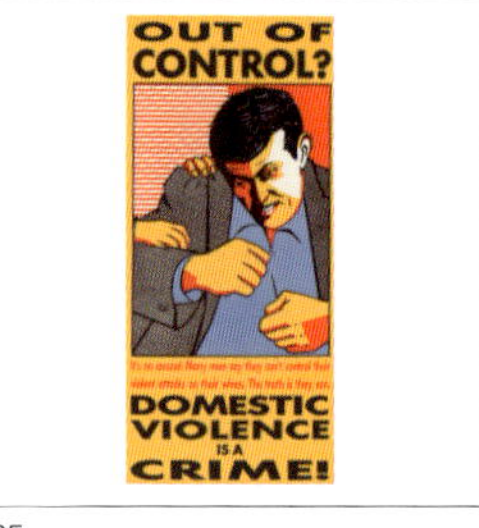

165

166

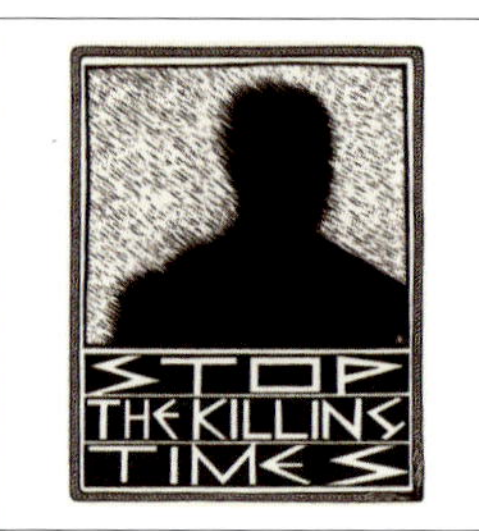


167

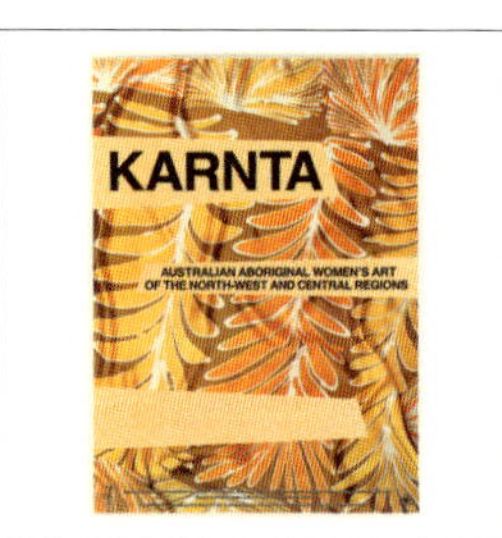


168

161 **Alison ALDER (**designer)
**THE IMPRESSIONISTS PTY LTD** (printer)
**Family Planning Association of NSW (FPA)** (client)

*FPA education information* 1988 Annandale, Sydney
offset-lithograph, printed in colour, on smooth white paper
printed image and sheet 76.0 x 51.0 cm
Gordon Darling Australia Pacific Print Fund 2008
2008.651

162 **Alison ALDER** (designer and printer)
**Public Broadcasting Association of Australia** (client)

*Yarn spinners* 1988 Annandale, Sydney
screenprint, printed in colour, from five stencils
on thin white wove paper
printed image and sheet 100.0 x 74.2 cm
Gordon Darling Australia Pacific Print Fund 2008
2008.652

163 **Leonie LANE** (designer)
**ROTARY OFFSET PRESS** (printer)
**Domestic Violence Advocacy Service** (client)

*I've survived domestic violence* 1988 Annandale, Sydney
offset-lithograph, printed in colour, on smooth white paper
printed image and sheet 66.0 x 34.0 cm
Gordon Darling Australia Pacific Print Fund 2008
2008.646

164 **Leonie LANE** (designer)
**ROTARY OFFSET PRESS** PTY LTD (printer)
**Domestic Violence Advocacy Service** (client)

*Stop domestic violence* 1988 Annandale, Sydney
offset-lithograph, printed in colour, on smooth white paper
printed image and sheet 66.0 x 34.0 cm
Gordon Darling Australia Pacific Print Fund 2008
2008.633

165 **Leonie LANE** (designer)
**ROTARY OFFSET PRESS** (printer)
**Domestic Violence Advocacy Service** (client)

*Out of control? Domestic violence is a crime* 1988 Annandale, Sydney
offset-lithograph, printed in colour, on smooth white paper
printed image and sheet 66.0 x 34.0 cm
Gordon Darling Australia Pacific Print Fund 2008
2008.632

166 **Alison ALDER** (designer and printer)
**Bernadette BOSCACCI** (printer's assistant)
born Australia 1969
**Co Media** (client)

*Undoing history—making a just future* 1988 Annandale, Sydney
screenprint, printed in colour, from three stencils
on thin white wove paper
printed image 47.4 x 62.6 cm
sheet 50.0 x 65.0 cm
Purchased from Gallery admission charges 1988
1988.809

167 **Michael CALLAGHAN** (designer)
**Peter CURTIS** (printer)
**Co Media** (client)

*Stop the killing times* 1988 Annandale, Sydney
screenprint, printed in black ink, from one stencil
on thin white wove paper
printed image 63.4 x 48.5 cm
sheet 65.0 x 49.9 cm
Purchased from Gallery admission charges 1988
1988.808

168 **Michael CALLAGHAN** (designer)
**PAUL COCKRAM** (film planner)
**PRINTCRAFT PTY LTD** (printer)
**Association of Northern and Central Australian Aboriginal Artists (ANCAAA)** (client)

*Karnta* 1988 Annandale, Sydney
offset-lithograph, printed in colour, on white wove card
printed image and sheet 63.4 x 45.0 cm
Gordon Darling Australia Pacific Print Fund 2008
2008.317

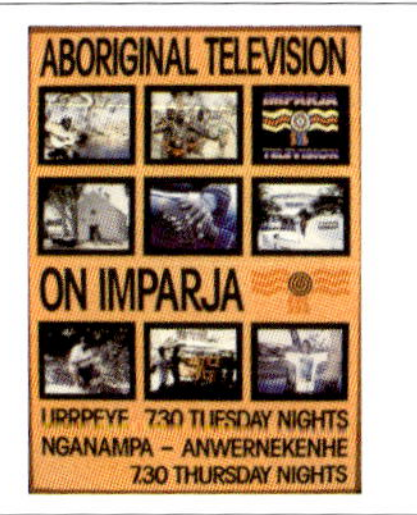


169

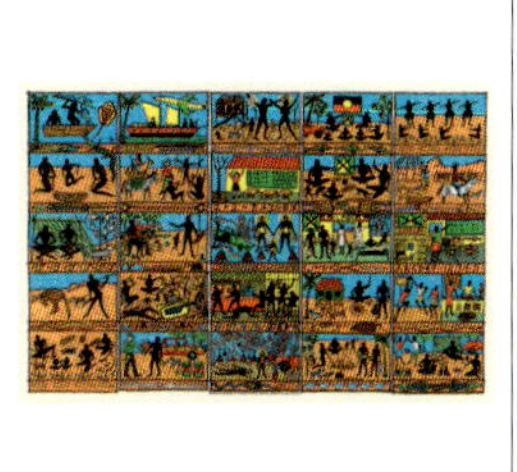

170

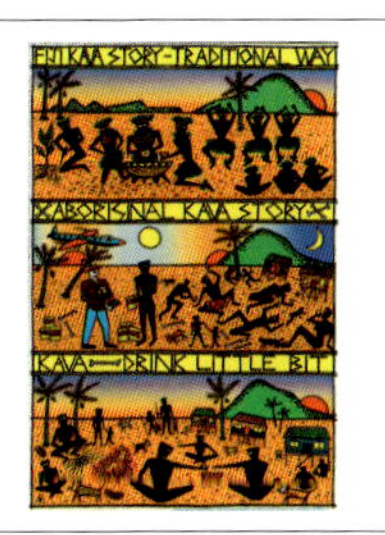


171

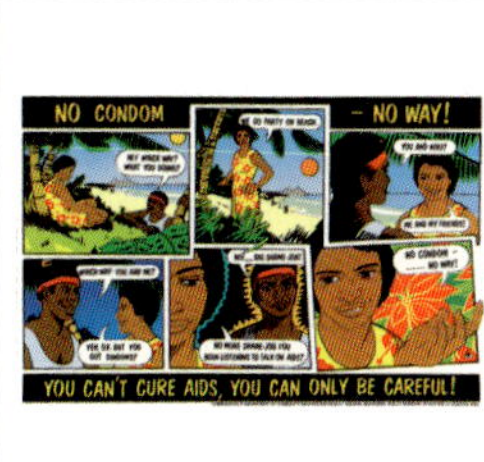


172

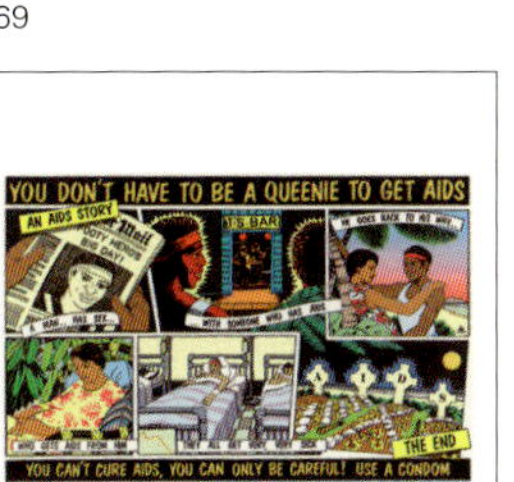


173

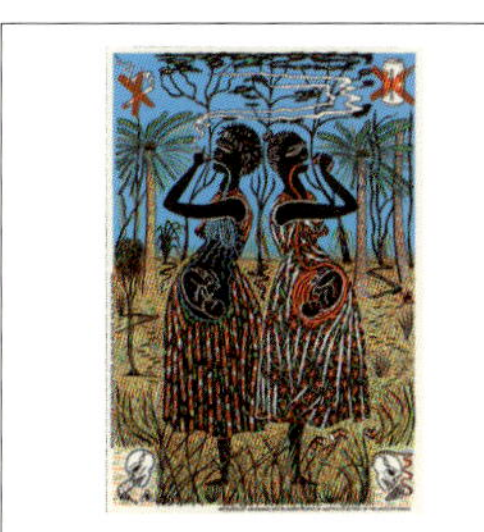

174

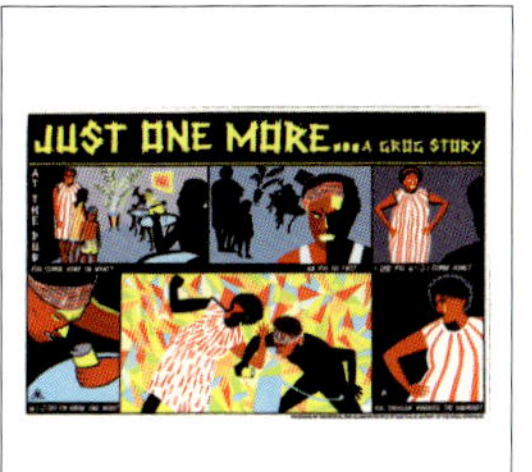


175

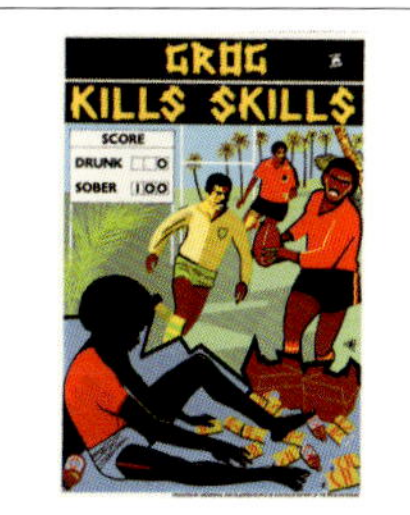


176

169 **Michael CALLAGHAN** (designer)
**PAUL COCKRAM** (film planner)
**PRINTCRAFT PTY LTD** (printer)
**Central Australian Aboriginal Media Association (CAAMA)** (client)
*Aboriginal television* 1988 Annandale, Sydney
offset-lithograph, printed in colour, on thin white wove paper
sheet 45.0 x 63.5 cm
Private collection

170 **Michael CALLAGHAN** (designer)
**Peter CURTIS** (printer)
**National Campaign Against Drug Abuse (NCADA)** (client)
*Big grog story* 1988 Annandale, Sydney
screenprint, printed in colour, from six stencils on thin white wove paper
printed image 101.4 x 151.4 cm sheet 109.6 x 160.0 cm
Gordon Darling Australasian Print Fund 1993
1993.1953

171 **Michael CALLAGHAN** (designer)
**Alison ALDER** (printer)
**National Campaign Against Drug Abuse (NCADA)** (client)
*Kava story* 1988 Annandale, Sydney
screenprint, printed in colour, from five stencils on thin white wove paper
printed image 91.2 x 60.6 cm sheet 92.0 x 61.4 cm
Gordon Darling Fund 1989
1989.629

172 **Stephen LEES** (designer)
**PAUL COCKRAM** (film planner)
**Alison ALDER** (printer)
**National Campaign Against AIDS (NACAIDS)** (client)
*No condom—no way!* 1988 Annandale, Sydney
screenprint, printed in colour, from four stencils on thin white wove paper
printed image 49.8 x 74.4 cm sheet 50.8 x 75.8 cm
Gordon Darling Fund 1989
1989.630

173 **Stephen LEES** (designer)
**PAUL COCKRAM** (film planner)
**Alison ALDER** (printer)
**National Campaign Against AIDS (NACAIDS)** (client)
*You don't have to be a queenie to get AIDS* 1988 Annandale, Sydney
screenprint, printed in colour, from four stencils on thin white wove paper
printed image 49.8 x 74.0 cm sheet 51.0 x 76.0 cm
Gordon Darling Fund 1989
1989.631

174 **Marie McMAHON** (designer)
**Alison ALDER** (printer)
**National Campaign Against Drug Abuse (NCADA)** (client)
*Pregnancy* 1988 Annandale, Sydney
screenprint, printed in colour, from five stencils on thin white wove paper
printed image 73.6 x 48.0 cm sheet 75.6 x 50.4 cm
Gordon Darling Fund 1989
1989.627

175 **Marie McMAHON** (designer and printer)
**Peter CURTIS** (printer)
**National Campaign Against Drug Abuse (NCADA)** (client)
*Just one more* 1988
screenprint, printed in colour, from five stencils on thin white wove paper
printed image 49.4 x 74.2 cm sheet 50.6 x 76.0 cm
Gordon Darling Fund 1989
1989.618

176 **Marie McMAHON** (designer)
**Peter CURTIS** (printer)
**National Campaign Against Drug Abuse (NCADA)** (client)
*Grog kills skills (football version)* 1988 Annandale, Sydney
screenprint, printed in colour, from four stencils on thick white wove paper
printed image 74.2 x 48.6 cm sheet 76.2 x 51.0 cm
Gordon Darling Fund 1989
1989.621

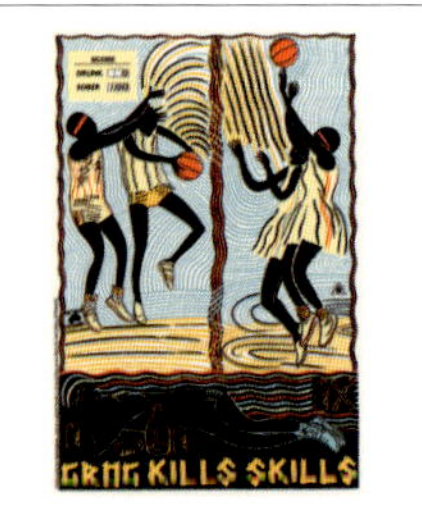

177

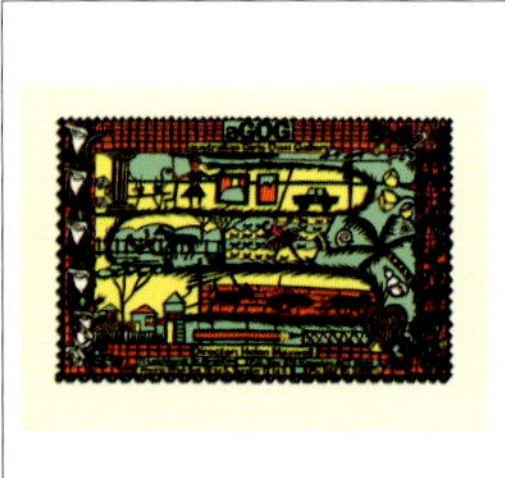

178

179

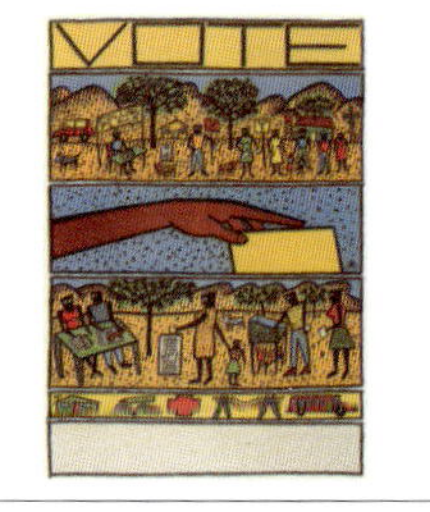


180

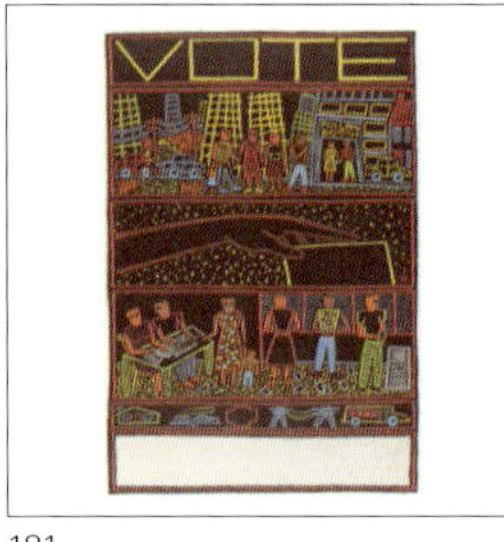


181

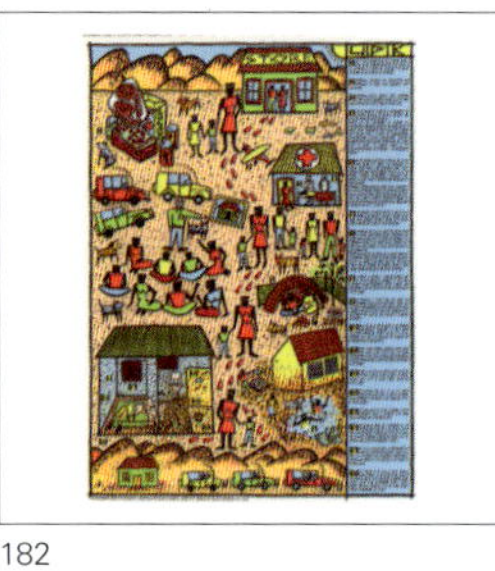

182

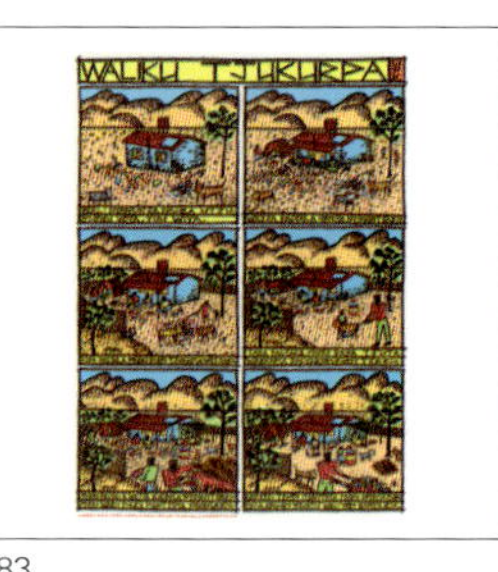

183

184

177 **Marie McMAHON** (designer and printer)
**Peter CURTIS** (printer)
**National Campaign Against Drug Abuse (NCADA)** (client)
*Grog kills skills (basketball version)* 1988 Annandale, Sydney
screenprint, printed in colour, from five stencils on thin white wove paper
printed image 73.0 x 48.4 cm
sheet 75.4 x 58.8 cm
Gordon Darling Fund 1989
1989.624

*178* **Alison ALDER** (designer and printer)
**Australian Girls Own Gallery** (client)
*aGOG* 1988 Annandale, Sydney
screenprint, printed in colour, from four stencils on paper
printed image 48.6 x 32.4 cm
sheet 60.4 x 85.6 cm
Gift of Helen Maxwell 1989
1989.986

179 **Michael CALLAGHAN (**designer)
**Alison ALDER (**designer and printer)
**Leonie LANE (**designer)
**PAUL COCKRAM (**film planner)
*Now we are ten* 1989 Annandale, Sydney
screenprint, printed in colour, from multiple stencils
printed image 99.8 x 74.0 cm sheet 101.8 x 76.2 cm
Gordon Darling Australia Pacific Print Fund 2008
2008.647

180 **Michael CALLAGHAN (**designer)
**P&R SCREEN PRINTING PTY LTD** (printer)
**Aboriginal and Torres Strait Islander Education & Information Service (ATSIEIS)** and **Australian Electoral Commission (AEC)** (clients)
*Vote [rural]* 1989 Annandale, Sydney
screenprint, printed in colour, from five stencils
printed image 96.4 x 66.2 cm sheet 98.8 x 68.0 cm
Gordon Darling Australia Pacific Print Fund 2008
2008.634

181 **Michael CALLAGHAN (**designer)
**P&R SCREEN PRINTING PTY LTD** (printer)
**Aboriginal and Torres Strait Islander Education & Information Service (ATSIEIS)** and **Australian Electoral Commission (AEC)** (clients)
*Vote [urban]* 1989 Annandale, Sydney
screenprint, printed in colour, from five stencils
printed image 99.0 x 66.8 cm sheet 101.0 x 68.8 cm
Gordon Darling Australia Pacific Print Fund 2008
2008.648

182 **Michael CALLAGHAN** (designer)
**Alison ALDER** (printer)
**Nganampa Health Council** (client)
*UPK/An average Anangu day* 1989 Annandale, Sydney
screenprint, printed in colour, from five stencils on thin white wove paper
printed image 92.0 x 65.9 cm
sheet 94.6 x 68.0 cm
Gordon Darling Australasian Print Fund 1993
1993.2259

183 **Michael CALLAGHAN** (designer)
**Alison ALDER** (printer)
**Nganampa Health Council** (client)
*Waliku Tjukurpa* 1989 Annandale, Sydney
screenprint, printed in colour, from five stencils on thin white wove paper
printed image 91.5 x 65.2 cm
sheet 94.6 x 67.4 cm
Gordon Darling Australasian Print Fund 1993
1993.2258

184 **Michael CALLAGHAN** (designer)
**SNAP ADS PTY LTD** (printer)
**Belvoir Street Theatre** (client)
*Greek tragedy* 1989 Annandale, Sydney
screenprint, printed in black ink, from one stencil on thin white wove paper
printed image 149.4 x 152.0 cm
sheet 99.8 x 102.0 cm
Gordon Darling Australasian Print Fund 1993
1993.1956

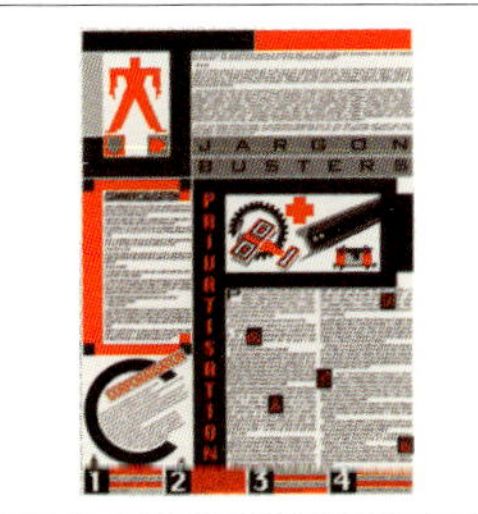

185

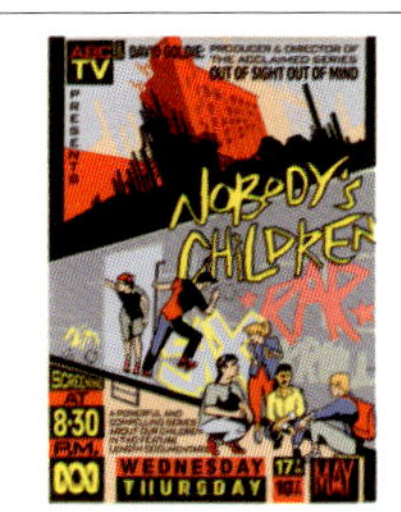

186

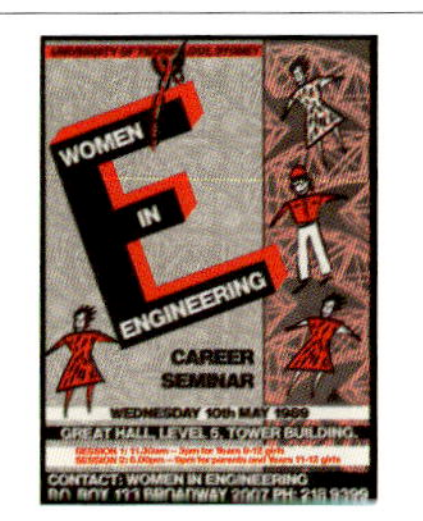

187

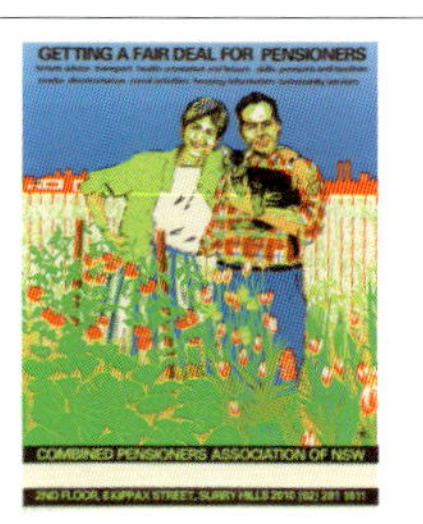

188

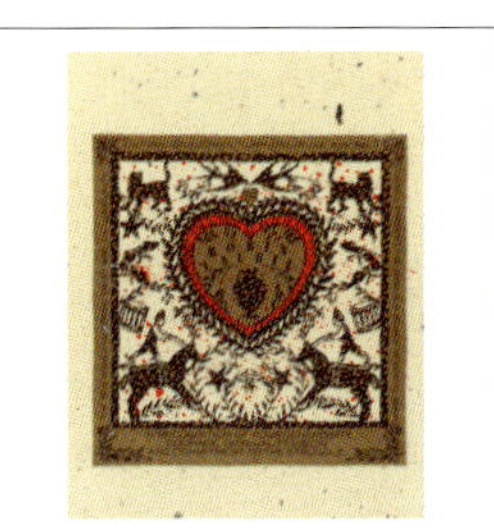
189

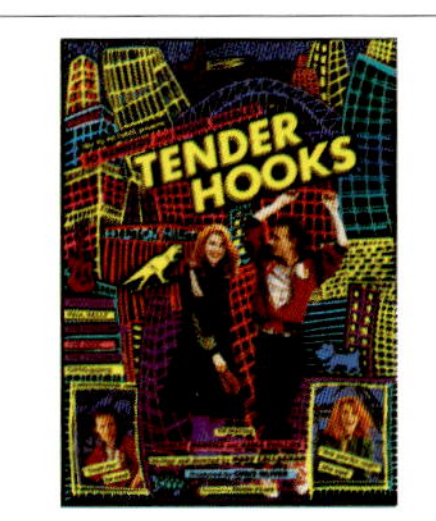

190

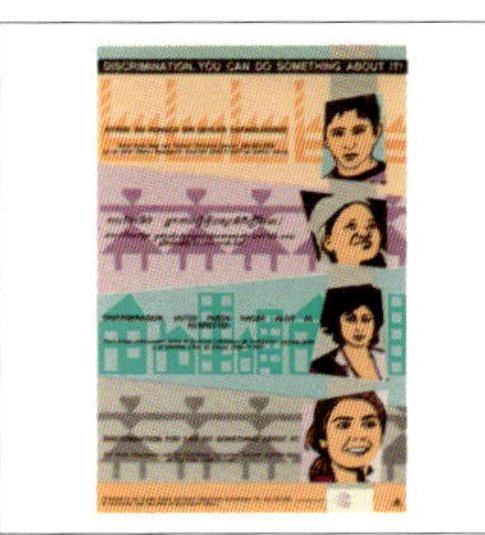

191

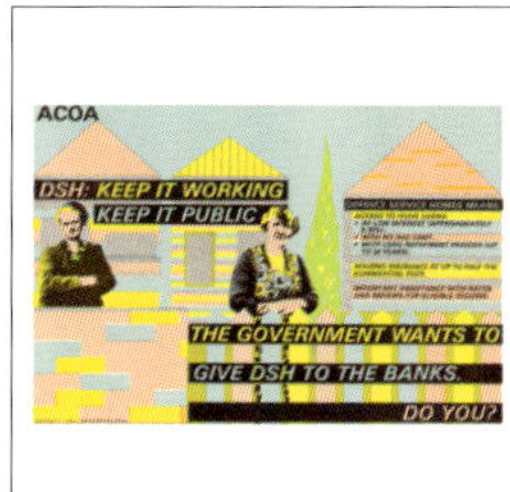

192

185 **Michael CALLAGHAN** (designer)
**THE IMPRESSIONISTS PTY LTD** (printer)
**Evatt Research Centre, Australian Public Service Federation** (client)
*Jargon busters* 1989 Annandale, Sydney
offset-lithograph, printed in colour, on thin white wove paper
printed image 58.6 x 41.0 cm
sheet 59.4 x 41.8 cm
Gordon Darling Australasian Print Fund 1993
1993.2256

186 **Vickie LEE** (designer)
**PRINTCRAFT PTY LTD** (printer)
**Australian Broadcasting Commission (ABC)** (client)
*Nobody's children* 1989
offset-lithograph, printed in colour, on smooth white paper
printed image and sheet 64.0 x 44.4 cm
Private collection

187 **Alison ALDER** (designer)
**PRINTCRAFT PTY LTD** (printer)
**Women in Engineering, University of Technology, Sydney (UTS)** (client)
*Women in engineering* 1989 Annandale, Sydney
offset-lithograph, printed in colour, on thin white wove paper
printed image and sheet 42.0x 39.6 cm
93.2253

188 **Leonie LANE** (designer and printer)
**Combined Pensioners Association of NSW** (client)
*Getting a fair deal for pensioners* 1989 Annandale, Sydney
screenprint, printed in colour, from four stencils on thin white paper
printed image and sheet 64.1 x 49.2 cm
Gordon Darling Australia Pacific Print Fund 2008
2008.315

*189* **Alison ALDER** (designer and printer)
**Visual Arts Board of the Australia Council** (client)
*Ros Bower Memorial Trust Award* 1989
screenprint, printed in colour, from three stencils on handmade paper
printed image 41.2 x 38.4 cm
sheet 63.2 x 46.8 cm
Gordon Darling Australia Pacific Print Fund 2008
2008.655

190 **Michael CALLAGHAN** (designer)
**PRINTCRAFT PTY LTD** (printer)
**Tru-Vu Pictures** (client)
*Tender hooks* 1989 Annandale, Sydney
offset-lithograph, printed in colour
printed image and sheet 83.0 x 58.6 cm
93.2257

191 **Alison ALDER** (designer)
**THE IMPRESSIONISTS PTY LTD** (printer)
**Human Rights and Equal Opportunity & Office of Multicultural Affairs** (clients)
*Discrimination—you can do something about it!* c. 1989
offset-lithograph, printed in colour, on smooth white paper
printed image and sheet 59.8 x 40.0 cm
Private collection

192 **Alison ALDER** (designer)
**MARTICH-OSTERMAN PRINTING & PUBLISHING PTY LTD** (printer)
**Administrative and Clerical Officers Association (ACOA)** (client)
*Defence service homes/DSH keep it working* 1989–90
offset-lithograph, printed in colour, on smooth white paper
printed image and sheet 39.3 x 57.5 cm
Gordon Darling Australia Pacific Print Fund 2008
2008.657

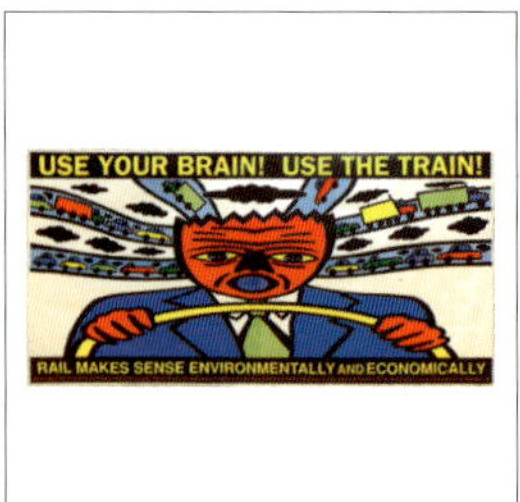

193

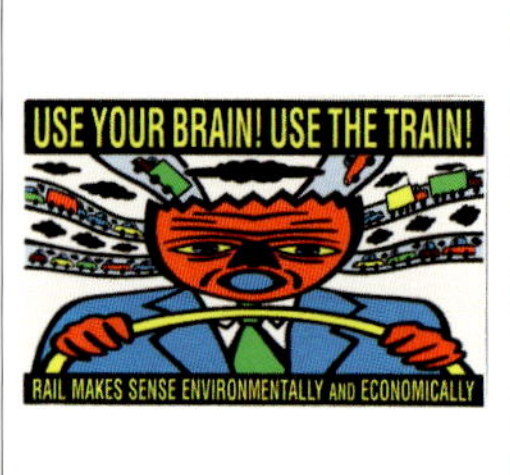

194

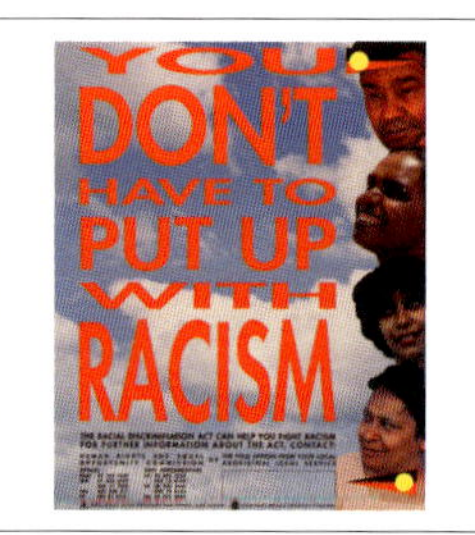

195

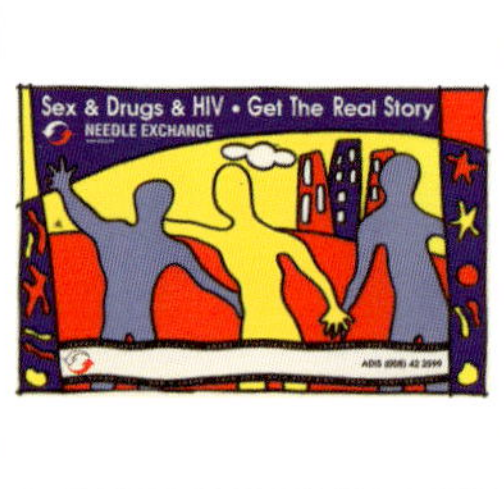

196

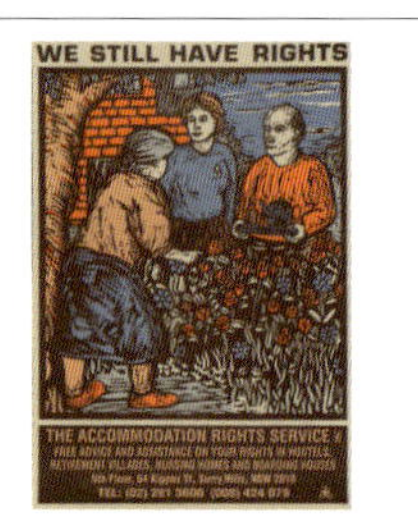

197

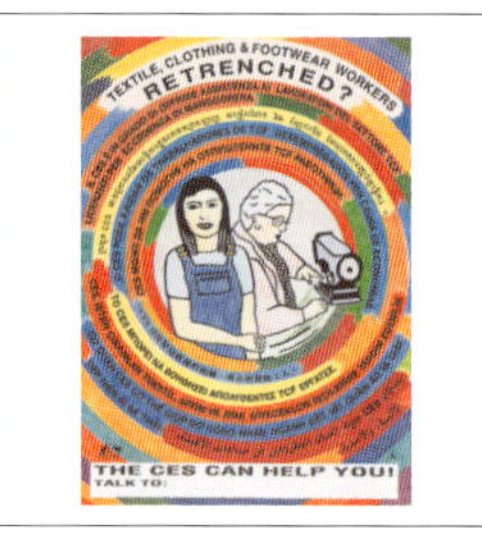

198

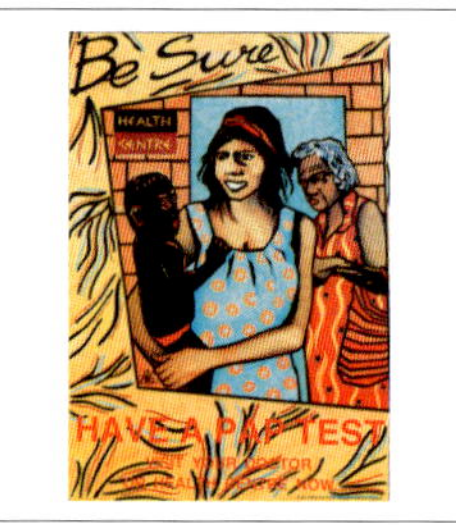

199

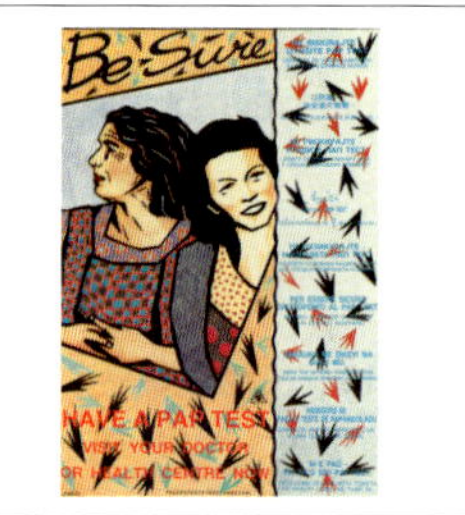

200

193 **Michael CALLAGHAN** (designer)
**Paul COCKRAM** (film planner)
**P&R SCREEN PRINTING PTY LTD** (printer)
**Australian Railways Union** (client)

*Use your brain, use the train* (billboard) 1990 Annandale, Sydney
screenprint, printed in colour, from four stencils
sheet 3003.0 x 5925.0 cm
Gordon Darling Australasian Print Fund 1993
1993.1950

194 **Michael CALLAGHAN** (designer)
**Paul COCKRAM** (film planner)
**P&R SCREEN PRINTING PTY LTD** (printer)
**Australian Railways Union** client)

*Use your brain, use the train* (poster) 1990 Annandale, Sydney
screenprint, printed in colour, from four stencils on paper
printed image 49.1 x 74.2 cm
sheet 50.8 x 75.8 cm
Gordon Darling Australasian Print Fund 1993
1993.1951

195 **Michael CALLAGHAN** (designer)
**PRINTCRAFT PTY LTD** (printer)
**Human Rights Equal Opportunity Commission** (client)

*You don't have to put up with racism* 1990 Annandale, Sydney
offset-lithograph, printed in colour, on smooth white paper
printed image and sheet 46.0 x 59.0 cm
Gordon Darling Australia Pacific Print Fund 2008
2008.319

196 **Alison ALDER** (designer)
**PRINTCRAFT PTY LTD** (printer)
**NSW Department of Health** (client)

*Sex & drugs & HIV* 1990 Annandale, Sydney
offset-lithograph, printed in colour, on smooth white paper
printed image 49.8 x 74.0 cm
sheet 50.2 x 74.4 cm
Gordon Darling Australia Pacific Print Fund 2008
2008.316

197 **Lawrence FINN** (designer)
born Australia 1969
**THE IMPRESSIONISTS PTY LTD** (printer)
**Accommodation Rights Service of NSW** (client)

*We still have rights* 1990 Annandale, Sydney
offset-lithograph, printed in colour, from multiple plates on white wove paper
printed image 57.5 x 39.0 cm
sheet 59.0 x 40.5 cm
Gordon Darling Australasian Print Fund 1993
1993.2254

198 **Alison ALDER** (designer)
**PRINTCRAFT PTY LTD** (printer)
**Commonwealth Employment Service (CES)** (client)

*Retrenched?* c. 1990 Annandale, Sydney
offset-lithograph, printed in colour
printed image and sheet 59.1 x 42.1 cm
93.2255

199 **Alison ALDER** (designer)
**PRINTCRAFT PTY LTD** (printer)
**NSW Womens Advisory Council** (client)

*Be sure—have a pap test [Aboriginal]* 1991 Annandale, Sydney
offset-lithograph, printed in colour, from multiple plates
printed image and sheet 72.3 x 48.8 cm
Gordon Darling Australasian Print Fund 1993
1993.2250

200 **Alison ALDER** (designer)
**PRINTCRAFT PTY LTD** (printer)
**NSW Womens Advisory Council** (client)

*Be sure—have a pap test* [*Migrant*] 1991 Annandale, Sydney
offset-lithograph, printed in colour, on white wove paper
printed image and sheet 72.4 x 48.8 cm
Gordon Darling Australasian Print Fund 1993
1993.2248

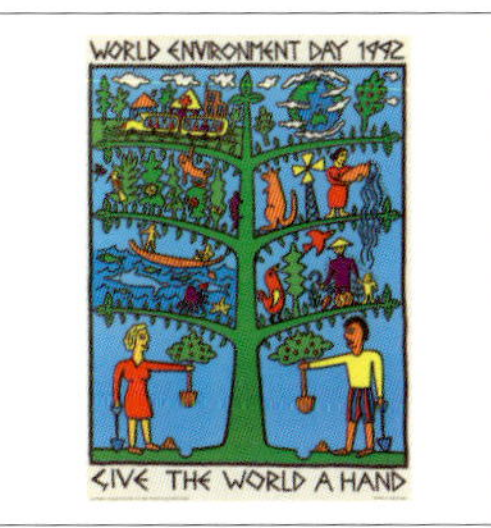

201

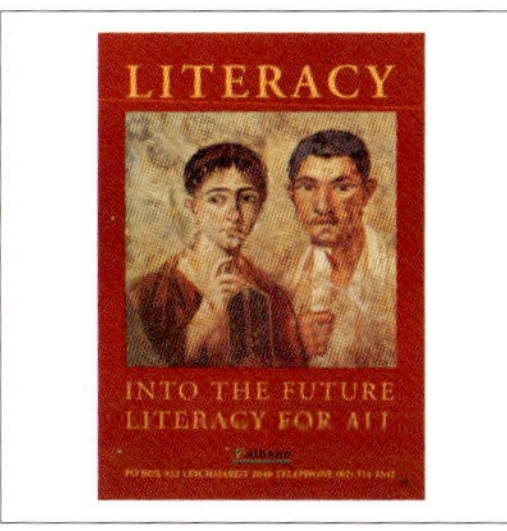

202

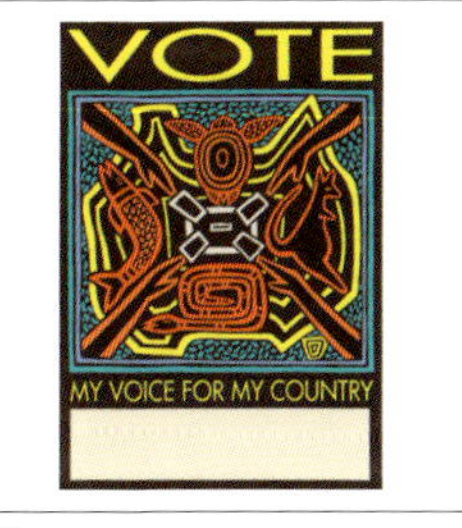

203

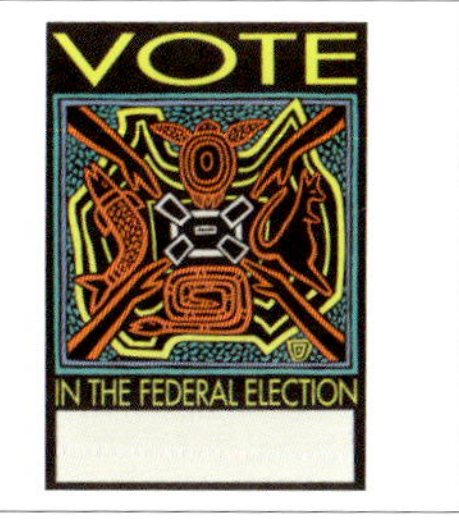

204

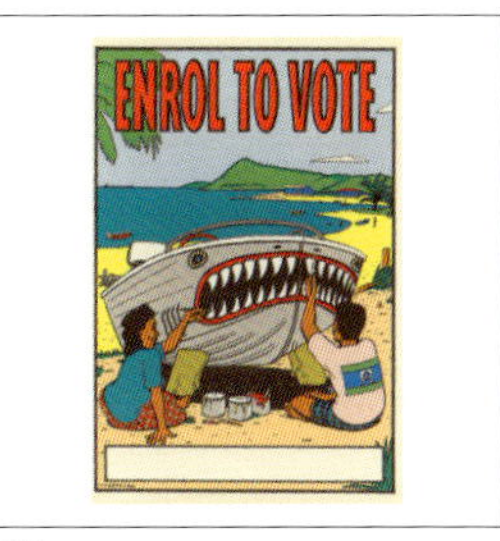

205

201 **Michael CALLAGHAN** (designer)
**THE IMPRESSIONISTS PTY LTD** (printer)
**Federal Department of Arts, Sport, Environment & Territories** (client)
*World Environment Day* 1992 Annandale, Sydney
offset-lithograph, printed in colour, on smooth white paper
printed image 58.0 x 41.0 cm
sheet 60.4 x 42.2 cm
Gordon Darling Australia Pacific Print Fund 2008
2008.320

202 **Michael CALLAGHAN** (designer)
**THE IMPRESSIONISTS PTY LTD** (printer)
**Adult Literacy and Basic Skills Action Coalition** (client)
*Literacy* 1993 Annandale, Sydney
offset-lithograph, printed in colour, on textured white paper
printed image and sheet 59.2 x 41.4 cm
Gordon Darling Australia Pacific Print Fund 2008
2008.298

203 **Michael CALLAGHAN** (designer)
**P&R SCREEN PRINTING PTY LTD** (printer)
**Aboriginal and Torres Strait Islander Education & Information Service (ATSIEIS)** and **Australian Electoral Commission** (AEC) (clients)
*Vote—my voice for my country* 1993 Annandale, Sydney
screenprint, printed in colour, from five stencils on smooth white paper
printed image and sheet 73.0 x 50.2 cm
Gordon Darling Australia Pacific Print Fund 2008
2008.300

204 **Michael CALLAGHAN** (designer)
**P&R SCREEN PRINTING PTY LTD** (printer)
**Aboriginal and Torres Strait Islander Education & Information Service (ATSIEIS)** and **Australian Electoral Commission** (AEC) (clients)
*Vote in the federal election* 1993 Annandale, Sydney
screenprint, printed in colour, from five stencils
printed image and sheet 73.0 x 50.2 cm
Gordon Darling Australia Pacific Print Fund 2008
2008.640

205 **Tony THORNE** (designer)
born Australia 1962
**P&R SCREEN PRINTING PTY LTD** (printer)
**Aboriginal and Torres Strait Islander Education & Information Service (ATSIEIS)** and **Australian Electoral Commission** (AEC) (clients)
*Enrol to vote* [*shark*] 1993 Annandale, Sydney
screenprint, printed in colour, from four stencils on thin white wove paper
printed image 72.2 x 48.5 cm
sheet 76.2 x 51.0 cm
Gordon Darling Australia Pacific Print Fund 2008
2008.627

# Selected references


Allison, Joy, 'Off the hoardings and into the gallery', *Off the hoardings and into the gallery: a survey of recent Australian political posters*, exhibition catalogue, Hobart: Tasmanian School of Art, 1982.

Annear, Judy, *Continuum '83: The 1st exhibition of Australian contemporary art in Japan*, exhibition catalogue, Japan, 1983.

Barnicoat, John, *A concise history of posters*, London: Thames and Hudson, 1972.

Bolton, Ken & Goodwin Christine, 'Truth rules – OK?', *Power to the people: Truth rules OK? revisited: An exhibition of political posters*, exhibition catalogue, Adelaide: Flinders University Art Museum, 1993, pp. 5–6.

Burn, Ian, *Working art: a survey of art in the Australian labour movement in the 1980s*, exhibition catalogue, Sydney: Art Gallery of New South Wales, 1985, pp. 9–15.

Butler, Roger, *The streets as art galleries – walls sometimes speak: poster art in Australia*, exhibition catalogue, Canberra: National Gallery of Australia, 1993.

Butler, Roger, 'Now we are ten', *Artlink*, vol. 10, no. 3, Spring, 1990, pp. 2–8.

Butler, Roger, 'Redback – a web of precedents, people and parallels', in *Redback Graphix: Now We Are 10*, Sydney: Redback Graphix, 1989, pp. 4–8.

Butler, Roger, 'Colin Little: poster maker', in *Colin Little retrospective*, exhibition catalogue, Canberra: Bitumen River Gallery, 1983.

Callaghan, Michael, Cullen, Gregor & McMahon, Marie, 'Redback Graphix', in *Eureka! Artists from Australia*, exhibition catalogue, London: Institute Contemporary Arts/ Arts Council of Great Britain, 1982.

Cater, Melissa, *Out of line: 25 years of women's posters*, exhibition catalogue, Sydney: State Library of New South Wales, 1995.

Cater, Melissa, *Women's Political Posters 1970–1990*, Masters of Arts Administration thesis, College of Fine Arts, UNSW, 1994.

Church, Julia, 'Alive & kicking: Redback Graphix – championing the vernacular in Australian art', *Imprint*, vol. 25, no. 1, 1990, pp. 1–3.

Church, Julia, *Pressing issues: contemporary posters from local co-operative presses*, exhibition catalogue, Melbourne: State Library of Victoria, 1990.

Dauth, Louise, 'Earthworks Poster Collective 1972–1979' in *Eureka! Artists from Australia*, exhibition catalogue, London: Institute Contemporary Arts/Arts Council of Great Britain, 1982, p. 38.

Dolan, Janey, Can Speaking Walls Cross Cultural Boundaries? Redback Graphix and Aboriginal and Islander Health, Honours thesis, Canberra: Australian National University, 1994.

Ewington, Julie, 'Right here, right now – Australia 1988', *Right here, right now – Australia 1988*, exhibition catalogue, Adelaide: Adelaide Arts Festival, 1988.

Ewington, Julie, 'Shocking diversity', *Shocking diversity: Some recent Sydney prints*, exhibition catalogue, Melbourne: Print Council of Australia, 1987, pp. 19–22.

Goldman, Shifra M., 'A public voice: fifteen years of Chicano posters', *Art Journal*, Spring, 1984, pp. 50–7.

Hall, Lee-Anne, 'Who is Bill Posters? An examination of six Australian socially concerned alternative print media organisations', *Caper 27*, 1988, pp. 1–23.

Kenyon, Therese, *Under a hot tin roof: art, passion and politics at the Tin Sheds Art Workshop*, Sydney: State Library of New South Wales Press, 1995.

Lavin, Maud (ed), *Graphic design in the mechanical age: selections from the Merrill C. Berman Collection*, London: Yale University Press, 1998.

Lupton, Ellen, *Design writing, research: writing on graphic design*, London: Phaidon Press, 1996.

Mara, Tim, *The Thames and Hudson manual of screenprinting*, London: Thames and Hudson, 1979.

Merewether, Charles, 'The art of serious dancing', in *Redback Graphix Posters 1979–1985*, exhibition catalogue, Wollongong: Wollongong City Gallery, 1987.

McMillan, Richard, 'Redback Graphix', *Art Monthly Australia*, 1987, no. 2, July, p. 19.

McQuiston, Liz, *Graphic agitation*, London: Phaidon Press, 1993.

Mann, Allan, 'Printed states', *Imprint*, 1997, vol. 32, no. 4, p. 24.

Poyner, Rick, *Design without boundaries: visual communication in transition*, London: Booth Clibborn Editions, 1998.

Russell, Allison, 'Revisiting the political poster', *Power to the people: truth rules OK?* revisited: an exhibition of political posters, exhibition catalogue, Adelaide: Flinders University Art Museum, 1993, pp. 3–4.

Stephen, Ann, 'Now We are 10: Let's read Redback' in *Redback Graphix: Now We Are 10*, Sydney: Redback Graphix, 1989 pp. 9–13.

Sutton, Peter (ed.), *Dreamings: The art of Aboriginal Australia*, Melbourne: Viking, 1988.

Taylor, Paul (ed.), *Anything goes: art in Australia 1970–1980*, Melbourne: Art & Text, 1984.

Taylor, Paul, 'Culture of temporary culture', *Australia: nine contemporary artists*, Olympic Arts Festival Los Angeles 1984, exhibition catalogue, LA: Los Angeles Institute of Contemporary Art, 1984, pp. 11–14.

Timmers, Margaret (ed.), *The power of the poster*, London: V&A Publications, 1998.

Vernon, Kay, 'Redback Graphix retrospective', *Art Monthly Australia*, 1990, no. 28, March, pp. 17–18.

Williamson, Clare, 'The revolution will not be televised: a social context for political posters', *Signs of the times: political posters in Queensland*, exhibition catalogue, Brisbane: Queensland Art Gallery, 1991.

Williamson, Clare, Political posters in Brisbane from the late 1970s to the early 1980s: their socio–political and cultural contexts, Honours thesis, Department of Art History, Bachelor of Arts, University of Queensland, 1989.

Yanker, G., *Prop art*, Darian House: New York, 1972.

# Index